Weaving Wellbeing into the Literac Curriculum for Ages 8–11

Combining literacy lessons with wellbeing, this accessible guide, full of practical lesson plans and photocopiable activities is the ideal resource for the busy primary school teacher.

The book is divided into five chapters, each one focused on an area that creates positive foundations for mental health and wellbeing: relationships, emotional literacy, sense of self, skills for learning and understanding how our brain influences our learning and behaviour. Popular children's books are used to develop a series of lesson plans that link to the literacy curriculum and include activities that focus on wellbeing to complement the literacy work being undertaken.

Using a range of teaching techniques that develop the key areas that impact mental health and wellbeing, this is the perfect resource for KS2 teachers looking to incorporate wellbeing into the literacy curriculum.

Alison Waterhouse has worked in mainstream, special education and the independent sector for the past 30 years. She now works as an Educational Psychotherapist and Educational Consultant for SEN and Wellbeing. She is involved in staff training, acts as an Adviser for a renowned Wellbeing Award and supervises Wellbeing Leads and Therapists working in schools.

Melanie Smith has over 25 years' experience in a variety of school settings. She currently works in Children's Services with a Local Authority supporting children, young people and parents.

Weaving Wellbeing into the Literacy Curriculum for Ages 8–11

A Practical Resource for Busy Teachers

Alison Waterhouse and Melanie Smith

Routledge
Taylor & Francis Group

LONDON AND NEW YORK

Cover image: © Getty Images

First published 2023
by Routledge
4 Park Square, Milton Park, Abingdon, Oxon OX14 4RN

and by Routledge
605 Third Avenue, New York, NY 10158

Routledge is an imprint of the Taylor & Francis Group, an informa business

British Library Cataloguing-in-Publication Data
A catalogue record for this book is available from the British Library

Library of Congress Cataloging-in-Publication Data
Names: Waterhouse, Alison, 1963- author. | Smith, Melanie K., author.
Title: Weaving wellbeing into the literacy curriculum for ages 8-11 : a practical resource for busy teachers / Alison Waterhouse and Melanie Smith.
Description: Abingdon, Oxon ; New York, NY : Routledge, 2023. | Series: Weaving wellbeing into the curriculum
Identifiers: LCCN 2022037639 (print) | LCCN 2022037640 (ebook) | ISBN 9781032345628 (hardback) | ISBN 9781032345611 (paperback) | ISBN 9781003322801 (ebook)
Subjects: LCSH: Language arts (Elementary)--Psychological aspects. | Language arts (Elementary)--Activity programs. | School children--Mental health.
Classification: LCC LB1576 .W264 2023 (print) | LCC LB1576 (ebook) | DDC 372.6--dc23/eng/20220922
LC record available at https://lccn.loc.gov/2022037639
LC ebook record available at https://lccn.loc.gov/2022037640

ISBN: 978-1-032-34562-8 (hbk)
ISBN: 978-1-032-34561-1 (pbk)
ISBN: 978-1-003-32280-1 (ebk)

DOI: 10.4324/9781003322801

Typeset in Avant Garde
by Deanta Global Publishing Services, Chennai, India

Contents

Contents

Weaving Wellbeing into Literacy

DOI: 10.4324/9781003322801-1

Introduction

IN THE BEGINNING...

The idea for this book came into being when Melanie and I were having coffee. Melanie is a brilliant teacher, possibly one of the best I have ever had the pleasure to work with. We would often joke about how wonderful it would be to own a bookshop together. We both love children's books but look at them from completely different angles. She is passionate about teaching literacy, and I am passionate about wellbeing. While catching up over a coffee one day we decided it would be brilliant fun to work together and write a resource for teachers, the sort of resource we wanted, but could never find, one that combined good teaching with wellbeing interwoven into the lesson – the *Golden Thread* series of books came into being and the idea started to grow.

So why do I love books? Good question. One of my first memories is of my mum reading after she had done the household jobs in the afternoon, I would sit down next to her on the settee and read as well. I have no memory of learning to read but just remember I could. Our house only had one bookcase and it was filled with a strange variety of books from Agatha Christie to Edgar Rice Burroughs – he wrote the Tarzan books. Victoria Holt, Lewis Carroll and Shakespeare. My dad didn't read – later it became obvious that he was very dyslexic as was I, but I didn't find that out for many years. By the age of 12, I had read every single one of the books and anything else I could get my hands on. I had been transported to wonderful places, met extraordinary characters and learnt how to escape from the world. My love of reading was ignited.

Melanie's memories about reading are linked to being told that she had finished her reading scheme at school. Up until that point she had had no idea she was following any scheme! It was the fact that now she had completed it and was a 'free reader', which had a profound effect on her as it opened doors that enabled her to discover a greater variety of genres and authors.

It was years later when I was working with very traumatised children in a special school in Kent that I started to understand the power of books and stories in helping children grow and heal. When children arrived at the school, they had experienced the very worst life and school could throw at them. They didn't like school, were stuck with learning and didn't trust anyone. Each child came to school for an hour a day for the first week to help them get used to the building, meet staff and start to settle. During this time, I worked with them on a 1:1 basis. As I got to know them, I went in search of 'their book'. Sometimes I would know exactly which book I wanted, but most of the time I needed to wander around the bookshops or second-hand shops. As I did, 'their book' would reveal itself.

Introduction

At other times, children would struggle in school, for a variety of reasons, often unknown. It was during these times that I would once more go in search of a book for them. One of the most important times when this happened was when a child who had been with us for several years really experienced huge difficulties. His anger and violence became very difficult to contain. He lived in a therapeutic children's home and to support him manage we created a part-time timetable for him for several weeks. During this time, I was privileged enough to be able to work with him. It was a really difficult and challenging time and so once more I went in search of a book to help me. I found it in a story called *Heads and Tales* by Barry Tutt. What an amazing book. Each day as he came into our small room to work with me, I read a chapter. While I read, he calmed and relaxed and played with a few small toy cars while he listened. The chapter then became the starting point for the work – either drawing or making something linked to the story we were reading. The story was about a small group of strange animals who found each other and lived in a forest. One day when they were out in the forest they came across a really, really scary animal called Pandemonium – the most dreadful creature in the whole forest. This of course was just what we needed because we needed to explore scary things and how to manage them. It was helped by the fact that the pictures in the book were brilliant and made us laugh.

My experience working with the children at school led me to train as an Educational Psychotherapist and it was during my training that I encountered the work of Bruno Bettelheim and his work on the Uses of Enchantment. Within his book, he explores the importance and irreplaceable value of fairy tales and how they can both educate and enable children to explore and understand their emotions. Bettelheim describes fairy tales as art that can 'both delight and instruct; their special genius is that they do so in terms which speak directly to children' (1977, p. 53).

Ever since I have used books to explore things, the things that are hard to talk about and hard to think about. I have used them to help friends, my staff teams, parents and of course children, and each time I do, they work their magic. Melanie still vividly remembers the first book I bought her – The *Tin Forest* and she still refers to it in times of change, hope and re-framing.

The books we have chosen to use as the basis for the work on literacy are all books that help children explore and think about difficult things. The *Teachers Resource* is divided into five chapters, each one focused on an area that creates positive foundations for mental health and wellbeing: relationships, emotional literacy, sense of self, skills for learning and understanding how our brain affects our learning and our behaviour.

Between 'One fine day' and 'That was the end of that', amazing adventures can happen, worlds can be explored and scary monsters beaten. Each storybook enables children and young people to explore and think about things within the safety of the story world. By helping them think about and manage these adventures we give them the tools to manage when life gets a bit bumpy for them, or we enable them to understand something in a different and healthier way without it being overwhelming. We as the storyteller are there to act as the guide and protector while they experience strange and dangerous places or places of fun filled with laughter and happy thoughts.

THE IMPORTANCE OF STORIES

Stories have been important since the beginning of time, they are part of every culture and have been told for generations around campfires, candles and gaslights, while holding their listeners enthralled. They have been used by adults to help teach children about their heritage and culture and the values that are important to their communities. They pass on their customs from generation to generation. Many years ago, teachers used to be taught how to tell stories as part of their training – something Melanie vehemently believes should still happen. A well-timed and well-told story ignites the imagination, evokes empathy, builds expectation, provides speculation and, if paused at just the right point in the narrative, can elicit cries of dismay from the audience that they must 'wait until the next instalment'. In fact, I can remember loving the story at the end of the school day when I was a child. My class teacher read this with great passion, and it transported us all to worlds like Never Land, The Shire and Alice's Wonderland.

Stories help develop language, vocabulary and how words feel, they support planning, organisation and empathy and they support children learning to listen and imagine. They are inclusive to all and when told well can capture everyone in the room and whisk them away to another place, leaving all their worries or struggles behind for a short time.

THE IMPORTANCE OF METAPHOR

Stories hold magic for children, they include symbolic language of mythical creatures, monsters, heroes and heroines, of terrifying challenges that have to be overcome and of evil that is defeated by a range of characters, from the small and weak to the brave and clever. Stories seem able to convey meaning, answer problems and solve challenges in ways that everyday communication isn't able to. Not only do stories take you on a journey but they are able to stimulate children's imagination and enable them to both play and create their own. Within play or their own writing, children get to project their own feelings, fears, dilemmas and anxieties into the characters contained on the page. They can experience how the characters might behave, being brave or clever, failing or losing something important. By experiencing these things within the safety of the story, they are practising how to manage the challenges they face at the moment or the ones they may face in the future.

Bettleheim stated that:

> when unconscious material is to some degree permitted to come to awareness and worked through in imagination its potential for causing harm – to ourselves and others is much reduced; some of its forces can then be made to serve positive purposes.
>
> *(1997, p. 7)*

Our traditional stories help children to explore difficult concepts or ideas through the use of metaphor rather than by addressing the issue directly. Separation, loss anxiety and fear are all explored through the characters of the stories, one step removed and therefore safe to think about and experience. They offer a forum to think, share and discuss without making the issues personal. Sometimes, if the stories are too direct, they are uncomfortable and the children can't let them in to hear. When working with a story, children take what they need, and it is not always what we think they need. Children can explore situations that they may not have experienced in the safety of the story and the storyteller. Others will take the belief that the dangers are always defeated, and this then becomes the hope that whatever they meet that is difficult means that it can be managed. Each story means different things to different people. We can often just enjoy the story without knowing why or how it may be working at a deeper level. Many children will return to a story again and again and this can help us understand, that for them, it is extremely important for some reason.

DEVELOPING THINKING SKILLS

Hearing stories enables children to set out on a voyage of discovery. They get to 'try on' character traits and behaviours and experience emotions within the safety of the story. They get to explore challenges and problems and see how others might experience or solve these. They are able to think, reflect and understand a range of experiences in the safety of the story and their imagination. The experience of a story leads them to experiment with their own, to set out on their own adventure, one of their making. To plan and work out what happens, what challenges they wish to experience, how they wish the story to unfold and how they want it to end. The thinking, reflection and re-working of a story can be incredibly good at supporting children in developing their thinking and planning, organisation and sequencing. All of these skills have been shown to be important in developing positive mental health and wellbeing.

EMOTIONAL LITERACY

Daniel Goleman's book *Emotional Intelligence* (1996) popularised the concept of emotional literacy, but since then, research has clearly demonstrated the importance of emotional literacy on our mental health and wellbeing. As teachers, one aspect of the work we engage with is how to support children develop the skills to both recognise and understand their emotions as well as being able to express or manage them effectively and appropriately. Stories are a really great vehicle for doing this. Stories provide a place to explore how different characters feel and why they may behave as they do. They provide a forum to think, reflect, discuss and share ideas and opinions. By allowing this 'looking in on another', children can explore emotions more fully and safely in the belief that it is another they are thinking about. For the adults involved, we can be aware of the projection that is being used and therefore work discreetly, staying in the story, to discuss the characters and not the child that we are supporting.

INTRODUCING THE STORY

A wonderful way to introduce the stories to the children for the first time is using a story box technique that is based on the Montessori-based approach to religious education called Godly

Plays. Godly Plays uses small wooden figures and objects to retell stories from the Bible. The storyteller moves the figures in silence and then tells the story in between the movements. An adaption of this method allows you as the teacher to tell the story while moving very simple symbolic figures on a story mat within a circle of children. The children watch you tell and re-enact the story without talking. You as the storyteller focus on the story, pausing at important parts as you move the symbols around the story mat. I tend to use a piece of material as my story mat. Sometimes, I use green other times blue or brown. It does mean that you need to have learnt the story as you don't have enough hands to turn the pages and act out the story with the figures! You could always get someone else to read as you act it out if needed or if you feel more comfortable that way.

Over the years, I have collected a range of very basic props that can tell the stories I wish to share. Children are amazing at being able to imagine a small symbol such as a simple stylised wooden person to represent a king or a wizard, or a wooden coloured block as a pig or a dragon. The simplicity of the figures means that the children use their imagination to create the story you are telling. Each child will imagine something slightly different.

Another important point is to set the scene for telling the story. I use a candle and small Tibetan symbols to help set the mood and allow the children to settle into the story circle. I then unfold the story mat or the material I have chosen and open up the box with all my figures or objects, laying them out to the side so I can find them easily. As you start, you can gently introduce the characters and the symbols you are using to represent them. If you need small figures, the Reception classes are always willing to share what they have.

At the end of the story, I set the timer for a minute to allow us all to think and reflect on what we have heard.

Once we have finished, I invite the children to take some time to explore the story or something it has made them think about on their own. Around the room, I have laid out tables with paints, plasticine, paper and crayons or pens, Lego, collage materials or other creative materials. I suggest to the children that they can explore something the story has made them think about using the materials. I ask them to do this on their own and quietly.

Once the children have finished, it is really useful to bring them back into the circle and explore some of the things the story has made them think about using questions such as the ones below.

1. If you could ask one character a question, what would you ask?

2. If you were able to give a character something, what would you give them?

3. What has the story made you think about?

4. Is there something that could have been done earlier?

5. How can you help one of the characters?

Once you have explored the story and the children have been given the time and space to reflect and share their thoughts, then you can engage with the different learning activities. It is completely up to you whether you start with the wellbeing lesson for each book or the literacy lessons.

Within each of the five chapters, we have included a book that can be used in assembly to promote one of the five key areas that form the foundations for positive mental health and wellbeing. Again, these can be used as a whole school assembly or as a class assembly.

Chapter 1

Relationships
KS2

KS2 BOOKS

One by Kathryn Otoshi

Dandylion by Lizzie Finlay

TrooFriend by Kirsty Applebaum

ASSEMBLY

Phileas's Fortune by Agnes de Lestrade and
   Valeria Docampo

DOI: 10.4324/9781003322801-2

To Explore Figurative Language

Learning Objective: To explore how idioms are used to express feelings and ideas
Success Criteria:
◆ Find the phrase where the literal meaning would be odd
◆ Read around the phrase to see what is happening before, within and after the sentence
◆ Replace the idiom with a literal phrase
◆ Re-read to ensure it makes sense

Pupils Can...	Discuss and evaluate how authors use language, including figurative language, considering the impact on the reader.
	Draw inferences from the author's use of figurative language.
	Identify how language can contribute to meaning.

Figurative meaning is when a word/symbol/icon is used to mean or represent something other than its typical definition.

An **idiom** is an expression that is not meant to be taken literally. For example, 'Get off my back!' is an idiom meaning 'Stop bothering me!'

One by Kathryn Otoshi
Pictures of idioms
Pictures of idioms with phrases

Colour and number idioms with meanings

www.shutterstock.com/search/idioms

www.oysterenglish.com/idioms-list.html

https://examples.yourdictionary.com/idioms-for-kids.html

https://lemongrad.com/idioms-with-meanings-and-examples/

TASTER: SYMPHONY IN SLANG

Play the short cartoon (three minutes). What is unusual about the conversation in this clip? Play from 1.44 onwards.

www.youtube.com/watch?v=mEeROUVzCHk

Tex Avery Screwball Classics Vol. 1: Symphony in Slang

BUILDING TASK: GUESS THE IDIOM

Show an idiom picture, e.g. **It's raining cats and dogs.** Ask the students if they know the expression. Obviously, it never rains animals, so what is the idiom representing? What is its hidden meaning?

Show an idiom where the meaning could possibly be worked out (with a bit of lateral thinking!) or has some historical context. For example:

Pulling someone's leg. Meaning: *teasing someone in a joking manner*

Origin: *pulling someone's leg is supposed to be all good fun. Originally it was a method of robbing someone by tripping them up.*

Cost an arm and a leg. Meaning: *extremely expensive.* Origin: *in the 1700s, it was fashionable to have one's portrait painted. Most people had just their heads and shoulders painted as it cost more if you wanted arms and legs in the picture!*

Get the sack. Meaning: *be fired from a job.* Origin: *In the 1500s, workmen would carry the tools of their trade around in a sack. The sack could be left securely at the worksite. If the boss did not like the work, he would give them their sack to leave and not come back.*

BUILDING TASK: IDIOM PICTIONARY

Students are given a selection of pictures and/or idioms to match up with the phrase. This could be a quick activity to share or could be played as a team game. Students are divided into teams. A member from each team must sketch a pictorial representation of an idiom for their team to guess.

MAIN TASK: HOW HAS THE AUTHOR USED IDIOMS IN HER WRITING?

Read the book *One* by Kathryn Otoshi to the children.

1. There are idioms within the story. Students should jot these down as they hear them – 'to be picked on'; 'to blow a fuse'; 'to feel blue'; 'to take a stand'; 'to stop in his tracks'.

2. Students identify the idioms within the story. They should re-write them, changing the idioms to more formal language.

3. In discussion, compare the original idiomatic story to their new version. What effect does the use of idioms have on the reader? Why do you think Otoshi chose to use idioms in her story? Is 'to blow a fuse' a good choice?

4. Working in pairs, partners should choose two idioms for each other. The challenge is to use these idioms in a very short story or a few linked sentences.

5. Using colour and number idioms, students should write sentences that make the definition clear, e.g. *Melanie was **feeling blue** as she had been upset by an argument with her friend. She hoped that the argument was **a one-off** and would not happen again.*

6. Call my bluff – create a game with an idiom and three meanings: one true and two false, but plausible. Challenge a partner/group to identify the correct meaning.

7. Etymology – the teacher chooses an idiom and creates a possible origin for the meaning. Students choose a different idiom to create their own fictional origin.

DIFFERENTIATION

✓ Students could be given pictorial representations of idioms with phrases and definitions to match, allowing some process of choice and elimination.

✓ Students could re-write only relevant parts of the story into more formal language.

✓ Students could be challenged to write their own idiomatic storyline.

✓ Students could research the origins of idioms and create a dictionary.

Teacher Tools and Techniques	
Emotional Literacy	Extended vocabulary on feelings
Developing Relationships	Talking partners
	Teamwork
Self-Development	Thinking out loud
Skills for Learning	Pictorial representations. Visualising
The Brain Learning and Behaviour	Reflection on characters' behaviour
	Lateral thinking

PHSE LINK (PSHE ASSOCIATION PROGRAMME OF STUDY FOR PSHE EDUCATION – KS2)

Recognise that feelings can change over time and range in intensity.

Recognise individuality and personal qualities.

To Explore Figurative Language

Learning Objective: To explore how colour is used to express feelings and ideas	

Success Criteria:

◆ Choose a colour and express what it reminds you of in nature

◆ Identify some feelings associated with the image/memory

◆ Link the colour to an emotion and/or character's action

Pupils Can...	Discuss and evaluate how authors use language, including figurative language, considering the impact on the reader.
	Draw inferences from the author's use of figurative language.
	Identify how language can contribute to meaning.

Figurative meaning *is when a word/symbol/icon is used to mean or represent something other than its typical definition.*

Symbolism *is when one idea, feeling, emotion or other concept is represented by something else like a picture, colour, object, animal or icon. Symbols reflect the figurative meaning of the picture, object, colour, etc.*

Resources	*One* by Kathryn Otoshi	Colour wheel Paint colour charts

TASTER: CROSS MY HEART

Ask the children to work with their Talking Partner. Show the class an outline of a heart – what is the first thing that comes into their head? Is it a feeling? A colour? An event? Or something else? Ask them to share what the heart made them think of with their Talking Partner.

Share another image – this time a cross X. With their talking partner, ask them to share three things that spring to mind when they saw the cross. Share together what the children thought about with the heart and the cross. Next, show a colour – model out loud your thinking to the class. For example:

'Green makes me think of freshly cut grass, new leaves, spring, the smell of the woods, soft grass underfoot, picnics and emeralds'.

MINI TASK: PAINT PALETTE

Show the children an example of a paint colour chart – share some of the unusual names used to describe the different colours. What colour do they think 'Elephants Breath' might be?

Elephant's breath *is described by the manufacturer as a warm mid-grey with a hint of magenta but can also look lilac depending on the light.*

Ask the children to work in small groups and give each group a selection of colours and cards with the paint names on them. Ask them to try and match them together. What do they notice about the names? Usually, they are named after natural things such as precious stones, animals, fruit, vegetables and so on.

Share some favourites: dromedary, hot flamingo, ocean surf.

Some colours can be a feeling: e.g. Surprise – pale orange, Happy – bright yellow, Attitude – dusky brown.

MINI TASK: COLOUR CAROUSEL

On each table place a large piece of plain paper – Flipchart or A3 and some markers. In the centre of the paper, place a colour card – a different colour for each table. Each group of children has two minutes to mind map as many words or phrases that the colour represents to them. Remind the children that it could be from the natural world (animal, vegetable, precious stone) or it could be an emotion or a feeling. After two minutes ask the children to move to the next table and continue adding to the previous group's words and phrases.

MAIN TASK: HOW HAS THE AUTHOR USED COLOUR IN HER WRITING?

1. Read the book *One* by Kathryn Otoshi to the children.

2. The author uses colours as characters. Explore with the children which colours she has used and what the colour tells us about the character.

3. Work with the class to model how they might find out about the character – colour, connotations, actions, speech, words and imagery.

4. Ask the children to work either with a partner or on their own and create a chart to show how each colour is used in the text and illustrations. It could be in the form of a mind map, colour wheel, chart or a form of their choosing.

5. Alternatively, provide them with a table to complete.

6. Share the ideas the children have come up with as a class. Compare ideas and differences.

7. Discuss why the author chose Red to be the character that picks on all the others.

8. Ask the children to think about themselves. If they were a colour, which colour would they want to be and why? Ask the children to write about why they would like to be the colour they have chosen and the characteristics that this colour and they have.

9. If some children are struggling to think about a colour to describe themselves, they could choose to write about a character from a story, e.g. Hermione Granger – if she were a colour what colour would she be and what characteristics would she have as that colour?

DIFFERENTIATION

✓ Use mind maps to link ideas.

✓ Provide students with a table template and one completed example to show expectations.

✓ Provide students with a colour chart and the usual emotions associated with them.

✓ Students could identify times when they have felt that emotion/colour, e.g. 'I am deep green when my little brother gets all my mum's attention'.

Teacher Tools and Techniques	
Emotional Literacy	Extended vocabulary on feelings
Developing Relationships	Talking partners
Self-Development	Thinking out loud
Skills for Learning	Mind maps
The Brain Learning and Behaviour	Reflection on characters' behaviour

PHSE LINK (PSHE ASSOCIATION PROGRAMME OF STUDY FOR PSHE EDUCATION – KS2)

Recognise that feelings can change over time and range in intensity.

Recognise individuality and personal qualities.

Exploring the Bystander Effect and the Impact It Can Have on Our Behaviour

Learning Objectives:	
To explore how the bystander effect can influence and affect our behaviour	
To explore ways to challenge the bystander effect and change our behaviour	
Success Criteria:	
◆ Explain what the bystander effect is	
◆ Give an example and suggest ways to challenge this	

Pupils Can...	Describe the bystander effect.
	Give an example of the bystander effect and how it can impact our behaviour.
	Give examples of ways of challenging the bystander effect.

The Bystander Effect *is also known as bystander apathy and is a social psychological theory that states that individuals are less likely to help a victim when there are other people present. It was first proposed in 1968 and was prompted by the murder of Kitty Genovese in which it was reported – incorrectly – that 38 people stood by passively and watched. Most of the research has been undertaken in the laboratory and has looked at a range of factors including the number of bystanders, group cohesiveness and diffusion of responsibility that reinforces mutual denial. Recent research has focused on 'real world' events captured on security cameras.*

One by Kathryn Otoshi	Counters/Blocks/Giant Lego
Character name cards	Impact Sheet on A3 paper
A4 paper	Counters

TASTER: HARM DOER, TARGET OR BYSTANDER?

Ask the children to work in small groups of four to six. Give each group the name cards of the characters – Red, Blue, Green, Yellow and One – and some plain paper. Ask one or two people to scribe for the group.

Ask them to put each card in the middle of the paper, working together, decide the different feelings each character was experiencing. Help the children understand that we can have a mixture of feelings, not just one at a time.

Ask the children to write the different feelings on the paper.

Once they have finished, share what the different groups have come up with and write the different feelings from the groups on the board under each character's label. Show the emotions over time – write them in order and show the variety of emotions that they all went through. This helps the children understand that our emotions change and do not stay forever. Label the colours Red – Harmdoer, Blue – Target and Green and the other colours – Bystanders. What name would they give One?

Discuss the terms harmdoer, target and bystander and create a definition with the children for each one.

BUILDING TASK: ACT IT OUT!

Ask the children to work in their groups and using the coloured counters/bricks/ giant Lego act out the story with a narrator reading it.

Ask the children to write additional parts to the story showing how the other colours were feeling watching Red be unkind to Blue and what stopped them from stepping in. This could be as thoughts or as a conversation between other colours. Share some of the scenarios and then ask the following questions:

- *How are the other colours feeling when Red is picking on Blue?*
- *What might happen in the future?*
- *What lesson is being learnt by the different characters?*

Record on the board and discuss the different points that come up.

MAIN TASK: IMPACT

1. Ask the children to work individually and draw a time when they experienced or they were aware of someone picking on another person. It can be something that they have experienced as a target or a bystander or it can be made up.

2. Ask each of the children to work in pairs and complete the Impact sheet to show the different feelings the harmdoer, target and bystanders experienced and possible ways the bystanders could have managed the situation.

3. Ask each pair to lay out their work on the table and then ask the children to move around in a Silent Exhibition and read the different scenarios. Ask the children to vote with a counter on the best way for the bystander to manage the situation.

DIFFERENTIATION

✓ Pair the children so that any non-writers are paired with children who are happy to read and write.

✓ Suggest that children can share their ideas with the group and not just record them in writing or drawing.

Teacher Tools and Techniques	
Emotional Literacy	Extending the language of emotions
Developing Relationships	Working in groups, developing empathy
Self-Development	Sharing thoughts and ideas with others that are valued and listened to
Skills for Learning	Problem-solving, sharing ideas, reflection
The Brain Learning and Behaviour	Understanding that we can choose how we behave in difficult situations

PHSE LINK (PSHE ASSOCIATION PROGRAMME OF STUDY FOR PSHE EDUCATION – KS2)

How to recognise and name different feelings.

How feelings can affect people's bodies and how they behave.

Ways of sharing feelings; a range of words to describe feelings.

About how people may feel if they experience hurtful behaviour or bullying.

Impact Sheet

Situation Description: *Describe the situation: where people were and what was happening.*

Person involved	What you observed: Facial expression and body language	How do you think the incident made them feel?	Other information
Harmdoer			
Target			
Bystander			

Formal and Informal Language

Learning Objective: To understand the difference between formal and informal language	

Success Criteria:

◆ Read the phrase – say it aloud

◆ Consider the genre (the text type)

◆ Consider where you might use the phrase (the audience)

◆ Consider why you might use the phrase (the purpose)

◆ Look for slang, contractions, abbreviations

◆ Look for ambitious vocabulary, passive or active voice

Pupils Can...	Recognise formal and informal vocabulary in texts that use language which is archaic or colloquial
	Explain why sentences are formal or informal, identifying specific words.
	Identify the audience for and purpose of the writing

Formal language is written for an audience you do not know personally. Formal writing is serious and uses more complex sentences.

Informal language is more casual and conversational. It is used when communicating with friends or family. It is used in texts such as personal emails, diaries or text messages.

Contractions are words made by shortening and combining two words. Words like can't (can + not), don't (do + not) and I'll (I + will) are all contractions.

Slang is vocabulary used between people who know each other well. It is very informal language and is mostly used in speech rather than writing. Slang can be a particular word but can also be a longer phrase such as an idiom.

	*Dandylion* by Lizzie Finlay Slang terms to sort.	Examples of formal and informal sentences and/or short extracts.

TASTER: SORTA SLANG!

Ask the children how many words they can think of that mean 'stole'.

Examples might include robbed, nicked, pinched, pilfered, filched or five-finger discount.

Give the children slang terms to sort into groups.

Give the children a word to find its slang terms.

BUILDING TASK: LET US CONVERSE

Using a thesaurus, children look up words and sort them into formal/informal. Children could sort the synonyms into degrees of formality. For example:

Talk – gossip, prattle, chatter, speak, converse, discuss, exchange, confer.

BUILDING TASK: WHAT'S UP?

Role-play formal/informal language for different situations.

◆ *You have been sick – how would you tell your friend, your teacher or the doctor?*

◆ *You believe you have had something stolen – how would you tell your friend, your teacher or the police?*

◆ *You are complaining about a meal you had at a restaurant – how would you describe it to your friend, the restaurant owner or a local newspaper?*

MAIN TASK: FORMAL OR INFORMAL?

1. As a class, list as many text types as you can.

Diaries, reports, newspapers, stories, explanations, letters, text messages, information leaflets, journals, recipes, instructions, email, etc.

Children consider the audience and purpose to decide whether each text type would be formal/informal/both.

2. With a learning partner, children compare a short formal and informal text. How many differences can they find? Gather differences as a class and group into formal or informal language.

3. Using the children's responses and any missing criteria, display the list of differences between formal and informal.

Formal	Informal
Ambitious vocabulary	Use of slang
Serious	Very chatty, friendly and can be funny.
Lengthier and more complex sentences	Use of abbreviations
Correct grammar and punctuation	Use of idioms and expressions – It was a piece of cake!
Passive voice	Active voice

4. Children are given sentences and/or short texts to sort into formal and informal language.

5. Read the book *Dandylion* by Lizzie Finlay to the class. Using some of the phrases from the book, have children change the phrases from formal to informal or vice versa

    'My mum knows I don't like tuna fish' **becomes** *'My mother is aware that I dislike the taste of tuna fish sandwiches'.*

    Please allow me to introduce you to…

    Please can he sit next to me?

    Apple-pie order had returned to Miss Gardner's class.

    We all need special people to come and stir up our lives for us.

    'What's happening, my little Dandy?'

    'I think it might be because you're like a weed'.

DIFFERENTIATION

✓ Children match up given formal sentences with given informal sentences.

✓ Children use a thesaurus or word bank.

✓ Children are given sentences that include only one difference to change, such as slang, abbreviations, or contractions.

Teacher Tools and Techniques	
Emotional Literacy	How we communicate our thoughts and feelings
Developing Relationships	Talking partners
Self-Development	Thinking out loud, use of language to communicate
Skills for Learning	Grouping/sorting, decision-making
The Brain Learning and Behaviour	Reflection on characters' behaviour and how they interact and communicate

PHSE LINK (PSHE ASSOCIATION PROGRAMME OF STUDY FOR PSHE EDUCATION – KS2)

Respecting the differences and similarities between people

Understand that different groups make up their community; what living in a community means

To Write a Letter Using Formal or Informal Language

Learning Objective: To write a formal or informal letter using the appropriate language features

Success Criteria:

◆ Consider the audience and purpose and decide whether your language will be formal or informal

◆ Use formal/informal criteria checklist

◆ Include:

  – address of writer

  – address of recipient

  – date

  – greeting

  – paragraphs for each point

  – closing

  – signature

Pupils Can...	Identify the audience and purpose, use the correct features of text type, use the correct degree of formality and use active/passive voice consistently.
	Identify the audience and purpose, use the correct features of text type and use language that matches the formality needed.
	Identify the audience and purpose of the writing and choose the correct features of the text type.

Formal language is written for an audience you do not know personally. Formal writing is serious and uses more complex sentences.

Informal language is more casual and conversational. It is used when communicating with friends or family. It is used in texts such as personal emails, diaries or text messages.

Contractions are words made by shortening and combining two words. Words like can't (can + not), don't (do + not) and I'll (I + will) are all contractions.

Slang is vocabulary used between people who know each other well. It is very informal language and is mostly used in speech rather than writing. Slang can be a particular word but can also be a longer phrase such as an idiom.

 **Resources**	*Dandylion* by Lizzie Finlay	Blank layout of the letter A letter that can be cut up and children can place back into the correct order

TASTER: WHO GETS WHAT?

With a talking partner, children discuss who might receive a letter and why. Gather responses as a class.

Ask the children to stand. One side of the room is designated as formal and the opposite side as informal. When you call out the name of the recipient of a letter, the children should move to the side of the room for the formality level required. It may be that the children decide the degree of formality could fall into both categories and therefore stay in the middle of the room.

Letter to –

a doctor, nan, the school office, the police, a restaurant manager, a friend, a pen pal, a parent, a teacher, a new employer, a politician, a sibling, a favourite actor/singer/author, a friend you have fallen out with, someone who has helped you, someone who has upset you.

BUILDING TASK: I'M ALL CUT UP!

With their talking partner, children discuss the features they think will be needed for a letter. Discuss and create a class list of criteria.

Children are given either a blank template of the layout of a formal and/or informal letter in which to write the features or are given a letter that has been cut up and needs to be placed back into the correct layout.

BUILDING TASK: DID IT SAY?

Refreshing the children's memory about the story *Dandylion*, ask the children what they think was inside the letter to the parents. What type of language do they think was used? Discuss the degree of formality in writing to parents. Show the class a school letter on headed paper. Why does the school have headed paper? Why might it be so formal?

Give the children a list of phrases that might have been in Miss Gardner's letter to the parents. On a scale of likelihood, do the children think the phrase or sentence was included in the letter?

Definitely not   Unlikely   Maybe   Likely   Definitely

Dear parents and carers,	*Staff will be there so no one acts bad and start trouble*
Hello everyone,	*The party will be the best thing since sliced bread*
It would be lovely if….	*The class will be organising a special event for …*
I would be grateful….	*The party will be amazing and the kids will have a lot of stuff to eat and do.*
Refreshments will be provided.	*Any contributions of food for the party will be gratefully received*
Come and have a laugh.	*Let's hope it won't be raining cats and dogs.*
Reply asap	*Staff will be dressed up too – LOL*

MAIN TASK: FORMAL OR INFORMAL?

1. Read *Dandylion* by Lizzie Finlay again.

2. As a class discuss how the characters might be feeling. Why might Miss Gardner decide to have a Wildflower Day?

3. First with a talking partner and then as a class, list the things that the children missed or might miss about Dandylion.

4. Reminding children of the layout, purpose and audience, either ask the children to

   – *write a letter to Dandylion saying why they miss him and asking him to come back to school. They might even include an apology and what they will do better next time (a bit of restorative justice/buddy support thinking!).*

   – *write a letter to parents in the role of Miss Gardner.*

DIFFERENTIATION

✓ Children given a formal letter to change to informal

Children given layout and sentence starters/prompt sheet for each paragraph such as

- *I would like you to come back to school because…*

- *It was great fun when we…*

- *Do you remember when…?*

- *We are having a Wildflower Day so…*

- *I'm sorry that I…*

Teacher Tools and Techniques	
Emotional Literacy	How we communicate our thoughts and feelings
Developing Relationships	Talking partners
Self-Development	Thinking out loud, use of language to communicate
Skills for Learning	Organisation, visual layouts
The Brain Learning and Behaviour	Reflection on characters' behaviour and how they interact and communicate
	Visual prompts

PHSE LINK (PSHE ASSOCIATION PROGRAMME OF STUDY FOR PSHE EDUCATION – KS2)

Ethnicity, family, gender, faith, culture, hobbies, likes/dislikes contribute to who we are.

Personal strengths, skills, achievements and interests contribute to a sense of self-worth.

Expressing feelings is important and can be expressed in different ways.

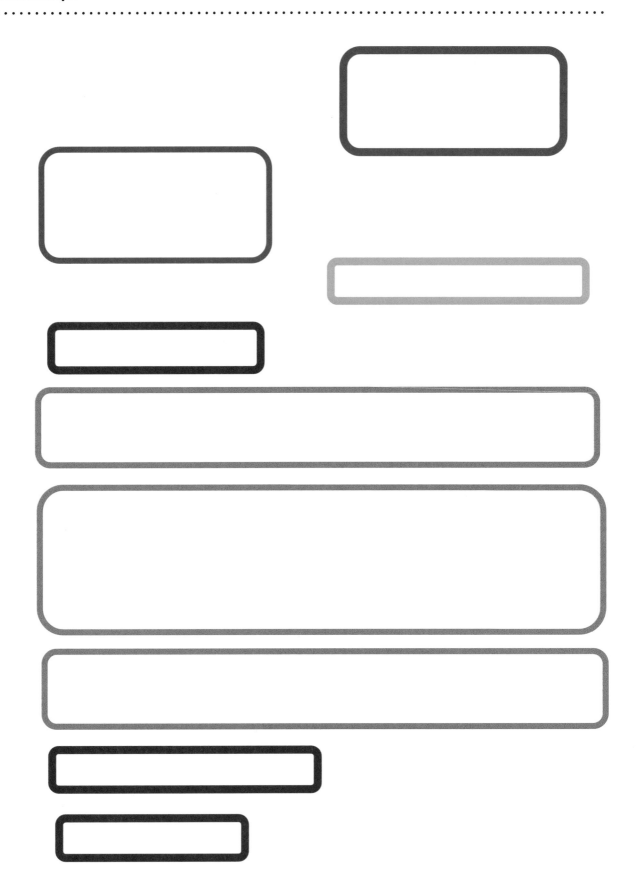

The formal layout of this letter is incorrect. Can you place the features into their correct positions?

Sender's address

Signature

Introductory Paragraph

Recipients address

Formal closure

Closing Paragraph

Date

Formal greeting

Main body of text

Miss Violet Pettle
220 Petunia Drive
Garden Park
Sussex

Master Dandy Lion
32 Begonia Road
Garden Park
Sussex

10th September 2021

Dear Master Dandy Lion,

I hope this letter finds you in good health. The staff and children are concerned by your absence from school and wish to express their desire for your return to the classroom and your studies.

The children in our class wish to convey their fondness for you and their regret that you may be troubled by their recent behaviour towards you. They have mentioned how much they miss your bright, sunny face and your boundless energy; school is less exciting without you. You have helped the pupils realise that everyone is unique and can offer something special to our community. Therefore, your peers would like to cordially invite you to a special day in your honour at school tomorrow.

I do hope you will be able to attend and look forward to greeting you at the school entrance tomorrow at 8:50am.

Yours sincerely,

V. Pettle

Celebrating Difference

Learning Objectives:
To develop an understanding that everyone is different and that it is our differences that make us special and unique
To develop an understanding of the importance of diversity

Success Criteria:
◆ Share ways in which we are all different
◆ Identify the skills and characteristics that make us special and unique.

Pupils Can...	Describe the skills we have.
	Give an example of special skills and characteristics of other young people we know.
	Describe what diversity means and why it is important to promote.

Celebrating Diversity includes acceptance and respect. It means not only understanding that each individual is unique, but also recognising our individual differences. These differences may be around race, ethnicity, gender, sexual orientation, socio-economic status, age, physical abilities, religious beliefs, political beliefs or other ideologies. Through the exploration of these differences in a safe, positive and nurturing environment, we can learn about others, understand different ideas, opinions and beliefs, celebrate differences and then truly understand diversity.

Resources

Dandylion by Lizzie Finlay	Adverts showing why a product is good.
Bag of stones – one for each child	Television advert
	Radio advert
Photos of children	Advert template

TASTER: STONES ARE ALL THE SAME!

Hold up a bag of stones and explain to the children that you've never really taken that much notice of stones, that they all look pretty much the same and that you think stones are a lot like people – pretty much the same.

Pass around the bag of stones and ask each child to take one. Tell each child to look carefully at their stone, get to know its bumps, scars and defects and make friends with it for about one minute or so in silence. Explain that you want them to get to know their stone well enough to be able to introduce their 'friend' to the group.

After a few minutes, tell the children that you'd like to start by introducing your 'friend' to them. (Share a story about your stone and how it got its lumps, bumps and scars.) Then explain that the other children in the class would like to meet their friends.

Ask the children to work with a partner and tell their partner about their special friend.

Once the children have done this ask for volunteers to stand and share their friend with the whole class. When enough students have introduced their 'friends' to the class, take the bag around to each person. Ask them to please put their 'friends' back into the bag.

Pose the statement 'all stones are the same'. Explore this with the children.

Mix up the stones and then lay them out on a table. Ask everyone to come up and pick out their stones.

After everyone has their stones explain that 'Perhaps stones are a little like people. Sometimes, we lump people as a group altogether. When we think, "they're all alike", we are really saying that we haven't taken the time or thought it important enough to get to know the person. When we do, we find out everyone is different and special in some way, just like our stone friends'.

BUILDING TASK: LEAVE A COMMENT

Ask the children to bring a photo of themselves to school or take photos of each of the children. If you have time, you might ask the children to draw or paint a picture of themselves.

Stick their picture onto a sheet of paper so that there is space around the picture to write things.

Ask the children to work in groups of six. Lay out the pictures on the table and then ask the children to move around the table and write something that they like, admire or believe that person is good at or that makes them special on each picture. Emphasise the importance of making the comment positive and that it is important that children do this. That everyone must feel safe that others will be focusing on the positive things.

Once the table has done this, you can ask tables to move so that each child can then write on another six pictures. Allow the children time to read all the different things that the other children have written about them.

MAIN TASK: ADVERT

1. Put the children into working pairs and explain that they are going to create an advert about their partner. The advert will need to highlight their skills, talents, characteristics and what makes them unique and special. Discuss the purpose of an advert.

2. Share a range of adverts from magazine or newspaper adverts. You might also like to show TV adverts or a radio advert.

3. In small groups ask the children to identify three specific things an advert does or has. This can include positive language, a special phrase, the use of fonts to highlight words or phrases and so on.

4. Come up with sentences that describe people together as a class and record them on the board. You can use staff as a focus.

   Mr Finn the fast football wonder
   Mrs Holland the snappy happy dinner lady
   Brighten up your day, spend time with Mrs Hay

5. Discuss catchphrases that can be used and share examples.
   For a great start to your day XXXXX drink
   You can't buy happiness, but you can drink it XXXXXX
   The chicken, the whole chicken and nothing but the chicken.
   XXXXXX quality never goes out of style.
   XXXXX Just do it.
   Naughty but nice.
   XXXXX Just pen happiness
   XXXXX the breakfast of champions
   XXXXX because you're worth it.

6. If needed, allow children to use the advert template

7. Share different aspects of the work as the children undertake the task. Focus on ways of working as well as what is being produced.

8. Ask children to put their advert on their table. Get the class to take part in a silent exhibition, walking around to look at how others have undertaken the task.

9. Share the ideas that they have seen and why they have liked them.
   Which advert particularly caught your attention and why?

Which advert do you think was most eye-catching?

Which was your favourite catchphrase?

What was your favourite sentence used to focus on the positives about someone?

DIFFERENTIATION

✓ Suggest that children can write or draw the things they admire about the other children's skills, talents or characteristics.

✓ Pair children up with other children who can scribe for them.

✓ Model how you focus on the talents and skills children have by giving examples.

✓ Allow children to use the advert template.

✓ Allow children to create a video/radio advert with another child instead of writing the advert.

Teacher Tools and Techniques	
Emotional Literacy	Being able to share positive things about individuals and hear positive things being said about themselves
Developing Relationships	Focusing on noticing positive traits and characteristics, skills and talents
Self-Development	Sharing things that individuals enjoy and are good at
Skills for Learning	Developing vocabulary and language to promote something
The Brain Learning and Behaviour	Focusing on the positive

PHSE LINK

To recognise what makes them special.

To recognise the ways in which we are all unique.

About personal identity – what contributes to who we are (e.g. ethnicity, family, gender, faith, culture, hobbies, likes/dislikes).

About diversity – what it means; the benefits of living in a diverse community; about valuing diversity within communities.

Name of Product — use a really eye catching font that is easily seen and read.

Picture

Chose the best picture you can to show the product in the best way possible

Catchy phrase — By using a catchy phrase you help people remember your product

5 Good Reasons — List the five good reasons why people should buy your product . Why should they buy this one and not any of the others?

Persuasive Techniques

Learning Objective: To identify some of the different ways that adverts can persuade or affect choice

Success Criteria:

◆ Highlight, underline or annotate

     – Catchy name of product

     – Slogans and wordplay

     – Hyperbole

     – Superlatives

     – Evaluative adjectives

     – Rhetorical questions

Pupils Can...	Identify the features and analyse the effect of an advertisement on an intended audience.
	Identify and describe the features of an advertisement.
	Identify key persuasive techniques in an advertisement.

Superlatives are used to describe an object which is at the upper or lower limit of a quality: 'The worst meal'; 'The biggest tower'; 'The smartest dog'.

Evaluative adjectives are words that show a judgement on the noun it is describing. It could be a negative or a positive judgement and effect: 'The awesome product'; 'The dreadful meal'.

Hyperbole is a figure of speech and is an exaggerated statement or claim not meant to be taken literally: 'It'll blow your mind'.

A *rhetorical question* is a question that is asked to create an effect or make a point rather than expecting an answer: 'Who could ask for more?'

Resources	*TrooFriend* by Kirsty Applebaum	Examples of brand logos, slogans or jingles. Poster adverts for products or services.

TASTER: STICKABILITY!

Give the children slogans to see if they can name the product or give them part of a slogan and see if they can finish it (there are some great quiz questions online as a resource). For example:

Because you're...

Vorsprung durch...

Loves the jobs...

Discuss with the children why these phrases stick. Is it the rhyme, length or wordplay? What makes it catchy? Is it easily memorable? Does it come as a jingle? Is it said by a cute animal like a meerkat?

Does it work? Ask the children to agree and place slogans on a sliding scale of one to ten for stickability effectiveness.

BUILDING TASK: LOGO SHOUT OUT!

Divide the room into groups or teams then show the children a variety of logos and see how many they can name. First to name wins a point. Logos could gradually appear a bit at a time. Discuss why businesses choose to have logos as part of their brand.

https://logosquiz.net/en/quizlogogame/united-kingdom

https://www.funkidslive.com/quiz/many-logos-can-get-right-logo-trivia-quiz-game/

BUILDING TASK: WHAT'S IN A NAME?

Ask the children to decide which name is better and ask them to think why the name was chosen.

For example:

Bugs Hare or Bugs Bunny?

Brian McDonald or Ronald McDonald?

Sesame Street or Sesame Boulevard?

Daisy Duck or Poppy Duck?

Show children some names of products and businesses that use wordplay as part of their branding. These examples have been found online. You may even be aware of some local businesses. For example:

Hairy Pop-ins (a dog sitting service)

Surelock Holmes (locksmiths – home security)

Lord of the Fries (fish and chip shop)

K9 Kutz (dog groomers)

MT Coffeepot (café)

Discuss the types of wordplay used such as puns, alliteration, abbreviations, rhymes, incorrect spellings and alphanumeric characters.

Give the children a number of pictures/photos/businesses and ask them to create a name for them. For example, what might they name their business if they were an electrician? What might they name their mascot for their football team?

Thinking about the book *TrooFriend* - if the class were creating their own AI classmate what might they be called?

MAIN TASK: SPOT THE TECHNIQUE?

1. As a class, look at a poster advert together. Can the children spot any of the techniques used in the taster or minitasks?

2. With a learning partner, look closely at the advert. What else do they notice? What do they like or dislike about the advert?

3. Gather the children's responses. They may have found rhetorical questions or looked at the use of colour and font. As a class, list and discuss some other useful devices and techniques that may have been used or that may be missing. List these as part of the success criteria.

Wordplay	Alliteration
	Pun
	Rhyme
	Alternate spelling
	Alphanumeric
Rhetorical question	
Logo/slogan	
Colour	
Font	
Superlatives	
Evaluative language	

4. Discuss the difference that colour might make to an advert. The class might consider the psychology behind colour or what might have 'stickability'.

5. Discuss the difference font type or size might make to an advert

Troofriend **TROOFRIEND** Troofriend *Troofriend*

Troofriend

6. Can the children spot any superlatives? If not, could they add any? Look for or add phrases such as most delicious, scrummiest, healthiest, best, friendliest, cheapest. Something that would suggest that this is the most it could be.

7. Look for evaluative adjectives in the class advert. If there are none, the teacher uses 'thinking out loud' to add one to the advert, e.g. 'The amazing nose-hair clippers!' 'The perfect potato peeler!'

8. Individually or with learning partners, children look at another example of an advert to spot and annotate the advert for the techniques used.

DIFFERENTIATION

✓ Children given familiar adverts to identify techniques.

✓ Reduce the number of techniques to identify or give them the techniques to match with the advert.

✓ Colour code and highlight techniques.

✓ Annotate and describe how the technique is effective.

✓ Improve the advert.

Teacher Tools and Techniques	
Emotional Literacy	Awareness of emotions in decision-making
Developing Relationships	Talking partners – agreement and compromise
Self-Development	Thinking out loud, use of language/ symbols to communicate, self-motivation
Skills for Learning	Grouping/sorting, decision-making, agreement, persuasion, annotation, colour coding
The Brain Learning and Behaviour	Use of emotive words that resonate and link to experiences and needs
	Targeting audience and purpose

PHSE LINK (PSHE ASSOCIATION PROGRAMME OF STUDY FOR PSHE EDUCATION – KS2)

Respecting the differences and similarities between people.

Understand that different groups make up their community; what living in a community means.

Identify some of the different ways information and data are shared and used online, including for commercial purposes

Recognise that people make spending decisions based on priorities, needs and wants, and what influences people's decisions.

Create a Persuasive Poster

Learning Objective: To design and create a persuasive poster to advertise a product	

Success Criteria:

◆ Include on your poster some or all of the following features (RAG highlight for differentiation)

◆ Catchy name of product

◆ Description of product

◆ Benefit to the buyer

◆ Slogans and wordplay

◆ Hyperbole

◆ Imperative and modal verbs

◆ Superlative or evaluative language

◆ Rhetorical questions

◆ Customer review or special offer

◆ Rule of three (may include repetition)

Pupils Can...	Use persuasive techniques and rhetorical devices, selecting appropriate grammar and vocabulary and understanding how such choices can change and enhance meaning.
	Use persuasive techniques and rhetorical devices with a particular purpose and target audience.
	Use simple persuasive and organisational devices.

Superlatives are used to describe an object which is at the upper or lower limit of a quality*:* *'The worst meal'; 'The biggest tower'; 'The smartest dog'.*

Evaluative adjectives are words that show a judgement on the noun it is describing. It could be a negative or a positive judgement and effect: *'The awesome product'; 'The dreadful meal'.*

Hyperbole is a figure of speech and is an exaggerated statement or claim not meant to be taken literally: *'It'll blow your mind'.*

A **rhetorical question** is a question that is asked to create an effect or make a point rather than expecting an answer: *'Who could ask for more?'*

Imperative verbs appear in **commands** – these are usually very short and direct. Imperative sentences look for the person to act, not to question the speaker: *'Tidy your room!' 'Buy this product'.*

Modal verbs are an auxiliary verb that expresses possibility or obligation. They include words like can, must, will, should, might, may and could. *'You should buy before they all go'. 'You must try this'. 'Every home should have one'.*

	*TrooFriend* by Kirsty Applebaum	Examples of poster adverts for products as templates or reference.

TASTER: REPEAT, REPEAT, REPEAT

Repetition is often used to emphasise an important point or to make what you are saying/selling more memorable. There are famous speeches for example that use repetition from Martin Luther King's 'I have a dream' speech to Greta Thunberg's 'How dare you' address to the UN. Advertising uses the same technique to emphasise a product's name or its quality. The more you repeat a tagline, a name or a quality, the more memorable it will become, e.g. *Touch the Rainbow – Taste the Rainbow. Maybe she's born with it, maybe it's Maybelline. You only get an oo with Typhoo.* However, some repetition of slogans may not necessarily be likeable. Some can be irritating… but memorable! Can the students think of adverts that repeat the product's name or slogan? Do they find them irritating or enjoyable?

What is their favourite or most annoying advert and why?

Look at the blurb on *TrooFriend* and the repetition used. I do not bully, I do not harm, etc. How is this effective?

BUILDING TASK: RULE OF THREE

The rule of three is a useful tool in persuasive writing as it can emphasise a point – strengthening your writing and making it more memorable. When advertising products, adjectives are often grouped in threes. Add alliteration and it's even more memorable! It doesn't just have to be adjectives; snappy straplines also work in that they use three words:

Beanz Meanz Heinz; Every Little Helps; Snap, Crackle, Pop; Just Do It; Reduce. Reuse. Recycle

Sweet, crisp and crunchy apples; soft, smooth, satin sheets; cute, cuddly and comforting koala bear.

Explore techniques in the straplines/list of adjectives such as the use of rhyme, onomatopoeia or alliteration.

Give the children an object such as a toy or a piece of fruit/veg. Can they come up with a Rule of Three to help sell the product – it could be three adjectives or a three-word strapline. Extend to giving bonus marks if they use alliteration, rhyme or onomatopoeia

BUILDING TASK: SHOULDA, COULDA, WOULDA

Imperative verbs are used in advertising to tell us what we should or need to do. They are usually positive exciting verbs that make us feel that we ought to do something. They often make the audience feel that they would be missing out if they did not do it. For example:

Explore new places. Create new adventures. Buy before they are all gone. Enjoy time with friends. Relax and recuperate. Play fun activities.

Imperative verbs begin a short instructive or command sentence. Can the students think of a sentence beginning with an imperative verb that would persuade someone to

◆ join their class?

◆ go to a theme park?

◆ join a club?

◆ buy a new brand of trainers?

◆ read their favourite book?

◆ visit a particular holiday destination?

Can the students make their sentence feel like the audience is missing out if they don't do it?

MAIN TASK: SELL, SELL, SELL

1. As a class, think about the book *TrooFriend*. Look at Chapter One and the description and advertising details for 'The Jenson and Jenson TrooFriend 560 Mark IV'. Which techniques can students identify?

2. Discuss with a partner their own Troofriend – it may be a pet or it could be TrooFriend 560 Mark V. Think about the qualities needed. What might attract the audience and persuade them to buy? Share with another pair, group or as a class. Students can design, draw and label the features of their new product.

3. Discuss essential elements for Success Criteria as a class. Students can design an advertising poster for their Troofriend.

4. Peer review – post-it evaluations. Display posters – students write positive notes and 'even better if' notes onto sticky notes to place on posters as feedback.

5. Think, pair, share – which techniques are key? Can the students use a Diamond 9 to prioritise effective techniques (use success criteria)? Most effective technique

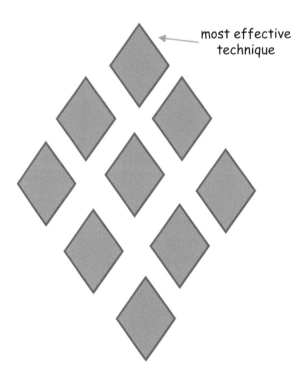

most effective technique

DIFFERENTIATION

✓ Consider RAG rating criteria
(Highlight – Red: must include. Yellow: should include. Green: could include.)

✓ Provide examples of effective adverts.

✓ Provide examples of adventurous adjectives to use.

✓ Annotate and describe how the technique is effective.

✓ Students could create a jingle to accompany their product.

✓ Students could plan a TV advert for their product using a comic strip template.

Teacher Tools and Techniques	
Emotional Literacy	Awareness of emotions in decision-making
Developing Relationships	Talking partners; think, pair, share; constructive feedback – agreement and compromise
Self-Development	Thinking out loud, use of language/symbols to communicate, self-motivation
Skills for Learning	Grouping/sorting, decision-making, agreement, persuasion, annotation, colour coding
The Brain Learning and Behaviour	Use of emotive words that resonate and link to experiences and needs Targeting audience and purpose

PHSE LINK (PSHE ASSOCIATION PROGRAMME OF STUDY FOR PSHE EDUCATION – KS2)

Respecting the differences and similarities between people.

Understand that different groups make up their community; what living in a community means.

Identify some of the different ways information and data are shared and used online, including for commercial purposes.

Recognise that people make spending decisions based on priorities, needs and wants, and what influences people's decisions – what makes something 'good' value.

Social Skills Support the Building of Positive Relationships

Learning Objective: To be able to define social skills and give examples
Success Criteria:
◆ Listen to another person giving their whole attention

Pupils Can...	Identify why social skills are important to building positive relationships.
	Listen to another person giving his or her whole attention and explain how this makes the person feel.
	Demonstrate the use of a variety of social skills in their interactions with others.

Social skills are the skills/competencies we use to communicate and interact with each other. They include both verbal skills such as language and use of words and non-verbal skills such as gestures, body language and our personal appearance, written skills and visual skills. Human beings need relationships with others and are thus sociable creatures. They have developed many ways to communicate their messages, thoughts and feelings with others. Developing social skills in children enables them to create healthier interactions in all aspects of life. Displaying respect, communicating effectively with others, being considerate of the feelings of others and expressing personal needs are all important components of solid social skills.

Resources	*TrooFriend* by Kirsty Applebaum Social Skills 6 category cards Social Skills cards iPad	Large sheets of card or sugar paper Plain paper Pens, pencils and felt tip pens Glue sticks Scissors

TASTER: LISTEN UP!

Introduce the children to the term Social Skills – ask them to work in pairs to come up with a definition. Share the definitions. Create a class one using their ideas and phrases.

Explain that one of the groups of social skills is Communication and that one of the most important skills within that group is active listening. Explain that you are going to play a game that involves them actively listening.

Telephone: A classic children's game that provides children with the opportunity to listen closely, reflect and repeat back what they think they heard.

Ask the children to sit in a circle. Explain that you are going to whisper a sentence into the ear of the person on your right who will then pass whisper the message into the ear of the person on their right and so on. The last person will say aloud the message that they have received. A good phrase to use is **'I want to know what it feels like to listen and what it feels like to be heard'.**

Simon Says: This classic game from childhood allows children to practice active listening skills by paying close attention to directions given by the lead person. If the lead person says 'Simon says put your hand up' the children follow the instruction. If the lead person just gives the direction 'Put your hand up', the children should ignore it. Those children who get this wrong are out of the game.

Popcorn Storytelling: In popcorn storytelling, the children sit or stand in a circle. Each 'player' takes a turn adding on to the story that the group is building together. The first person can start with 'Once upon a time there lived a great big hairy dog…' and the next person has to use their active listening skills to incorporate what they just heard in order to add to the story.

20 Questions: In 20 Questions, the person who is 'it' thinks of an object. The other players then have to guess what the object is. The catch is that they can only ask 20 yes or no questions to figure out the clue! This is a great game to get children to think about the information they have heard. When it is their turn, they have to put it all together and then ask a question that will give them more information until someone correctly guesses the object.

MINI TASK: SKILLS IDENTIFICATION.

Ask the children to work in groups (four to six). Give them the six category cards that make up Social Skills: Communication, Respecting yourself and others, Friendship, Participation, Resolving conflict and Collaboration.

Ask them to put the social skills cards that fit into each category with the correct group, e.g. *Communication would have the social skills cards body language, facial expressions, conversational skills, active listening, the language we use and thinking before we speak.*

Ask each person in the group to choose one skill they believe they are good at.

Ask each of the group members to write down the names of all the people in their group and then write one skill that they feel each person is strong in. Then ask each person from the group to share one skill they feel they would like to work on. Share what people have chosen and create a chart to show what they are each working on.

MAIN TASK: ROLE-PLAY

1. Divide the children into six groups and give each group one of the six categories: Communication, Respecting yourself and others, Friendship, Participation, Resolving conflict and Collaboration.

2. Ask each group to come up with a short role-play to demonstrate as many of the skills in this category as possible. They will then perform this for the other groups who will then try to spot the skills.

3. Once each group has had time to both create and then share their role-play, ask them to come up with a poster to show all the skills in their category. One way to do this effectively is to ask each person in the group to draw and write a short description of one skill. Collectively, they can then arrange the pictures and writing on a large sheet of card to come up with their poster.

4. After the work on social skills has been completed, start to notice the efforts and skills children are using and make this a focus of the class – 'Catch the social skills in action' and note them down – celebrating at the end of the week. You might like to introduce certificates for the person who manages to try out the most social skills each week.

DIFFERENTIATION

✓ Ask for volunteers in each group to act as a scribe so that only children who feel confident recording on paper are asked to do this. This will enable all children to take part in the various activities.

✓ If children feel uncomfortable performing, ask them to film or take pictures of the group working/highlighting each of the skills they are focusing on.

✓ Make sure that you are able to notice all children trying out their social skills.

Teacher Tools and Techniques	
Emotional Literacy	Role-paly scenarios
Developing Relationships	Collaboration in groups
Self-Development	Reflection on their own social skills
Skills for Learning	Goal setting
The Brain Learning and Behaviour	The importance of active listening in building relationships

PHSE LINK (PSHE ASSOCIATION PROGRAMME OF STUDY FOR PSHE EDUCATION – KS2)

About how people make friends and what makes a good friendship.

About the importance of friendships; strategies for building positive friendships; how positive friendships support wellbeing.

What constitutes a positive healthy friendship (e.g. mutual respect, trust, truthfulness, loyalty, kindness, generosity, sharing interests and experiences, support with problems and difficulties); that the same principles apply to online friendships as face-to-face relationships.

Communication

Respecting Yourself and Others

Friendship

Participation

Resolving Conflict

Collaboration

Relationships

Team Building and Collaboration
Respect
Encouragement
Accepting the ideas and opinions of others
Flexibility
Problem-solving
Constructive feedback
Supporting others

Resolving Conflict
Active listening
Being open to new ideas
Understanding points of view
Compromise
Problem-solving
Recounting
Persistence

Participation
Taking part and having a go
Including everyone
Working together
Building your confidence
Resilience
Focusing and concentration

Friendship
Being able to welcome the ideas of others
Being kind
Being thoughtful
Acknowledging when you have made a mistake
Positive feedback
Respecting confidences
Co-operation
Interactions

Respecting Yourself and Others
Co-operation
Sharing and taking turns
No bullying
No putdowns
Celebrate difference
Treating people equally
Being assertive
Empathy

Communication
Active listening
Body language
Facial expressions
The language we use
Thinking before you speak
Conversational skills

Active listening
Body language
Facial expressions
The language we use
Thinking before we speak
Conversational skills
Co-operation
Sharing and taking turns
No bullying
No putdowns
Celebrate difference
Treating people equally
Being assertive
Empathy
Interactions
Co-operation

Respecting confidences
Positive feedback
Acknowledging when you make a mistake
Being kind
Being thoughtful
Welcome new ideas
Taking part
Having a go
Working together
Resilience
Focusing and concentration
Active listening
Being open to new ideas

Understanding points of view
Compromise
Problem-solving
Recounting
Persistence
Respect for others
Encouragement
Accepting the opinions and ideas of others
Flexibility
Supporting others
Constructive feedback
Problem-solving
Thinking outside the box

Primary Assembly:

Who is the Assembly for?
Children in KS1 and KS2.

What is the Focus?
The power of words.

Objectives
Words are powerful, and we can choose to use them for good or to cause harm.

Key Message
Words are very powerful and we are in charge of the words we use.

Involvement of Children
Words that change how we feel.

High, medium and low value words.

Words to give their best friend.

Resources
A selection of words written on individual pieces of paper.

A dictionary.

Famous people and quotes that they said.

Phileas's Fortune by Agnes de Lestrade.

Introduction
Explain to the children that by saying a couple of words you can change how they feel. Ask them to show how they are feeling at the moment with their thumbs. Use the phrase No Playtime and ask them to show you now.

Use the phrase *Extra Homework* and then *Longer Playtime*.

Walk up to one of the members of staff and compliment them on what they are wearing. Then walk up to another member of staff and say something unkind about what they are wearing.

Explain that your words can affect how people feel.

Main Event
Read the story *Phileas's Fortune* and then hand out the pieces of paper with the words on. Ask children to share some of the words they have and then to say if they are a high value, medium value or low value word.

Ask children for words in each category and see what they come up with. What might be the most valuable word?

Finale
Ask children to choose a word that they would like to give to their best friend.

Ask the children to think about how they could kindly remind people if they heard them use words that might harm.

Collect different phrases and ways of kindly helping people think about their words.

Chapter 2

Emotional Literacy
KS2

KS2 BOOKS

It's All about Bodd by Linda Wheeler and Tom Lawley

What Do You Do with a Problem? by Kobi Yamada and Mae Besom

The Worry Tree by Marianne Musgrove

ASSEMBLY

The Invisible by Tom Percival

DOI: 10.4324/9781003322801-3

Descriptive Poem

Learning Objective: To describe emotions using figurative language	

Success Criteria:

◆ Choose an emotion

◆ Use the five senses to help describe the emotion

◆ Compare with another object using a simile, metaphor and/or personification

◆ Use a range of precise descriptive adverbs and adjectives

◆ Use a colour/symbol to represent your emotion

Pupils Can...	Make comparisons through precise, expressive vocabulary choices and figurative language.
	Make comparisons using similes, metaphors and personification, and using verbs and adverbs for effect.
	Make comparisons using similes and metaphors.

Figurative language is the use of words, phrases and ideas that go beyond the literal understanding to suggest a meaning and help the reader create a mental image. Figurative language uses devices such as similes, metaphors, personification, onomatopoeia and hyperbole.

Similes are phrases that compare one thing to another thing of a different kind. It helps the reader understand the characteristics or qualities of the object/character/feeling they are describing. Similes can involve comparative words – 'like' and 'as', for example, 'The puppy had eyes like chocolate buttons' and 'He was as quiet as snowfall at night'.

A *metaphor* is a word or phrase that compares one thing to another thing of a different kind. It helps the reader understand the characteristics or qualities of the object/character/feeling they are describing. It can be directly compared using 'is', for example, 'The moon is a shiny marble against a sea of black night sky'.

Personification is when something non-human is given a human quality, ability or emotion. It is a type of comparison and helps the reader understand a description by giving it recognisable behaviours and feelings, for example, 'The daffodils danced and turned their happy faces towards the sun'.

Inference is using facts and logical reasoning to draw a conclusion or opinion, for example, 'The dog ran in circles wagging his tail' – we can infer that the dog is happy or excited.

 **Resources**	*It's All about Bodd* by Lindy Wheeler and Tom Lawley	Objects or pictures of objects (e.g. fruit and veg)
		Mirrors
		Vocabulary mats/thesaurus
	Examples of emoticons	Feeling poem to up-level

TASTER: EMOTICON MATCH

Show the children examples of favourite emoticons/emojis. Can the students name the feelings that these represent? How do they know? What can they infer?

 Worried, concerned, fearful, anxious, unsure, perturbed, bothered, troubled.

Students could write as many synonyms as possible for a particular emotion and then order them according to the strength of feeling.

BUILDING TASK: PULL A FACE!

Choose a feeling that the students have not used. You can choose more adventurous words such as *relieved, lethargic, enthused* or *discombobulated.*

Model a feeling and design an emoticon as a class. Ask students to think about times that they may have felt this emotion and to 'make the face'. Give them mirrors or work with a partner to help them see how their face changes or their body feels.

Students can be given a selection of emotions to design a brand-new emoticon.

BUILDING TASK: WHAT IS IT?

Read the book with the class. How does Bodd describe his emotions?

Feelings sit in his stomach

Problems are insurmountably tall

Anger grows

Anger creeps up the dark stairs at the back of his mind

Anger is an enormous volcanic eruption of rage

His spark has gone out

His feelings take a dive

He is in a cold, dark tower

Discuss with the class the use of figurative language. The writer has compared the emotions to other things and even to a person! Can they identify where metaphor and personification have been used? What does it mean that he is 'in a cold, dark tower'? Is he really in a tower or does the writer want us to think about what that might feel like? Is it effective?

MAIN TASK: WHAT IS IT LIKE?

1. As a class, discuss how and when we describe something as we use our senses. What it feels, smells, tastes, looks and sounds like. Explain that using comparisons helps the reader to create a mental image of what you are describing.

2. Give the students objects to describe without using its name. For example, a piece of fruit. Can they describe it using their senses but not actually use its name? Ask the children to share their descriptions with each other. Can they improve their description with more adventurous and precise vocabulary? For example, rather than green, is it emerald? Rather than bumpy, is it gnarled or pitted?

3. Remind the children about Bodd and how he described his emotions. He used comparisons. He likened his anger to an erupting volcano. With the class, choose an emotion to model using comparisons. Use the senses to help describe. Children can work in partners to think of a comparison for each sense one at a time and share. A class poem can build up gradually. Start with simple comparisons and up-level (modelling thinking aloud techniques) with precise adjectives and adverbs, with some personification.
Anger is (look) an erupting violent volcano *spilling its guts across the ground*
Anger is (sound) seagulls screeching *incessantly making my ears bleed*
Anger is (smell) *acrid* burning rubber
Anger is (touch) sharp, spiky hawthorns *creating an impenetrable barrier*
Anger is (taste) chilli sauce *attacking your throat*
Anger is (colour) *blood*-red

4. Children can perform their poems leaving out the emotion – can the rest of the class identify the emotion being described?
The pleading, chocolate-brown eyes of an abandoned puppy
The slow, low tone of a violin echoing around the empty room
Damp earth and musty clothes
Rough, torn, ragged cotton shielding a skeletal form
Sour lemon drops biting at your cheeks
Lead grey

DIFFERENTIATION

✓ Give children a thesaurus or vocabulary mat.

✓ Reduce the number of techniques to include.

✓ Give children a completed poem to improve and up-level.

✓ Students choose from a range of feelings, some of which are more challenging than others.

✓ Students complete the comparisons pictorially as a mind map.

✓ Children can perform and record their poems.

Teacher Tools and Techniques	
Emotional Literacy	Recognition and awareness of emotions
	Exploring and explaining emotions
Developing Relationships	Talking partners – agreement and compromise
Self-Development	Thinking out loud, use of language/symbols to communicate, self-motivation, recognising motivators and triggers
Skills for Learning	Thinking out loud, decision-making, agreement, collaboration
The Brain Learning and Behaviour	Use of emotive words that resonate and link to experiences and needs
	Human tools to self-soothe and train your brain and body to relax

PHSE LINK (PSHE ASSOCIATION PROGRAMME OF STUDY FOR PSHE EDUCATION – KS2)

Strategies and behaviours that support mental health – good quality sleep, physical exercise/time outdoors, being involved in community groups, doing things for others, clubs and activities, hobbies and spending time with family and friends can support mental health and wellbeing.

Recognise that feelings can change over time and range in intensity.

Everyday things that affect feelings and the importance of expressing feelings.

A varied vocabulary to use when talking about feelings and how to express feelings in different ways.

Descriptive Narrative

Learning Objective: To use showing not telling in our descriptive writing

Success Criteria:

◆ Consider how the subject/character moves, acts, speaks

◆ Consider body language

◆ Use verbs and adverbs for effect (shouted/muttered – dawdled/marched – angrily/ hesitantly)

◆ Use relative clauses to add further information

◆ Use precise vocabulary

◆ Use figurative language

Pupils Can...	Make comparisons through precise, expressive vocabulary choices and figurative language.
	Make comparisons using similes, metaphors and personification, and using verbs and adverbs for effect.
	Make comparisons using similes and metaphors.

Figurative language is the use of words, phrases and ideas that go beyond the literal understanding to suggest a meaning and help the reader create a mental image. Figurative language uses devices such as similes, metaphors, personification, onomatopoeia and hyperbole.

Similes are phrases that compare one thing to another thing of a different kind. It helps the reader understand the characteristics or qualities of the object/character/feeling they are describing. Similes can involve comparative words – 'like' and 'as', for example, 'The puppy had eyes like chocolate buttons' and 'He was as quiet as snowfall at night'.

A *metaphor* is a word or phrase that compares one thing to another thing of a different kind. It helps the reader understand the characteristics or qualities of the object/character/feeling they are describing. It can be directly compared using 'is', for example, 'The moon is a shiny marble against a sea of black night sky'.

Personification is when something non-human is given a human quality, ability or emotion. It is a type of comparison and helps the reader understand a description by giving it recognisable behaviours and feelings, for example, 'The daffodils danced and turned their happy faces towards the sun'.

Inference is using facts and logical reasoning to draw a conclusion or opinion, for example, 'The dog ran in circles wagging his tail' – we can infer that the dog is happy or excited.

	It's All about Bodd by Lindy Wheeler and Tom Lawley	Pictures/photos of food/meals to be described Pictures/photos of settings or characters to be described

TASTER: NOT JUST ANY BURGER...

Show the students a picture of a delicious meal such as a burger meal, a pizza, an elaborate cake, unusual fruit or something similar. Can the students describe what they see? It can be delicious or disgusting!

Model an example with the class on how to improve their sentences

The huge burger looked delicious. This sentence tells us rather than shows us.

Burger patties, enveloped by sesame toasted buns, dripping in luscious sauce and bedded on crisp, green salad, sat temptingly. It was willing me to pick it up and sink my teeth into the juicy tower of delight. My mouth salivated and my eyes widened as I hungrily looked at the meal in anticipation.

BUILDING TASK: HOW DO YOU KNOW?

Explain to the students that writers often use the 'Show don't Tell' technique to help the reader build a better mental picture. The reader must use inference to conclude how a subject is feeling or what a setting is like. Demonstrate to the children how they use inference from body language and facial expressions every day. For example, go out of the classroom and re-enter by marching in and slamming books on the table. What can the children infer about your mood? Repeat but this time come in slumped, head down and mumble a 'Good Morning'. What can they infer about your mood now? Role-play body language stances. Ask the class to pose and use a facial expression for the following:

◆ *Just fallen over and severely injured your knee*

◆ *In a busy shopping centre and you are lost and confused*

◆ *Your puppy is missing*

◆ *You're in a spooky house at night and you hear noises*

In groups, have one member hold a pose and the rest of the group describe what they notice about body language and facial expression.

BUILDING TASK: WHAT DO YOU INFER?

This activity could be through pictures, photos, book illustrations or written descriptions. For pictures, you could choose images for surprise, shock, grief, feeling tired, fear, love, delight.

◆ *With fists clenched and gritted teeth, he stormed into the room searching for his foe.*

◆ *His eyes squinted slightly beneath his furrowed brow; his head tilted to one side as he tried to understand what was happening.*

◆ *'Not now!' she yelled as she turned sharply, pushed me aside and ran out of the room.*

◆ *Her eyes were tingling and a lump rose in her throat. She bit her lip and turned her head away from her teacher.*

◆ *He slumped into the room, plonked himself down in the chair and folded his arms defiantly.*

◆ *As he sniffed the air, his nose wrinkled and his lip curled. 'What was that stench?'*

◆ *Bright white light flashed across the dark sky like a knife slashing a tear through a curtain of silk.*

◆ *The timid, trembling dog slouched under the table with his ears flattened and his eyes lowered.*

MAIN TASK: WHAT IS IT LIKE?

1. As a class, look at a picture that allows for a subject's character to be explored. Alternatively. You could look at a setting to describe. Use an internet search for emotive scenes.

2. Choose one picture to work on as a class. What can you infer from the picture? Is it a beautiful setting with a relaxed atmosphere? Is it a delighted hamster enjoying life and celebrating the beauty of nature and being alive? Work on describing the picture as a class using the success criteria. Model thinking aloud when up-levelling. 'This reminds me of… I could add a simile or metaphor in here'.

3. Students can identify one of the sentences of which they are most proud to share with a learning partner. They then choose one sentence that they believe needs further development and can improve together.

DIFFERENTIATION

- ✓ Give children a thesaurus or vocabulary mat.

- ✓ Reduce the number of techniques to include.

✓ Students start with a mind map to help plan their writing.

- – Describe the body language:

- – Describe the facial expressions.

- – What are they saying to each other/ how are they saying it?

- – How are they moving?

- – What sounds, smells and tastes are there?

✓ Give students a picture with a planned structure. For example:
The hamster *verb, adverb* in the middle of the *adjective, adjective* wildflower.

Teacher Tools and Techniques	
Emotional Literacy	Recognition and awareness of emotions
	Understanding how facial expressions, tone of voice and body language give clues to how others are feeling or coping.
Developing Relationships	Talking partner's constructive criticism
	Agreement and compromise, modelling
Self-Development	Thinking out loud, use of language/ symbols to communicate, self-motivation, recognising motivators and triggers
Skills for Learning	Thinking out loud, decision-making, agreement, collaboration
	role-play. modelling
The Brain Learning and Behaviour	Use of emotive words that resonate and link to experiences and needs
	Modelling – auditory and kinaesthetic learning

PHSE LINK (PSHE ASSOCIATION PROGRAMME OF STUDY FOR PSHE EDUCATION – KS2)

Recognise that feelings can change over time and range in intensity.

Everyday things that affect feelings and the importance of expressing feelings.

A varied vocabulary to use when talking about feelings and how to express feelings in different ways.

Personal behaviour can affect other people.

Respect the differences and similarities between people and recognise what they have in common with others, for example, physically, in personality or in background.

Dealing with Feelings

Learning Objective: To further develop emotional literacy
Success Criteria: ◆ Describe a range of emotions   ◆ Understand how to manage these emotions using the Human Toolkit

Pupils Can...	Use a range of emotional words to describe how someone might feel.
	Describe how an emotion may cause us to behave and why.
	Show a clear understanding of emotions and the way they can affect our thinking and behaviours as well as how to use a range of tools to support ourselves.

*The term **Emotional Literacy** has developed over the past 60 or so years and has been a gradual evolution. To more fully understand the term emotional literacy, it is useful to understand how this development has happened.*

In the 1930s, Edward Thorndike, an American psychologist, first described the concept of 'social intelligence'. He stated that this was the ability to get along with other people. This was the first time that this concept of social interaction started to be defined and thought of as important. This was followed by David Wechsler, another psychologist, who, in the 1940s, emphasised that factors other than intellectual ability were influential in intelligent behaviour and were essential to a successful life. His philosophy stated that intelligence was 'the global capacity to act purposefully, to think rationally, and to deal effectively with [one's] environment'.

In the 1950s, a humanistic psychologist called Abraham Maslow described how people can build emotional strength and develop their ability to effectively handle and control emotions.

This strand of knowledge was not expanded further until the 1970s when Howard Gardner, a Harvard developmental psychologist, published a book called Frames of Mind. *Within his book, he argued that intelligence should have a much boarder definition. He proposed a theory of multiple intelligences. He proposed that the new intelligences of interpersonal (the ability to understand people) and intrapersonal (involves access to own feelings and the ability to use these to operate efficiently) should be added to the linguistic and mathematical ones that were prominent at the time. By identifying human abilities such as emotions, self-awareness, empathy and social skills, and by putting them next to the traditional intelligences of literature and numeracy, Gardner made it possible for teachers to incorporate them into their teaching. From this emerged the theory that people may be emotionally intelligent*

Later in 1985, Wayne Payne introduced the term emotional intelligence in his doctoral dissertation entitled 'A study of emotion: developing emotional intelligence; self-integration; relating to fear, pain and desire'. This was then followed by an article published in Mensa Magazine by Keith Beasley in 1987. Mr Beasley used the term 'emotional quotient' for the first time.

In 1990, psychologists Peter Salovey and John Mayer publish their landmark article, 'Emotional Intelligence', and then in 1995, the concept of emotional intelligence was popularised by Daniel Goleman's book Emotional Intelligence: Why It Can Matter More Than IQ.

Within the UK, emotional intelligence has taken its place alongside other terms, notably that of emotional literacy. For some, the word literacy is preferred over intelligence as it states the ability to be articulate about feelings and the intention to empower young people and not just teach them. When the terms are explored, they appear very similar. This can be seen by comparison of Goleman's definition of emotional intelligence and with Katherine Wear's definition of emotional literacy in her book Developing the Emotionally Literate School *(2004), where she describes emotional literacy as:*

The ability to understand ourselves and other people, and in particular to be aware of, understand and use information about emotional states of ourselves and others with competence. It includes the ability to understand, express and manage our own emotions and respond to the emotions of others in ways that are helpful to ourselves and others.

(Weare 2004, p. 2)

	*It's All about Bodd* by Lindy Wheeler and Tom Lawley	Emotions for Call My Bluff words
	The Book of Human Emotions by Tiffany Watt Smith	Comic strip template
		Emotion action sheet

TASTER: CALL MY BLUFF!

Working in pairs, ask the children to write down or show with emojis as many feelings as they can.

Share what the class has identified.

Share some of the more unusual ones and ask children to draw an emoji and write a definition so that you can create a display around the classroom.

Play Call my Bluff as a class using emotions that the children may not know.

BUILDING TASK: EMOTIONS ZOO

Ask the children to choose an emotion and draw a picture of what they believe it might be like. Demonstrate this with the emotion Love. Help the children think of a colour and shape that the word love evokes in them and describe it. Draw how it might look.

Once the children have drawn their emotion, ask them to write a brief description about it as if it was a label in an Emotions Zoo. For example:

Love is one of the bigger emotions that we can find in the zoo. It is bright red with pink and gold sparkles. Love is very powerful and uses its sparkles to light up the world in which the human lives. It is often full of energy and enjoys playing with people. Love lives inside the human heart and makes the heart pound and gives the human a fluttering feeling in their tummy. When Love is around, the human feels like everything is good and that they are safe. When Love disappears, humans notice how horrible it is without the light that Love shines on them and they often feel lonely.

Share with the children the comic strip template and ask them to draw a story about their emotion. Ask them to show how the emotion arrives, the effect it has on the human and the different ways it might make the human behave.

MAIN TASK: EMOTION IDENTIFICATION

◆ Ask the children to work in pairs. Ask them to choose an emotion. You might write different emotions on paper and hand them out for the children to open or for the children to choose.

◆ Ask the children to complete the Emotions Action Sheet. Explain that when emotions arrive, they make us feel a feeling and then they cause us to do something - an action. Each emotion can cause a range of actions depending on the person who experiences them. For example:

Emotion: Thirsty. Feelings: dry throat, tongue sticking to teeth, mouth dry. Some emotions then cause others to arrive – thirsty might make a human feel cross and hot or irritated. Behaviours: Useful behaviour – go and get a drink OR ask for a drink OR have some fruit. If we ignore emotions, then we can behave in an unhelpful way. We might get cross with people and upset people because we can't get a drink or don't have one.

◆ Read the book to the children again. As a group collect the Human Tools and write them on the board.

- Belly breathing.

- Stretch yawn and shake.

- Talk about feelings.

- Write about how you feel or draw a picture.

- Have a good cry or have a good laugh.

- Be grateful and be kind.

- Exercise.

- Time out.

- Think about the actions you could take, mindfulness.

- Take a walk in nature.

- Get a hug or give a hug.

◆ Divide the class up into groups to help create the Great Class Human Toolkit. Give each group one of the tools and ask them to:

- Draw a picture.

- Write instructions about how to do this.

- Design a symbol to represent the tool.

- Create a cartoon picture or a story to show the strategy/tool in action.

- Create a label for the board where you will display the toolkit.

- Create a short sketch to show the tool in action.

- Share personal extracts of what happened when the children tried this tool.

DIFFERENTIATION

- ✓ Ask children to create an emotional words and emoji matching game.

- ✓ Support children by creating groups where they can work or be supported by others.

✓ Ensure that children who need support in starting or understanding an activity have a Learning Buddy to help them get going and answer any questions.

✓ Use the Emotions Action Sheet provided for those children who need extra support. This can then be completed by them with a partner or in a small, supported group.

Teacher Tools and Techniques	
Emotional Literacy	Developing vocabulary
Developing Relationships	Working in pairs, small groups or with a Learning Buddy
Self-Development	Understanding how emotions can make them feel and then behave
Skills for Learning	Planning and organisation of thinking and then tasks
The Brain Learning and Behaviour	Understanding that worries are part of the brain's way of keeping us safe and that we can learn a range of ways to help us manage

PHSE LINK (PSHE ASSOCIATION PROGRAMME OF STUDY FOR PSHE EDUCATION – KS2)

Recognise that feelings can change over time and range in intensity.

Everyday things that affect feelings and the importance of expressing feelings.

A varied vocabulary to use when talking about feelings and how to express feelings in different ways.

Personal behaviour can affect other people.

Respect the differences and similarities between people and recognise what they have in common with others, e.g. physically, in personality or in background.

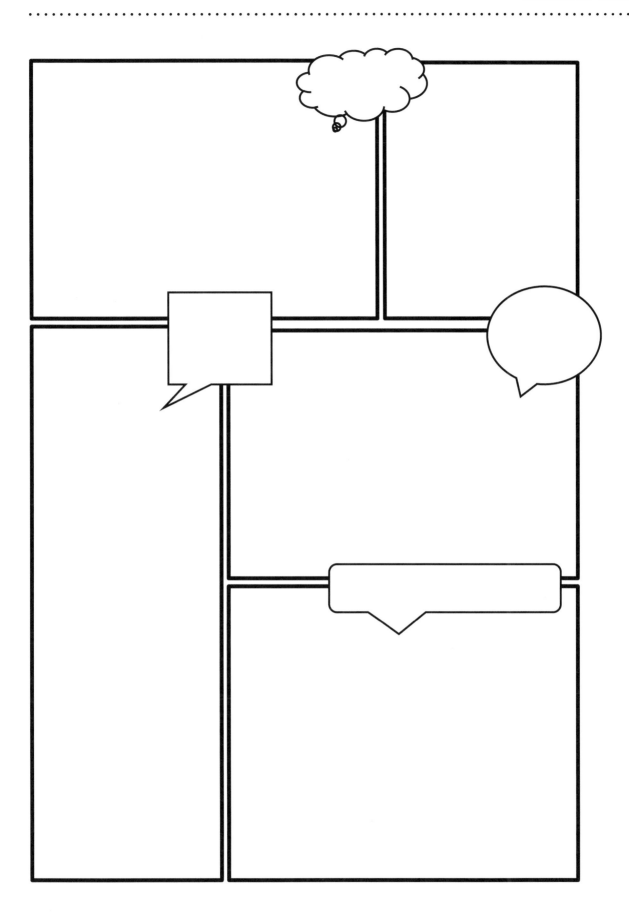

Emotions Action Sheet

Emotions Picture

Feelings emotion created

Which is the best option and why?

Option 1

Option 2

Option 3

Description of Emotion

Responding to a Dilemma

Learning Objective: To respond constructively to a problem/dilemma
Success Criteria: ◆ Give advice/point of view   ◆ Use of causal conjunctions, e.g. so, because, when, if, that, while, but…   ◆ Second person   ◆ Adverbial phrases – time, place, manner and reason   ◆ Informal language and style   ◆ Sympathetic tone

Pupils Can…	Present a reasoned view and explore more than one possible outcome or view on an issue. Use causal conjunctions, and adverbs for degrees of possibility – perhaps, surely, clearly.
	Explore the expression of different views through discussion, role-play and drama. Choose a balanced and objective viewpoint and use conjunctions, causal conjunction and adverbials.
	Explore how different views might be expressed/explained/justified.

Causal Conjunctions *are words and phrases that are used to introduce a cause, reason or explanation for a given action within a sentence. They are connecting words that explain the outcome of an action or an event, for instance, 'because', 'due to', 'as a result of' and 'if' are all causal conjunctions that link an action to its supposed cause.*

Informal language *is used when writing in a friendly and relaxed way. It is conversational and chatty in style and often uses abbreviations, contractions and slang.*

Sympathetic tone *is an expression of pity or sorrow for someone else's misfortune. A show of understanding and support between people. 'I understand it must be difficult…' 'It must feel like…' 'I know you must be…' 'Let's take this one step at a time'.*

 Resources	*What Do You Do with a Problem?* by Kobi Yamada and Mae Besom	Collection of 'Would you rather…?' questions Example of an Agony Aunt letter

TASTER: WOULD YOU RATHER?

Play a quick question-and-answer game. Students are offered two options. They need to choose between A or B very quickly. They can hold up whiteboards or move to one side of the classroom.

Would you rather:

Eat six Brussel sprouts or six spicy chilli chicken wings? Hold a stick insect or a rat? Feed an alligator or feed a pigeon? Time travel to the future or to the past? Have the super-power of invisibility or be able to fly? Be a famous singer or a famous inventor? Be a bird or a fish?

Aim to have questions that raises debate on the consequences of their choice, e.g. Upset your friend or upset your mum?

BUILDING TASK: FORTUNATELY, UNFORTUNATELY

Model with the class the game of Fortunately, Unfortunately. Start with the teacher being the negative thinker and the class as the positive thinker. For example:

This morning I was late for school.

Fortunately, the teacher was late too so did not see me.

Unfortunately, the secretary knew I was late.

Fortunately, the secretary had lots of jobs to do and forget to tell the teacher.

Unfortunately, one of my friends asked me why I was late in front of my teacher.

Fortunately…

With a partner play the game starting with 'This morning, I lost my wallet', 'This morning, I found hidden treasure in my garden' or something similar.

BUILDING TASK: WHAT WOULD YOU DO?

In the story, 'What do you do with a problem?' we do not find out what the actual problem is. What might the problem be? What might his options be?

As a class, look at a couple of problems – what choices could they make?

You see a friend steal something. Do you...

A: Speak to them and tell them why it is wrong and to give it back?

B: Tell a trusted adult?

C: Join them and share what they have taken?

D: Pretend you did not see it?

You are being bullied. Do you...

A: Tell a friend but ask them not to say anything?

B: Tell an adult?

C: Keep it to yourself?

D: Face your bully and fight back?

As a group, discuss the consequences of each action. Share responses as a class. Is there any other possible action they could take?

MAIN TASK: AGONY AUNT

1. Ask the class if they know what an agony aunt is. Share an example and explain that an agony aunt is a person, usually a woman, who gives advice to people with personal problems. The letters are usually published in magazines or newspapers. However, the agony aunt may also be on the radio or TV.

2. Decide whether you wish the class to respond to a particular problem/dilemma in a written form or orally – such as a 'phone-in' or 'live TV'.

3. Students choose a problem/dilemma and, with a learning partner, think about possible actions that could be taken. Students decide whether to advise a particular course of action or to give a couple of options. However, their advice must be reasoned and mention

possible consequences and resolutions. They may advise against a certain action but must also explain why they advise against it.

Some examples include

- You are arguing a lot with your sibling

- You know that your friend has been stealing

- You see someone destroying a friend's piece of work

- You cheated on a spelling test and feel guilty

- You told your parent an untruth

4. Children can role-play a phone-in or live TV episode. It may include a question-and-answer session.

DIFFERENTIATION

✓ Give students sentence starters for their reply:

- *I understand that you must be feeling…*

- *I suggest you…*

- *If you do this, you…*

- *After you should feel…*

- *Good luck with…*

✓ Give one piece of advice.

✓ Give options and justify reasoning.

✓ Give students an agony aunt response and ask them to identify strengths and improvements.

✓ Students can perform and record their role-play.

Teacher Tools and Techniques	
Emotional Literacy	Recognition and awareness of emotions
	Exploring and explaining emotions
	Understanding actions will have consequences – positive and negative
Developing Relationships	Talking partners – agreement and compromise
	Sympathy and empathy
Self-Development	Thinking out loud, considering options, self-motivation, recognising motivators and triggers
Skills for Learning	Thinking out loud, decision-making, agreement, collaboration, problem-solving
The Brain Learning and Behaviour	Intrinsic and extrinsic rewards

PHSE LINK (PSHE ASSOCIATION PROGRAMME OF STUDY FOR PSHE EDUCATION – KS2)

Everyday things affect feelings and the importance of expressing feelings.

Increasing independence may bring new opportunities and responsibilities.

There are reasons for following and complying with regulations and restrictions.

The importance of seeking support and how to seek help or advice.

Strategies to respond to hurtful behaviour - experienced or witnessed.

Personal behaviour can affect other people.

Discuss and debate topical issues, respect other people's points of view and constructively challenge those they disagree with.

Would you rather…	
Eat six Brussel sprouts or six spicy chilli chicken wings?	Be a bird or a fish?
Save the bees or save the whales?	Be a famous singer or a famous inventor?
Hold a stick insect or a rat?	Tell a fib or upset someone's feelings?
Time travel to the future or to the past?	Upset your teacher or your friend?
Have a hand half its size or twice as big?	Have extra eyes in the back of your head or an extra eye on the end of your little finger?
Be the best player on a team that loses a lot or the worst player on a team that wins?	Walk through knee-deep snow or knee-deep water?
Swim with sharks or ride a tiger?	Have a saucepan stuck on your head or your feet stuck in mud?
Wash the dishes or dry the dishes?	Visit a castle or climb a mountain?
Be hairy all over or completely bald?	Be able to read or be able to do maths?
Be the youngest or oldest in the family?	Have the super-power of invisibility or be able to fly?
Have a brother or a sister?	Feed an alligator or feed a pigeon?

Agony Aunt Examples

Dear Agony Aunt,

I'm hoping that you can help me. I feel so bad and just don't know what to do. I told my mum that I was staying behind after school to do homework club. She said she was really proud of me because I don't often do my homework and she was so happy that I was beginning to take my schoolwork seriously (especially as we have assessments coming up). But my problem is that I lied. I actually went round to my friend's house to play on the Xbox. Now, I feel so guilty because I keep seeing my mum's happy face and she keeps asking me questions about the work. I don't want to disappoint her. What should I do?

From Hazel

Dear Agony Aunt,

What should I do? Everything is a mess. I am so unhappy. Life at home with my sister is unbearable as we argue all the time. She vis annoying and irritating. I would like a room of my own, but I have to share with my little sister, who just won't stop touching or moving my things. She takes my clothes, she reads my diary, she tells lies about me to my mum – she's horrible. Just yesterday, she told Mum that I hit her and she pretended to cry. I didn't touch her! I tell her she's mean and horrible and that no one likes her, but she just won't stop.

From Emily

Dear Agony Aunt,

I have a best friend called George; we have been friends since Reception Class. He is great at football and we often play football in the park after school. George also helps me with my classwork as he is better at maths than me. I like George but I'm not sure I can be his friend anymore. Yesterday, we had a new boy in the class. The new boy is new to our country and doesn't speak much English. I asked him to play football with me and George at playtime. He is an amazing footballer, even better than George. George got angry and called the new boy some names and used very unkind words about how he looks and where he was born. I didn't join in but I also didn't stop George either. I don't know what to do next.

From Finley

Dear Agony Aunt,

I can't believe it! I saw Rebecca cheating on the spelling test. She thinks no one saw her, but I did. She had the words written on her arm and she kept rolling up her sleeve to check – she pretended she was hot or had an itch. She got 20/20 and Miss Markham was so pleased that she gave Rebecca 5 Dojo points and gave her a certificate to take home. I only got 6/20. Should I tell everyone about Rebecca cheating?

From Robert

Dilemma Story

Learning Objective: To write a story that includes a dilemma
Success Criteria:
◆ Use chronological order
◆ Include a build-up of a problem
◆ Include characters' feelings
◆ Include a resolution where the main character has learnt something or changed
◆ Use third person
◆ Use of causal conjunctions, e.g. so, because, when, if, that, while, but…
◆ Use adverbial phrases – time, place, manner and reason

Pupils Can...	
	Write narratives in the third person and in the past tense. Write events in chronological order supported by adverbials and prepositions. Narratives may include flashbacks. Use descriptions, including settings, which are developed through adverbials for time, manner, place or reason. Write descriptions of characters, setting and atmosphere that are developed through precise vocabulary choices, e.g. adverbs, adjectives, precise nouns, expressive verbs and figurative language. Make greater use of inference. Use dialogue to convey characters' thoughts and move the narrative forward. Write a resolution linked to the introduction and include a moral.
	Write narratives in the third person and the past tense. Write events in chronological order supported by adverbials and prepositions. Use descriptions, including settings, which are developed through adverbials, e.g. under the creaky, wooden stairs. Use language choices that help create detailed and vivid mental images, e.g. precise nouns, adjectives, adverbs, expressive verbs and figurative language. Write a resolution linked to the introduction and includes a moral.
	Write narratives in the third person and the past tense. Write events in chronological order supported by adverbials and prepositions. Use descriptions, including settings, which are developed through adverbials, e.g. under the creaky, wooden stairs. Use vocabulary choices that help create a realistic mental image, e.g. adverbs, adjectives, precise nouns. Show how a character has changed.

Causal Conjunctions *are words and phrases that are used to introduce a cause, reason or explanation for a given action within a sentence. They are connecting words that explain the outcome of an action or an event, for instance, 'because', 'due to', 'as a result of' and 'if' are all* **causal conjunctions** *that link an action to its supposed cause.*

Resources

What Do You Do with a Problem? by Kobi Yamada and Mae Besom

Collection of 'Would you rather…?' questions

Example of an Agony Aunt letter

TASTER: WOULD YOU RATHER CONTINUED

Play a quick question-and-answer game. Students are offered two options. They need to choose between A or B very quickly. They can hold up whiteboards or move to one side of the classroom.

https://conversationstartersworld.com/would-you-rather-questions-for-kids

Children create their own 'Would you rather?' questions to ask the class.

BUILDING TASK: WHAT'S YOUR PROBLEM?

Read the book *What Do You Do with a Problem?* again.

As a class or in groups, students think about what the problem may be. How does the problem make the character feel? How does the child behave?

The problem seems to be living – it is following the child, almost swallowing him. How does the problem behave? If the problem could talk, what do the students think it might say?

BUILDING TASK: CONSCIENCE ALLEY

In the story, *What Do You Do with a Problem?* we do not find out what the actual problem is. What might the problem be? What might his options be?

As a class look at a couple of problems – what choices could they make?

◆ *My friend has a new pen which I really want. Her parents buy her anything she wants and I know that if it went missing, they would buy her another one. Should I take it?*

◆ *I'm so angry. Life is so unfair. I work really hard. I deserve to get some reward. The teacher left their Dojo page open and I could easily add some Dojo points.*

◆ *Nobody notices me. I never get any attention. I feel so ignored and worthless. If I do something wrong or unkind someone will have to pay me some attention then!*

◆ *I forgot to study my spellings for the test today. My friend is always getting his spellings correct, I could sit next to him and copy his answers. I'm sure he won't mind.*

Have the class make two lines facing each other. Either choose a child to be the main character or be the character yourself and walk between the lines. As the character walks down the 'aisle/ alley' each member of the line gives their advice. You could have one side giving reasons why the character should do the action and the other side giving an opposing opinion. When the character reaches the end of the alley, they must make a decision.

MAIN TASK: IT'S SUCH A DILEMMA!

1. With the children look at the structure of the book *What Do You Do with a Problem?*

— *Introduction of character and setting:* the character was ok one day and the next he had a problem.

— *What is the problem and build-up:* the problem starts to grow and the child does all sorts of things to make the problem go away. His imagination runs away with him, and he becomes really worried about it. The problem seems like a huge monster.

— *Takes action:* The character realises that he can't run away from it and decides to face the problem monster.

— *Consequences of action:* He finds that the problem isn't that big after all.

— *Moral:* He discovers that problems can be helpful as you can learn from them.

2. Children choose a dilemma/problem to write their own story. Using the same structure, they plan their story.

— *See someone stealing*

— *See someone bullying*

— *See someone cheating*

— *Arguing with siblings all the time*

— *Find an injured animal*

- *Told a fib to a parent*

- *Told a secret or asked to keep a secret*

3. Children draft their dilemma stories. Encourage them not to use too many characters. Encourage the students to think about a character's feelings.

4. Peer review stories – use success criteria checklist.

   Take one sentence and improve with your learning partner.

   Find two adverbs that could be changed or moved within the sentence for effect.

   Find three verbs that could be more precise.
   Find four adjectives that could be improved.

DIFFERENTIATION

- ◆ Students given a more basic structure. *Problem – action – consequence.*

- ◆ Use a comic strip to help plan their writing – graphic novel.

◆ Plan and write a joint/group story.

◆ Role-play part of their story to help them think about feelings and actions.

Teacher Tools and Techniques	
Emotional Literacy	Recognition and awareness of emotions
	Exploring and explaining emotions
	Understanding actions will have consequences – positive and negative
Developing Relationships	Talking partners – agreement and compromise
	Sympathy and empathy
Self-Development	Thinking out loud, considering options, self-motivation, recognising motivators and triggers
	Morals and values
Skills for Learning	Planning, draft and improve, constructive criticism, decision-making, agreement, collaboration, problem-solving
The Brain Learning and Behaviour	Intrinsic and extrinsic rewards

PHSE LINK (PSHE ASSOCIATION PROGRAMME OF STUDY FOR PSHE EDUCATION – KS2)

Everyday things affect feelings and the importance of expressing feelings.

Increasing independence may bring new opportunities and responsibilities.

There are reasons for following and complying with regulations and restrictions.

The importance of seeking support and how to seek help or advice.

Strategies to respond to hurtful behaviour – experienced or witnessed.

Personal behaviour can affect other people.

Discuss and debate topical issues, respect other people's points of view and constructively challenge those they disagree with.

Problems, Problems Everywhere

Learning Objective: To develop the skills needed to deal with a problem
Success Criteria: ◆ Describe a problem and a process that could be used to solve it.

Pupils Can...	Describe a problem that they have had to solve.
	Describe how having a problem can make them feel and who they can talk to if they needed help.
	Show a clear understanding of how problems can make them feel and share a process to help them out.

*The World Health Organisation defines **wellbeing** as 'the state in which an individual realises his or her own abilities, can cope with normal stresses of life, can work productively, and is able to make a contribution to his or her own community'. Wellbeing involves having positive self-image and self-esteem.*

***Resilience**, which is directly related to wellbeing, is about having the ability to cope with and adapt to new situations. Having a sense of resilience and positive wellbeing enables children and young people to approach other people and situations with confidence and optimism, which is especially important for young people given the enormous changes that occur with the transition into adolescence and adulthood. Resilience and being able to manage, cope and adapt to new situations are linked to the ability to manage those challenges. This includes problem-solving. The ability to problem-solve supports children and young people to think through situations, consider consequences and choose the best options. It can also include the ability to reframe and think of problems as challenges that offer opportunities to grow and develop skills.*

Resources	*What Do You Do with a Problem?* by Kobi Yamada and Mae Besom	Problem cards Problem-solving worksheet Character and their problem sheet

TASTER: OPPORTUNITIES EVERYWHERE

Ask the children to share problems that they have had to manage this week.

List the problems on the board and ask them to identify the opportunity that the problems gave them.

For example: *I forgot my packed lunch. Opportunity: To develop my speaking-up voice, as I had to go and ask the secretary to phone my mum.*

Give each of the children a problem card and ask them to identify the opportunity that the problem has given the person concerned. Share the opportunities that they have identified.

BUILDING TASK: PROBLEM CHARACTERS

Share the story with the children and ask them to think of their own Problem Character. Ask the children to draw, paint or make their 'Problem Character'. Once they have completed them, put on a Silent Exhibition. Ask the children to place their Character on their desk. Once they have done this, they walk around the room and view the different ways the other people in their class have interpreted the problem.

Give the children three post-it notes each and ask them to write a positive comment for three people and leave it on their desk. No piece of work can have more than three comments.

MAIN TASK. PROBLEMS AND SOLUTIONS

1. Ask the children to identify a problem from a story that a character has to sort out.

    For example: *What should the three bears do with Goldilocks when they find she has broken into their house and broke Baby Bear's chair?*

2. Ask the children to work in small groups (between four and six children). Give each child a Problem-Solving Worksheet. Ask them to share the problems that they have identified and the opportunity that these problems have given the characters.

3. Around the problem they have identified are a range of 'possible solutions'. Ask each child to ask the people in their group for a possible solution and add them to the sheet.

4. Ask them to come up with two possible solutions of their own.

5. It is important at this stage to encourage really creative ways of solving the problem. These creative ways may not be practical, however, everything is allowed at this stage as they may add to the creative process of finding a good solution.

6. Once they have filled in all the Possible Solutions ask them to discard any that are dangerous or may result in somebody being hurt physically, emotionally or psychologically. You can give examples to help the children understand.

7. For example: *Goldilocks Possible Solutions:*

    – *Lock her in the cupboard*

    – *Tie her up and take her home to her parents*

    – *Go and talk to her parents and explain what she has done*

    – *Leave her in bed and when she wakes up explain how upset Baby Bear is and that she needs to pay for the damage*

    – *Wake her up and tell her off*

    – *Destroy her*

    – *Call the police and report the damage she has done.*

    Explore the solutions with the children. Cross off the ones that can cause damage. Once these have been crossed off, explore the ones that are left. For each one write the consequence that would/could happen if that solution were to be used. Under the consequence, they can write the Opportunity this solution offers.

    Goldilocks Example:

    Go and talk to her parents. Her parents would know what she has done and might help her understand how wrong it is to break into someone's house and how bad Baby Bear would have felt about his chair. They may offer to pay for the damage. On the flip side, they may not want to know and not talk to Goldilocks.

    This solution offers the opportunity to help Goldilocks learn about respect in the future and the opportunity for her parents to support her in learning what is right and wrong.

8. Once the consequences have been explored and the opportunity identified, the children can then choose the preferred option.

9. Share the problem-solving work with each other.

DIFFERENTIATION

✓ Support children with a learning difference by putting them with Learning Buddies or in groups with an adult to support them.

✓ Pair children together and give them three of the Character Problems to choose from.

✓ Instead of writing on the Problem-Solving Sheet, they could draw pictures or choose to talk about the solutions they have identified.

✓ In the Silent Exhibition, the children could be offered the choice of giving the pieces of work a star rating instead of writing something.

Teacher Tools and Techniques	
Emotional Literacy	Developing problem-solving skills
Developing Relationships	Working in pairs, small groups or with a Learning Buddy
Self-Development	Understanding how problems can make us feel and a variety of ways of thinking about them and finding the best solution
Skills for Learning	Planning and organisation of thinking and then tasks
The Brain Learning and Behaviour	Understanding that worries are part of the brain's way of keeping us safe and that we can learn a range of ways to help us manage

PHSE LINK (PSHE ASSOCIATION PROGRAMME OF STUDY FOR PSHE EDUCATION – KS2)

Develop problem-solving strategies for dealing with emotions, challenges and change, including the transition to new schools.

Manage setbacks/perceived failures, including how to reframe unhelpful thinking.

Story Character Problems

Jack and the Beanstalk
Should he sell the cow for a packet of beans?

Snow White
Should she eat the apple from her stepmother?

The Three Little Pigs
What should they do when the Wolf knocks on their door?

The Three Billy Goats Gruff
Should they cross the bridge with the Troll underneath?

Little Red Riding Hood
Should she walk through the forest?

Rumpelstiltskin
Should she tell the King she can't really spin straw into gold?

Cinderella
Should she tell her stepmother that she went to the ball?

Aladdin
Should he set the genie free from the lamp for helping him?

Sleeping Beauty
Should she marry the prince?

The Gingerbread Man
Should he let the fox take him across the river?

Problem Cards	
You have left your PE kit in Mum's car	You have lost a very special party invitation
You have broken your little sister's toy doll	You have forgotten your dinner money
You have argued with your best friend and now they are not talking to you	You have argued with your dad and have stomped upstairs and are missing your favourite TV programme
You have forgotten a friend's birthday	You have forgotten to feed the dog
You have forgotten to do your homework.	You kicked the ball over the fence after Dad told you not to play in the garden
You have broken Gran's best china cup	You have taken Mum's new shoes for a dressing-up game and got glitter on them
You have got paint on the carpet	You have eaten Mum's special biscuits that Dad brought you to give her for Mother's Day
You have found your best friend's rubber in your pencil case.	You were playing with your little sister and you have drawn on Mum's tablecloth
You can't find the new notebook your mum brought you for school	You told Dad you could do your homework and now you have found you can't

You saw someone take another child's toy and put it in their bag	When your teacher went out of the room, one of your friends took their pen
The head has told all the children in school that if they see another child being unkind, they must go and tell her. You saw someone from your class being unkind to their younger brother on the way to school.	Your class teacher has asked everyone to write down who they would like to share a room with on the PGL trip. You know that no one wants to share with one of the girls in your class and she is very upset by this.
When you got home, you found one of your friends had hidden another child's football boots in your bag	Your friend has a party at the weekend, they have been saying they are going to make fun of one of the girls going
Your friend wants you to take a packet of sweets from the sweet shop	On the bus you catch to school you watch as one of the children in your class is being picked on
You have been invited to a party with your friends. You don't know what to wear. You really want to borrow your sister's top but she is not there to ask.	Your friends all tease you about the trainers you have. You really want a new pair, but Dad says the ones you have can last a bit longer.

As you walk around town with your friends, you see a child from your class being threatened by some of the older kids from your school. They look to you for help.	Mum wants you to have a healthy packed lunch, but all your friends eat biscuits and chocolate bars and you don't want them to pick on you.
You have been playing your new computer game all morning. Dad reminds you that you promised to walk the dog. Your best friend has just come to join the game.	Your best friend has just told you that they have been saving up for a present for their mum's birthday and that they are going to town to buy it. They want you to cover for them.
One of your friends tells you that an older child at their club is picking on them and saying that if they don't pay them, they will beat them up.	You have just started at your new school and are really worried about getting lost and being late for your maths lesson. The teacher has already put one child in detention for being late.
You are moving house and that means you have to change schools. Your new teacher has asked you to bring something about yourself to share with the other children in your class.	Your mum has asked you to choose four friends to come to a pizza and film night for your birthday but you have six good friends and you don't want anyone to be left out.

Problems	

Problem Solving

Consequence

Consequence

Consequence

Solution

Solution

Solution

Solution

Problem

Solution

Solution

Solution

Consequence

Solution

Consequence

Character Description

Learning Objective: To describe a character	

Success Criteria:

◆ Describe physical characteristics

◆ Describe character personality traits

    – *How they feel*

    – *What they do*

    – *What they say*

    – *How they change*

◆ Use descriptive vocabulary

    – *adjectives*

    – *adverbs*

    – *similes*

    – *metaphors*

◆ Expand your ideas by using relative clauses

Pupils Can...	Record details retrieved from the text about characters, places, events and ideas. Identify and summarise evidence from a text to support and justify their reasoning. Understand when it is useful to quote directly, paraphrase or adapt.
	Establish what is known about characters in narrative by retrieving details from the text to back up their understanding.
	Answer simple retrieval and inference questions. Identify key sentences and words in texts that show important information about characters, places and events.

A **Protagonist** is the main character of a story who is involved in a struggle of some kind. This could be a struggle against someone or something. The struggle may even be against their own emotions.

An **Antagonist** is an enemy or a foe. They are actively hostile to someone or something.

Explicit information is information that is clearly stated and there is no question about its meaning.

Implicit information is information that is implied or suggested. Information is understood through clues and 'reading between the lines'.

Inference is using clues from a text to draw a conclusion

Relative clause is used to give additional information about a noun. These clauses begin with a **relative** pronoun like 'that', 'which', 'who', 'whose', 'where' and 'when'.

|  | *The Worry Tree* by Marianne Musgrove | Chosen extracts from the book which help describe the character |

TASTER: I SAW AN ALIEN

As a class or in groups, play the 'I saw an alien…'. A student chooses a characteristic to describe an alien, the next student repeats the description and adds to it and so on.

I saw an alien with scarlet ears – I saw an alien with scarlet ears and a bobbly nose – I saw an alien with scarlet ears, a bobbly nose and piercing green eyes on antennae – I saw…

To add a further challenge the descriptions could be alphabetical.

I saw an angry alien – I saw an angry, bemused alien – I saw an angry, bemused, crusty alien…

BUILDING TASK: WHO AM I?

Read a description of a character – can the children identify who you are describing? For example, you could read a description of *The Gruffalo*. Children could draw what you are describing. A good source for descriptions is www .literacywagoll.com.

Children are given an image of a fictional character and with a partner describe the picture for their partner to visualise or draw. How long before they can work out who the character is? Ensure children know that their clues are describing appearance, e.g. describing their outward appearance, what they are wearing, holding or doing but not clues such as 'Her teacher is Miss Honey!' or 'His last name is a type of bird and rhymes with barrow!'

BUILDING TASK: WHAT'S IN A NAME?

Explain to the students that some writers use names that give clues to the character's personality. The name is chosen specifically to indicate whether the character is positive, negative or neutral. A good example of this is Roald Dahl's characters - think of Miss Honey and The Trunchbull.

Honey implies sweet and nice. Honey is good for you. On the other hand, Trunchbull sounds harsh, solid, immoveable.

Give the children some famous fictional names and, using connotations and associations, have them categorise into positive, negative or neutral characters.

Cruella de Vil, Harry Potter, Mr Wormwood, Augustus Gloop, Veruca Salt, Willy Wonka, Slugworth, Mugglewump, Mr Bumble, Scrooge, Pip, Tiny Tim, Fezziwig, Pumblechook, Darth Vader, Remus Lupin, Dorothy Gale, Desdemona, Ariadne, Juliet Jennifer Jones

Students could match these names to images of the characters. What do they think Desdemona would look, act, sound like?

MAIN TASK: CHARACTER DESCRIPTION

1. Collect information together about one of the main characters in the story, *The Worry Tree*. Together record what the character looks like and their personality traits.

Covered in blotches and a rash, which occur when she is stressed.

Extremely short fringe that is exactly 1 ½ cm long which she finds really mortifying.

Ensure you include examples that you can expand on using relative clauses or figurative language.

Exasperated by her sister as she rolls her eyes towards heaven like she is asking for divine intervention.

Storms round the house like a bubbling, volatile, volcano ready to erupt.

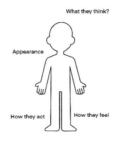

What they think?

Appearance

How they act   How they feel

A paper chain of people with personality traits written on each figure in the chain.

2. In pairs, students discuss and record their thoughts about one of the characters. They can then share with another pair. What do they agree on? What differences are there?

3. Students can share their descriptions with the class – can the other students guess which character they are describing?

4. Students can record and animate their descriptions using audio animate apps.

DIFFERENTIATION

✓ Choose a format that may be more suitable – a mind map, concertina book, audio recording device or a silhouette to write inside and annotate.

✓ Provide vocabulary word mats for character traits and adjectives to describe physical features. A thesaurus would be useful to encourage adventurous vocabulary.

✓ Challenge the children to include a target number of features, i.e. two similes, three adverbs, four double adjectives.

✓ Supporting text can be pre-chosen at an appropriate level for students to elicit information.

✓ Students can compare different characters.

Teacher Tools and Techniques	
Emotional Literacy	Recognition and awareness of emotions, naming feelings
	Exploring and explaining emotions
	Understanding that emotions change in intensity and over time
Developing Relationships	Agreement and compromise
	Sympathy and empathy
	Picking up on cues
	Understanding others
Self-Development	Thinking out loud, considering options, self-motivation, recognising motivators and triggers
Skills for Learning	Thinking out loud, decision-making, agreement, collaboration, problem-solving, inference

The Brain Learning and Behaviour	Intrinsic and extrinsic rewards
	Neuroplasticity

PHSE LINK (PSHE ASSOCIATION PROGRAMME OF STUDY FOR PSHE EDUCATION – KS2)

Recognise individuality and personal qualities.

Identify personal strengths, skills, achievements and interests and how these contribute to a sense of self-worth.

Understand that everyday things affect feelings and the importance of expressing feelings.

Strategies and behaviours that support mental health – good quality sleep, physical exercise/time outdoors, being involved in community groups, doing things for others, clubs and activities, hobbies and spending time with family and friends can support mental health and wellbeing.

Character Profile

Learning Objective: To complete a character profile
Success Criteria:
◆ Decide on the format of your profile
◆ Decide on Character and Character type for your profile
◆ Highlight explicit information from the text (What you know because it is clearly stated)
◆ Highlight implicit information from the text (What and how you know because it's implied/inferred. Speech, actions, tone)
◆ Support your choice/opinion using evidence from the text
◆ Expand your ideas by using relative clauses

Pupils Can...	Record details retrieved from the text about characters, places, events and ideas. Identify and summarise evidence from a text to support and justify their reasoning. Understand when it is useful to quote directly, paraphrase or adapt.
	Establish what is known about characters in narrative by retrieving details from the text to back up their understanding.
	Answer simple retrieval and inference questions.
	Identify key sentences and words in texts that show important information about characters, places and events.

Character types are described as static, dynamic, flat or stock.

Explicit information is information that is clearly stated and there is no question about its meaning.

Implicit information is information that is implied or suggested. Information is understood through clues and 'reading between the lines'.

Inference is using clues from a text to draw a conclusion.

Relative clause is used to give additional information about a noun. These clauses begin with a **relative** pronoun like 'that', 'which', 'who', 'whose', 'where' and 'when'.

	*The Worry Tree* by Marianne Musgrove	Chosen extracts from the book that help describe the character

TASTER: WORD CHAIN

Give the children a descriptive word chain to complete. This could be colours, textures or emotions. The last letter of each word needs to be the first letter of the next word in the link. As a challenge, give the children a target number of words to have in their chain.

Examples to start with:

Azure-ebony-yellow-white-earth-hazelnut-teal…

Smooth-hard-damaged-dull-luxurious-sunken-neat-thorny

BUILDING TASK: WHO'S WHO?

Using given sentences taken from the text, ask the children to think about which character is being described.

Holding her was like hugging a warm loaf of bread.

She could feel her skin itching and prickling. She stared at her apple as if it was the most interesting apple in the world. I'm taping my hair to my head. It's all about experimentation – you never know what might happen.

How do they know who it is and what does it tell us about them?

BUILDING TASK: CHARACTER TYPE

Explain to the children that stories often have different character types

◆ *STATIC – stays the same throughout the story*

◆ *DYNAMIC – character that changes due to events*

◆ *FLAT – background character – don't know much about them*

◆ *STOCK – stereotypical*

Ask the students to think about the characters in *The Worry Tree*. Which category do they think each character might come under? You could give the students characters from well-known stories to help embed the idea of character types such as Cinderella, the wicked stepmother, Batman, Sherlock Holmes, Miss Honey, Trunchbull, Matilda, Ned Flanders.

MAIN TASK: CHARACTER PROFILE

1. Ask the class to agree on the information that you would need to create a full picture of your character.

Appearance, Age, Character type, Personality traits, Interests, Background, Aspirations, Occupation/Education, etc. In what order would they place these categories? Would they include how the character has changed and developed through the story?

2. Model using an extract from the text to show how this could be used as part of the profile. Ensure your example includes a relative clause to expand on your idea.

*Juliet heard Mum's footsteps in the corridor, followed by the sound of boxes being **shoved** about. Mum **poked** her head into the lounge room looking an odd shade of purple. **Eggplant purple** thought Juliet.*

Discuss the use of interesting and precise verbs – what does 'shoved' imply? Discuss the use of similes and the student's understanding of mood associated with a purple face. What does this tell us about Mum?

Taped to the door of Dad's study was a large piece of paper bearing the words of Thomas Edison: TO INVENT, YOU NEED A GOOD IMAGINATION AND A PILE OF JUNK.

What does this tell us about Dad – his job, interests, thoughts.

Dad is highly creative and enjoys spending time experimenting. He has a room that is filled with rubbish which suggests he doesn't mind mess and collects unwanted materials just in case they might be useful. Dad, who likes his own space to do his work, is aware that other people might not understand why the room may be untidy and disorganised, so has placed a type of humorous warning on the door.

3. Limit the choice of characters to be used for the profile. Tables could be set up within the class with relevant information/evidence on each table for each character. Students use their knowledge of the story, text extracts and discussion with a learning partner or table group to complete their profiles. When using extracts from the book, students will find it helpful to highlight and annotate.

DIFFERENTIATION

✓ Limit the number of categories for the profile

✓ Choose a format that may be more suitable – a mind map, concertina book, audio recording device or a table/chart that includes a column heading for evidence.

✓ Supporting evidence can be pre-chosen at an appropriate level for students to elicit information. Include vocabulary mats with adjectives that describe appearance or emotions.

✓ Students can compare characters.

✓ A chart or story graph could be completed showing how a character has changed throughout the story. How has Juliet changed from the beginning of the book compared to the end? How has she managed her feelings?

Teacher Tools and Techniques	
Emotional Literacy	Recognition and awareness of emotions, naming feelings
	Exploring and explaining emotions
	Understanding that emotions change in intensity and over time
Developing Relationships	Agreement and compromise
	Sympathy and empathy
	Picking up on cues
Self-Development	Thinking out loud, considering options, self-motivation, recognising motivators and triggers
Skills for Learning	Thinking out loud, decision-making, agreement, collaboration, problem-solving, inference
The Brain Learning and Behaviour	Intrinsic and extrinsic rewards
	Neuroplasticity

PHSE LINK (PSHE ASSOCIATION PROGRAMME OF STUDY FOR PSHE EDUCATION – KS2)

Everyday things affect feelings and the importance of expressing feelings.

Strategies and behaviours that support mental health – good quality sleep, physical exercise/time outdoors, being involved in community groups, doing things for others, clubs and activities, hobbies and spending time with family and friends can support mental health and wellbeing.

The importance of seeking support and how to seek help or advice.

Strategies to respond to hurtful behaviour - experienced or witnessed.

Recognise that feelings can change over time and range in intensity.

Getting On and Falling Out

Learning Objective: To develop an understanding of conflict and the strategies needed to resolve differences within friendships groups
Success Criteria:
◆ Share ways to help friends manage conflict

Pupils Can...	Listen to friends and think about the things that have upset them.
	Help people problem-solve ways that can help them solve conflict.
	Share a range of strategies that can help friends resolve conflict.

Conflict Resolution: Children often find themselves in difficult situations that lead to conflict/arguments with their peers. The inability to resolve conflict without resorting to violence is symptomatic of children's inability to handle confrontation. Teaching children how to resolve conflict in a peaceful way can help reduce incidents of violence and criminal behaviour later in life.

Conflict resolution involves allowing both parties to express their points of view and provide ways to co-create acceptable solutions. The most effective ways teach and use a variety of components to achieve this outcome, including problem-solving skills, effective communication and listening skills and critical and creative thinking skills.

The Worry Tree by Marianne Musgrove	Ground rules and prompts
	Collage materials
Different points of view sheet	Paints or felt tip pens
Restorative scripts	Large sheets of paper

TASTER: FAMILY TREE

Read the story to the children. If they could ask one person in the book a question, what would that question be? Record the questions and explore the possible answers. Help children to understand that their answers are their points of view.

1. Explore the book and create a Family Tree for Juliet. Ask the children to write a brief description of each of the family members.

2. Explore their ideas of a family and the different types of families. Help them distil this down to the components. This may include a group of people who look after, care for and love each other. Families do not necessarily live together or have to be biologically related.

3. Discuss the types of things that families might do – go on holiday, look after each other if they are ill, share special days together, help with problems or celebrate special events. In addition, help the children understand that families often argue or disagree with each other or ignore each other and can be unkind to each other. Help them understand that this 'rupture' in relationships can be mended. Explore the ways that family relationships can rupture – arguments, fighting, etc. Help the children to explore how the rupture can be repaired.

BUILDING TASK: SHARE A WORRY

Read the chapter about the Worry Tree being uncovered.

Discuss the animals that lived in the tree and the worries that they worried about. Can the children think of any worries that wouldn't be looked after by one of the animals?

Ask the children to create their own worry tree. This could be a drawing, painting or collage. Ask them to design and make their own animals to go on the tree and share what they will worry about. The children could use the animals from the story or create their own. Alternatively, as a class, a tree could be created and then groups of children make the animals to put on the tree.

MAIN TASK: CONFLICT RESOLUTION

1. In the book, Juliet becomes very fed up with the way Gemma and Lindsay behave. Ask the children to work in groups and share how each of the girls may be feeling and why. Groups of three or six work well as then they can explore how each of the children may feel and share what they have come up with. Complete the sheet showing the different points of view.

2. Share what they have found.

3. Explain that conflict resolution is a way of helping people solve their differences or arguments. It focuses on the fact that everyone has a different view and that everyone needs to be listened to and heard. By doing this, each person feels that they have been able to tell their story. After this, the people involved are invited to share how they were feeling and what they were thinking. This then leads to a problem-solving period where the participants are asked to think of solutions to the difficulty that can be accepted by all.

4. Share the restorative script with the children and explore:

Why they think it starts by asking each of the participants what has happened.

Why they think it asks the participants about how they were feeling and what they were thinking.

Ask the children to think about how the mediators – people who help the conflicted parties come together, should behave and act.

— *Impartially*

— *Calmly*

— *Good listeners*

— *Good at summing up*

— *Well organised*

— *Empathetic*

— *Non-judgementally*

— *Compassionately*

5. Ask the children to work in their groups. Ask them to role-play the child from the story that they explored in the previous activity. Act out the mediation process and explore the ways that it could be solved. You may need to join two groups together so that there are the three girls from the story but also two mediators and one to record what the solution is that the role-players come up with.

6. Stop and ask children to present to each other at different points, highlighting the important aspects such as points of view, problem-solving, active listening, impartiality, etc.

7. Come together as a class and explore what the children have learnt and what they will take away with them.

DIFFERENTIATION

✓ For some children working in pairs can be supportive when working.

✓ Children could be provided with a blank family tree to complete instead of asking them to draw and make their own. They can then concentrate on drawing the family and identifying three words to describe each of the family members. For some children, family trees are difficult and can cause strong emotions, i.e., if children are adopted or fostered. If you have children in your class who are fostered or adopted, you would need to talk to them about this activity before you undertake it and offer them options. One option may be to look at a well know family tree – the Royal Family or a story family tree – The Weasleys from Harry Potter.

✓ Children can be supported in mixed-ability groups or with small groups supported by an adult.

✓ For children who struggle with acting or role-playing, they could be asked to take photos of the other groups working for a class display.

Teacher Tools and Techniques	
Emotional Literacy	To develop a range of vocabulary linked to anxiety and how it can make people fee
Developing Relationships	To work with other people both in pairs and small groups Listening to the ideas of others and co-creating work
Self-Development	To understand that anxiety is a normal human feeling that is experienced when people are feeling threatened or unsafe
Skills for Learning	Developing strategies to work with others and manage the learning task
The Brain Learning and Behaviour	To develop a range of strategies to support themselves deal with anxious feelings

PHSE LINK (PSHE ASSOCIATION PROGRAMME OF STUDY FOR PSHE EDUCATION – KS2)

Identify common features of family life.

About growing and changing from young to old and how people's needs change.

That friendships have ups and downs; strategies to resolve disputes and reconcile differences positively and safely.

About how people may feel if they experience hurtful behaviour or bullying.

That hurtful behaviour (offline and online) including teasing, name-calling, bullying and deliberately excluding others is not acceptable; how to report bullying; the importance of telling a trusted adult.

Ground Rules Prompt

◆ Welcome everyone to the room.

◆ Can we just start by reminding everyone that you have each agreed to attend this meeting.

◆ As Peer Mediators/Mediators we would like to remind you that we will not be taking sides.

◆ We will not be judging what is right or wrong.

◆ Our job is to help you sort things out for yourselves.

◆ We will do this by taking turns to ask you questions.

◆ We will listen to what you have to say.

◆ There are two ground rules: First, we will all listen with respect (no bullying, name-calling or put downs).

◆ Second, what is said in this meeting stays here. We will not go out and tell everyone else what has been said. The only exception is that if we hear something that means you are at risk of harm, we will have to share this with a member of staff.

Restorative Enquiry Script

These questions are asked to each of the participants in a session on their own so as they can be asked if they are willing to attend a meeting with the other people as a way of solving the conflict.

Can you start by telling us in your own words what happened? (Prompt if needed: when? Why? Where?)

What were you thinking at the time?

What were you feeling at the time?

What had happened before between you and…?

What were your thoughts then?

What has happened since the incident?

What have you been thinking?

What have you been feeling?

Who else has been affected?

Are you willing to have a meeting with… to sort this out?

Restorative Mediation Prompt

MEDIATOR 1

Welcome and Ground Rules

MEDIATOR 2

Asks Person A

Can you start by telling us in your own words what happened? (Prompt if needed: when? Why? Where?)

What were you thinking at the time?

What were you feeling at the time?

What had happened before between you and…?

What were your thoughts then?

What has happened since the incident?

What have you been thinking?

What have you been feeling?

Who else has been affected?

MEDIATOR 2

Asks Person B the same questions as they asked Person A

MEDIATOR 1

Asks person **A**

What do you need to help sort this out?

Asks Person **B**

What do you need to help sort this out?

Listen to common ground and summarise, for example:

'So you are both saying that you need…'

'We have heard you both say that…'

Asks Person **A**

What can you do to help move this forward?

Ask person **B**

What can you do to help move this forward?

Summarise agreement

So A you are agreeing to…

So B you are agreeing to…

Ask if they want the agreement written down. If yes, write the agreement and invite them to sign it.

Make arrangements to follow up and talk to them both about how their agreement and their relationship are going.

Restorative justice is an approach to justice that focuses on the needs of the victims and the offenders, as well as the involved community, instead of just punishing the offender. Victims take an active role in the process, while offenders are encouraged to take responsibility for their actions, 'to repair the harm they've done—by apologising, returning stolen money or community service'. It provides help for the offender in order to avoid future offences. Restorative justice that fosters dialogue between victim and offender shows the highest rates of victim satisfaction and offender accountability.

Retributive justice is a theory of justice that considers punishment, if proportionate, to be the best response to crime. When an offender breaks the law, s/he thereby forfeits or suspends her/his right to something of equal value.

'Let the punishment fit the crime' is a principle that means the severity of penalty for a misdeed or wrongdoing should be reasonable and proportionate to the severity of the crime. The concept is common to most cultures throughout the world. However, the judgement of whether a punishment is appropriately severe can vary greatly between cultures and individuals.

Primary Assembly:

Who is the Assembly for?

Children in KS1 and KS2.

What is the Focus?

We can all make a difference in the world in which we live.

Working together with people within our community can be very powerful.

We are responsible for the community in which we live.

Objectives

To support children understand that they have the power to make a difference in both the community in which they live and in other people's lives.

Involvement of Children

Questions about the story.

Small group to act out sketch.

Come up with ways to make a difference in and around school.

Key Message

You can make a difference to the world in which we live.

Introduction

Read the story to the children. Ask why they think some people may be invisible in the story?

Explore the ways that Isobel decided to make a difference.

Main Event

Act out a short sketch of an incident in the playground when a child is being left out/picked on/teased or bullied.

Show onlookers watching with some turning away and playing – as if the distressed child is invisible.

Ask the children to think about ways that they could make a difference. Collect a variety of things that could be done both in the playground and in the classrooms.

Finale

Watch the video https://www.youtube.com/watch?v=QUGQ-fMgVSQ

Ask the children to think about the small ways that they can make a difference to the school environment – litter/being kind to others/picking up coats in the cloakroom putting bags on pegs etc.

Resources

The Invisible by Tom Percival.

YouTube clip: Make a difference

https://www.youtube.com/watch?v=QUGQ-fMgVSQ

Chapter 3

Understanding Self
KS2

KS2 BOOKS

Can I Build Another Me? by Shinsuke Yoshitake

The Map of Good Memories by Fran Nuño and
Zuzanna Celej

Maybe by Kobi Yamada and Gabriella Barouch

ASSEMBLY

Your Thoughts Matter by Esther Pia Cordova
and Mariya Elizarova

DOI: 10.4324/9781003322801-4

Notes

Learning Objective: To write notes
Success Criteria:
◆ Decide on key information
◆ Don't worry about complete sentences
◆ Include diagrams and bullet points
◆ Use abbreviations, acronyms and symbols
◆ Combine facts with opinion
◆ Consider audience and purpose *(will you be able to use them as a plan for writing later)*

Pupils Can...	Identify key information. Condense and paraphrase information. Use a range of techniques to write notes. Use organisational and presentational devices.
	Identify key information. Summarise the information within the text. Use abbreviations and symbols to write notes. Use organisational and presentational devices.
	Identify and highlight key information. Summarise orally the information within the text. Use simple organisational devices.

Text Speak is a form of written communication used in text messages over digital devices such as mobile phones. This text uses abbreviations, symbols and pictures and does not follow standard grammar.

An **Abbreviation** is a shortened form of a word, e.g. anon for anonymous, sis for sister.

An **Acronym** is formed from the initial letters of other words and pronounced as a word, e.g. ASAP for as soon as possible.

An **Anecdote** is a very short story about a personal event or incident in the past that is interesting or amusing.

Can I Build Another Me? by Shinsuke Yoshitake

TASTER: TEXT TALK

Ask the children if they have ever sent or received a text message. Discuss how texts are different to speech or other written correspondence. For some, grammar and spelling can be a nightmare. Spelling, punctuation and grammar rules do not seem to apply!

Ask the children to look at the messages below. What is the message exchange and what techniques have been used to get the message across?

Hi BFF. Want 2 meet @ the park?

IDK. I need 2 ask mum

OK. Pls let me no.

Mum sed 2mro

That'd B gr8

C U L8r

Give the children a piece of writing that they can convert to text. It could be a nursery rhyme or a poem.

BUILDING TASK: REDUCE AND REVERSE!

Part of the skill in writing notes is to identify the key information. Give the students a few sentences. For each sentence, give the children a small sticky note. They should condense the information onto the sticky note. This can only be achieved if they are writing just key information. Children should identify the key information by underlining the key words and phrases in the sentence and then writing these onto their sticky note.

In 1464, Leonardo da Vinci designed a robot that resembled a knight and was controlled by ropes and wheels.

Most robots do not look like humans and are designed to complete jobs instead of people.

A robot is a machine that can be operated or controlled by a person or a computer programme.

Robots are also used in factories. These industrial robots complete tasks such as building cars or they move materials and objects around from one place to another.

Robots are useful because they can complete dangerous tasks and therefore not risk human lives. Better for a robot to defuse a bomb than a person!

Robots have been used to go into space. Five robots have been sent to Mars. In 2020, a robot called Perseverance landed on the Red Planet (Mars). This robot sends information back to earth helping scientists to better understand the planet.

For example, industrial robots are used in factories and complete tasks such as building cars or moving materials around from one place to another.

Industrial Robots factories building cars moving materials

Ind rob factories cars moving mat

Can they turn their notes into complete sentences again without referring to the original texts? This could be completed as an oral or written task.

BUILDING TASK: ANECDOTALLY SPEAKING

Look at the book again. Share the page of the profile of the boy titled MY FACE AND BODY. The labels on the diagram are notes of what makes the boy unique and special. Parts of his body remind him of feelings and some remind him of incidents.

Explore with the children that the boy has written notes on specific things that have happened to him, e.g. being scratched or a scar from falling off his bike. How might he have fallen off his bike – did he hit a bump or did his wheel fall off? It would be interesting to know more.

Explain that an anecdote is a very short story of a personal event or incident in the past that is interesting or amusing. Encourage children to share with each other an anecdote of a time when they hurt themselves. What happened? How did they feel? Do they have a scar? Did they break a bone?

For an extra challenge, can they re-tell their partner's anecdote to another student/the class?

MAIN TASK: MIND MAP YOUR UNIQUENESS

In *Can I Build Another Me?* the boy, Kevin, creates a fact file page and then labels a profile picture of himself with notes about his features, abilities and things that have happened to him.

1. Ask the students to complete an All About Me page similar to that of Kevin's. Agree as a class on which subheadings would be useful. 'Weight' may be something that could be removed. They may wish to include likes and dislikes, favourite teacher, favourite dinner.

2. Children draw a profile picture of themselves. Around the outside of their picture, they should make notes on some of their features. Children could write something about each of the features Kevin has labelled and make it personal to themselves.

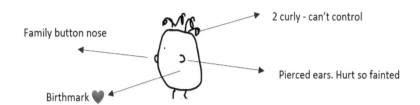

Family button nose

2 curly - can't control

Pierced ears. Hurt so fainted

Birthmark

Encourage the children to think of features in terms of

- what they look like (cute nose – button)
- find unusual about their features (curly uncontrollable hair)
- an incident of which it reminds them (Knobbly knees. Competition)
- what happens to this feature at certain times (swollen lips 🐡)

3. Ensure students are thinking about notes and not writing whole sentences. Are there any abbreviations used?

4. Share profile maps with a partner. Partner A looks at the profile map of partner B and asks a question about one of the notes. Partner B expands on the notes orally to partner A. Change roles and share Partner B's profile map.

5. In larger groups or as a class, can Partner B relate and share the anecdote/information of Partner A?

6. Choose one of the labels from a profile map and expand the notes further.
   For example, *pierced ears. Hurt so fainted*

   Birthday treat. 8 yrs old. Bedford town centre. Nervous. Sis teased. Called names.
   Chose earrings -round, gold stud. Steri-wipe. Blue dot on ear. Machine-like gun. Hot, sweaty,
   dizzy. Pierced ear. Fell 2 floor. Sis LOL.

DIFFERENTIATION

✓ Increase or decrease the number of subheadings and labels to be produced.

✓ Create a model exemplar as a class of one of the adults in school.

✓ Further work on general acronyms could be explored, especially those used widely, e.g. P.O., ASAP, WWF, WWW, UN, B&B, ASBO, BBC, LOL.

Teacher Tools and Techniques	
Emotional Literacy	Awareness of emotions in decision-making
	Understanding past events as learning opportunities
	Recognising and naming strengths and uniqueness
Developing Relationships	Talking partners – agreement and compromise
	Cooperation
	Listening and valuing the opinions and experiences of others
Self-Development	Thinking out loud, use of language/symbols to communicate, self-motivation, awareness of strength and areas for development
	Verbalising ideas
Skills for Learning	Thinking out loud, use of language/symbols to communicate
	Grouping/sorting, decision-making, agreement, sequencing, identifying information, understanding cause and effect, synthesising
	Speaking and listening
The Brain Learning and Behaviour	Targeting audience and purpose
	Communicating ideas

PHSE LINK (PSHE ASSOCIATION PROGRAMME OF STUDY FOR PSHE EDUCATION – KS2)

Personal identity; what contributes to who we are (e.g. ethnicity, family, gender, faith, culture, hobbies, likes/dislikes).

Recognise individuality and personal qualities.

Identify personal strengths, skills, achievements and interests and how these contribute to a sense of self-worth.

Respect the differences and similarities between people and recognise what they have in common with others, e.g. physically, in personality or in background.

Autobiography

Learning Objective: To write an autobiographical account
Success Criteria: ◆ Include a clear introduction about yourself ◆ Choose a memorable anecdote to describe ◆ Use first person ◆ Use the past tense ◆ Include my thoughts, feelings and actions ◆ Use temporal (time) connectives and adverbial phrases ◆ Include details such as date and place ◆ Include a reflection *(What did you learn from the experience? How do you feel now?)*

Pupils Can...	Make links between their own experiences and the events and information they encounter in texts. Write informally, recounting personal or imagined experiences, swapping appropriately between tenses. Use emotive language and precise descriptive language. Adapt degrees of formality and informality to suit the form of the text. Create cohesion across paragraphs using a wider range of cohesive devices, which can include adverbials.
	Express and articulate personal opinions, feelings and emotions. Write informally using the appropriate tense. Recount personal or imagined experiences using some emotive language to engage the reader. Create cohesion within paragraphs using adverbials
	Recognise and use narrative language. Use emotive language. Write informally in the first person. Use tenses mostly correctly. Use paragraphs to organise ideas. Use expanded noun phrases effectively. Use fronted adverbials.

*An **autobiography** is a retelling of a person's life written by that person.*

*An **anecdote** is a very short story about a personal event or incident in the past that is interesting or amusing.*

***Descriptive language** is used to help the reader visualise what a character or setting is like. It can engage the reader and help them feel part of the narrative and connect to the text. It often includes figurative language alongside adjectival phrases to help the reader to imagine in their mind's eye.*

| Can I build Another Me?
by Shinsuke Yoshitake | Template for autobiographies. |

TASTER: HOW MANY WORDS WILL IT TAKE?

Explain to the children that they will hear key words associated with a noun. They should try and guess the noun in the shortest number of key words given, e.g. *animal, paw, bark - could be guessed correctly as dog.* It took three key words, therefore they have three points. Complete several examples until the children understand the nature of the game.

Split the class into two teams. A member of team A is given a noun to describe, *using key words*, to ***their team***. The aim is to guess the noun in as few key words as possible.

A member of team B is given a different noun to describe to ***their team***, *using key words only.* Their team should try and guess the noun in as few key words as possible. The winner of the game is the team with the least points.

Suggested nouns: *cat, glasses, water, teacher, tree, sun, hand, pen, ball, book, curtains, house, owl, fire, steps, paint, towel, TV, mobile phone, computer, flower, fish, pool, mountain, sea, etc.*

BUILDING TASK: NOTE AN ANECDOTE

Using their profile map and the extended note they made from the main task on note writing, students should write up their notes into a full description of the event. This could be modelled to the class and the success criteria for descriptive autobiographical writing built up as the class task proceeds.

Alternatively, show them the completed anecdote and ask them to annotate, picking out techniques, parts they like and what needs improving.

> Choose one of the labels from own profile map and expand the notes further.
> E.g *Pierced ears. Hurt so fainted*
> *Birthday Treat. 8yrs old. Bedford town centre. Nervous. Sis teased. Called names. Chose earrings-round, gold stud. Steri-wipe. Blue dot on ear. Machine like gun. Hot, sweaty, dizzy. Pierced ear. Fell 2 floor. Sis LOL.*

As an 8th birthday treat my mum had promised to take me to have my ears pierced. It was something I had been looking forward to for ages. My sister had her ears pierced already and I remember feeling very jealous of all the beautiful dangly earrings she wore. I thought she looked like a princess with all her jewellery and I loved how her earrings bounced around as she moved her head. The shop where they pierced ears was in Bedford Town Centre which was a bus ride away. On the bus I was getting more and more nervous, especially as my sister teased me about how much it was going to hurt. I started to well up a little and my voice cracked when I told her to stop it – that was enough to make my sister call me 'chicken'!

Not long after, we arrived at the shopping centre and I hesitantly went in with my mum and sister. I was allowed to choose which studs I wanted (dangly ones were not allowed until your ears had healed) so I picked out some simple, plain, gold ones. Disappointing. The shop assistant cleaned my ears with a steri-wipe, which felt cold and wet. It smelled of hospitals. She took out a blue felt tip and placed a dot on each of my earlobes. Mum checked that the dots were in the right place for the holes to be made. Then, horror! In the hand of the shop assistant was what looked like a gun with two pincers. It had part of the earring placed in one of the pincers. As she came nearer to me, I could feel myself getting hotter, my back started to sweat and my hands became very sticky. There was a loud buzzing in my brain and I felt very nauseous. The pincers of the gun were placed around my earlobe and I could hear my sister doing a countdown 3…2…1… The next thing I remember was waking up dazed on the floor of the shop. My mum's face was looming over me and she looked concerned. However, my sister was completely different. She was on the floor too – rolling with laughter. I had fainted. That is why, to this day, I only have one ear pierced!

Children should take their extended notes and write up an anecdote using the agreed success criteria.

BUILDING TASK: INTRODUCTIONS AND REFLECTIONS

Think about how you could hook in a reader for your autobiography. What would you like your reader to know? Compare these openings. Which would want to make you read on?

◆ *My name is Victoria and I was born in East London in 1987.*

◆ *I was born in East London in 1987 and my parents called me Victoria; however, the family always use my nickname, Vixie.*

◆ *I was called Vixie from the very start, although my full name is Victoria. I am only called by the name Victoria when I am in trouble! I was born in the East End of London, within the sounds of Bow Bells, so I am a real cockney.*

https://www.literacywagoll.com/biographies.html contains a couple of autobiographies. One of a superhero and one of David Beckham.

Looking at the autobiography introduction for a **Superhero**, what facts do we learn about the writer? What else would we like to know? Is this a good example of an introduction?

Next look at the excerpt from David Beckham's autobiography. He shares an anecdote with the reader about a particular match he played. The last paragraph has a reflection – a thought about his experience and how it has affected him. What has he learnt from this experience? Children could look back at their anecdotes. Is there something that they could reflect on? Have they learnt anything from the experience?

MAIN TASK: SHORT AUTOBIOGRAPHY

Explain to the class that they will be writing their own autobiographical account. They have already looked at writing up anecdotes as part of their building skills – they could include this in their autobiography. They will need to think about how they plan their autobiography and how they design it.

1. Decide as a class some of the subheadings they could use. What will need to be included, e.g. place of birth, date of birth, family, school, favourite things, likes and dislikes. (These are some of the things they included in the fact file they made.) They may want a subheading for their anecdote and another for their reflection. Do they want to write it as a narrative or complete it as a fact file page? Share some templates with the children.

2. Children decide and plan the information under their subheadings They may wish to include more than one anecdote.

3. Encourage the children to reflect on their anecdote and what they have learnt from this event. It may be that they are just recording a memory, so they may need to think about whether they would have done something differently. Alternatively, they could write about their wishes for the future.

4. Children complete their autobiographies, referring to the success criteria as they work. Partway through they should highlight a sentence they are particularly pleased with and share it with a partner. They should also identify a sentence that they would like to amend and improve. With their partner, could they edit and improve?

5. Once completed, share autobiographies with a partner. The partner should identify five facts from the autobiography that they did not know about their classmate.

DIFFERENTIATION

✓ Children choose a template.

✓ Children design their own template.

✓ Work with a scribe.

✓ Record as a Q&A exercise on audio/visual equipment rather like an interview.

Teacher Tools and Techniques	
Emotional Literacy	Awareness of emotions in decision-making
	Understanding past events as learning opportunities
	Recognising and naming strengths and uniqueness
Developing Relationships	Talking partners – agreement and compromise
	Cooperation
	Listening and valuing the opinions and experiences of others
Self-Development	Thinking out loud, use of language/symbols to communicate, self-motivation, awareness of strength and areas for development
	Verbalising ideas
Skills for Learning	Thinking out loud, use of language/symbols to communicate, grouping/sorting, decision-making, agreement, sequencing, identifying information, understanding cause and effect, synthesising
	Speaking and listening
The Brain Learning and Behaviour	Targeting audience and purpose
	Communicating ideas

PHSE LINK (PSHE ASSOCIATION PROGRAMME OF STUDY FOR PSHE EDUCATION – KS2)

About different feelings that humans can experience.

How to recognise and name different feelings.

About ways of sharing feelings and a range of words to describe feelings.

About things that help people feel good (e.g. playing outside, doing things they enjoy, spending time with family, getting enough sleep).

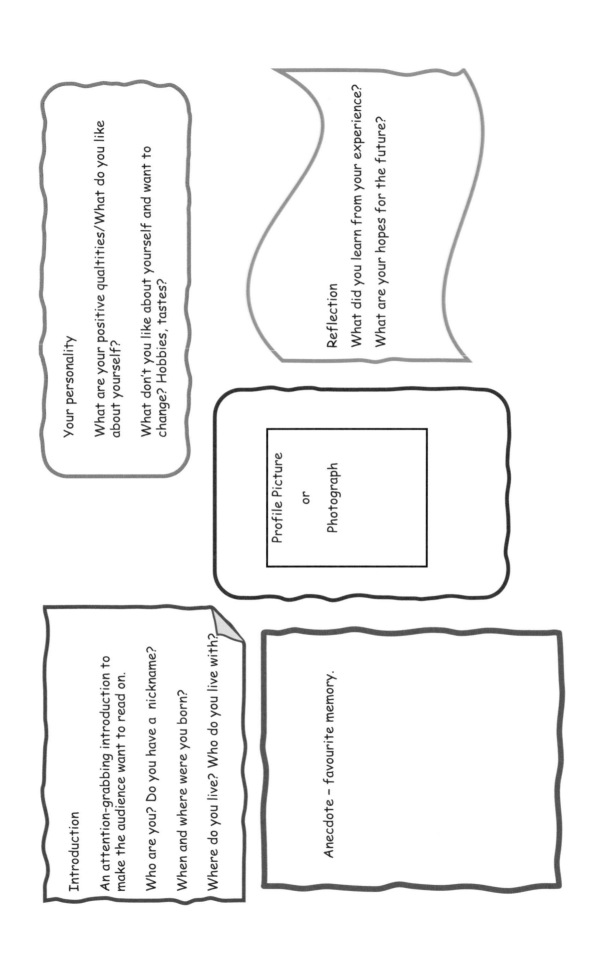

Your personality

What are your positive qualitities/What do you like about yourself?

What don't you like about yourself and want to change? Hobbies, tastes?

Reflection

What did you learn from your experience?

What are your hopes for the future?

Profile Picture

or

Photograph

Introduction

An attention-grabbing introduction to make the audience want to read on.

Who are you? Do you have a nickname?

When and where were you born?

Where do you live? Who do you live with?

Anecdote – favourite memory.

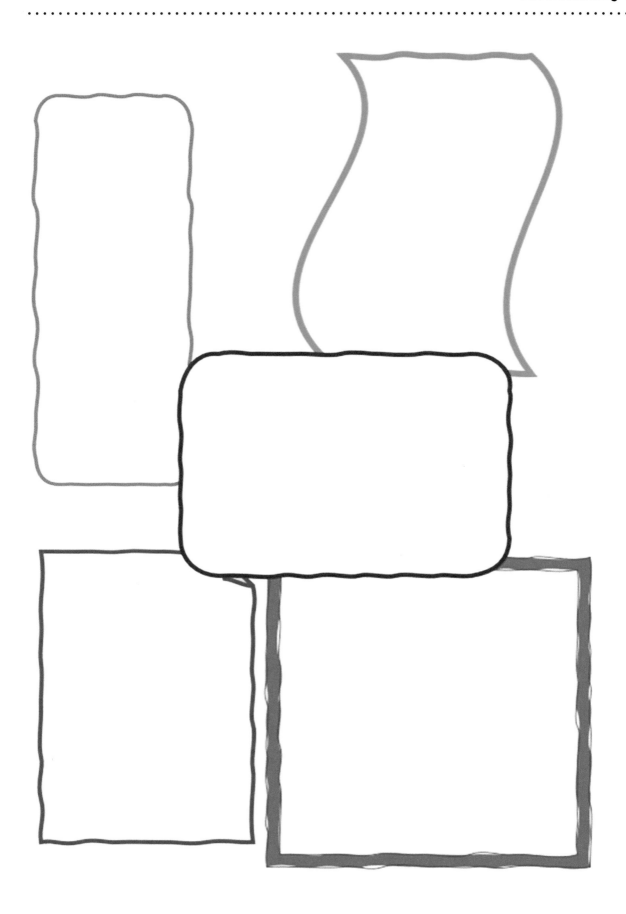

My Autobiography

My Personal Details

Name
Place of Birth
Date of Birth
My parents chose my name because.....

My Family

My Characteristics

My Favourite memory

The Future

When I am older I hope.....

Title	
Introduction My personal details, family, friends, pets	
My Characteristics How would I describe myself? What am I proud of?	
Favourites Things Things, places, activities, music, films	
Special Memory What is one of my favourite memories?	
Reflection What have I learned? What are my hopes and dreams for the future?	

Autobiography

What is your name?	
Where were you born?	
When were you born?	
Who do you live with?	
Name five things that best describe you.	
Name two things you like to do.	
What is your favourite subject at school?	
Name your favourite book.	
What is your favourite TV programme?	
What is your favourite animal and why?	

What are you most proud of?	
What is your favourite memory?	
Where was your best holiday?	
If you could have an unusual pet, what would it be?	
What job would you like to do in the future?	

All about Me

Learning Objective: To develop a greater understanding of how we decide what to believe about ourselves	
Success Criteria:	
◆ Talk about our strengths and skills as well	
◆ Share the things we would like to work on and improve	

Pupils Can...	Describe the skills they have.
	Give examples of a skill that they have developed over time.
	Describe what self-awareness is and why it is important to development and wellbeing.

How we see and understand ourselves is a personal construction created by the interactions and experiences we have had during our lives. How we think about ourselves impacts on how we interpret the world around us and the way we interact with others.

Self-awareness *is how a person consciously knows and understands their own character, feelings, motives and desires. Self-awareness is about stepping back and observing your thoughts and feelings as you experience them. It can be as simple as noticing the emotions you experience when in certain situations or how you feel when you are with certain friends. It can be being aware of your thoughts when you experience something scary or difficult or when you are faced with new situations. It can also be a more complex awareness of how your thoughts affect your emotions, bodily sensations and behaviours. For example, you might notice yourself feeling stressed about a test you have that day. You might experience butterflies in your stomach, which might lead you to miss breakfast. This may then mean that you feel sick. This sick feeling may make you feel like you can't do the test which may influence the way you focus and concentrate. This of course will have an impact on your results, which may then feed the belief that you don't do well on tests.*

Self-awareness is becoming aware of the parts of your internal world that might otherwise get buried, pushed aside or go unnoticed.

Awareness of these aspects of yourself is the first step to change and growth. After all, you can't change what you don't know about.

Resources	*Can I Build Another Me?* by Shinsuke Yoshitake. Large sheets of paper Books on different types of trees Weather symbols – computer and printer to print weather symbols, if needed iPad to take photos	Russian dolls set Journey map Art materials Small figure child, parent and robot Large piece of coloured cloth to act as the stage for the figures when acting out the story

TASTER: INSPIRATION

Read and share the book *Can I Build Another Me?* with the children. It can be a lovely experience if the story is acted out with small figures while it is being read. The children sit in a circle and the person reading the story sits alongside the person acting out the story in front of them using small figures.

At the end of the story, ask the children what it has made them think of. Explore their ideas together. Explain that you have set up a range of activities around the classroom. Explain what they are and then ask the children to choose one of the activities that the book has inspired them to do.

Activities:

1. *Likes and Dislikes*

2. *About my Face and Body*

3. *Things I Can Do and Things I Can't*

4. *My Younger Self Is Still Inside*

5. *My Family*

6. *Ever Changing Feelings*

7. *Inside my Head*

For each of the activities, use a picture of that part of the story from the book to remind the children and a range of art materials so that they can create something that the book has inspired them to explore. For example, Likes and Dislikes – the children take a large sheet of paper and using other smaller pieces make pockets all over it. In the pockets, they could put drawings or notes on things they like or dislike.

When the children have finished. ask them to lay their work on the table and create a Silent Exhibition. With a Silent Exhibition, the children walk around looking at each other's work in silence. You can give post-it notes to the children and encourage them to write notes to each other about an aspect of the work that they like.

BUILDING TASK: WEATHER FEELINGS

Share the My Journey map with the children. Point out how the artist has used a weather symbol to show how they felt about a part of that journey. Ask the children if this helps them understand the person whose journey it is. Explore the types of weather symbols they could use, and what they might show. For example, *sunshine could show a happy time, a rainbow might show a magical experience and a tornado might illustrate a really bad time.*

Explain that you would like them to create their own journey map. The map needs to include important things that they have done, learnt or experienced over their life. This might include a special birthday party, a holiday or a special present they have received. It may also include the not-so-good things: a time when they fell and broke a bone, the time when a family pet died or a time when they moved house and changed schools and lost friends.

While the children are working, create a journey map of your own for them to see and talk about.

Take time out for children to share something, ask a question about how to do something or have a look at each other's work.

MAIN TASK: WHAT WOULD HANG ON MY TREE?

1. Share the last part of the story with the children – I'm no one but me. Look at how the children have trees coming out of their heads and how all the trees are different.

2. Share the pictures of different types of trees with the children.

3. Ask the children to draw their head with a tree growing out of it as the children in the book have done.

4. Explain that you would like them to decorate their tree with pictures of things they like/enjoy/ are good at. Their tree can be any colour and have leaves and/or flowers on it if they would like. It is their special tree.

5. When all the trees are completed, create an exhibition and focus on how wonderful it is to have such amazing trees, each of which is special and different.

DIFFERENTIATION

✓ By acting out the story with figures as well as encouraging children to listen, you can include children with differences in concentration and language needs.

✓ By asking children to choose a way of creating something inspired by the story itself, you are enabling children to use the skills and abilities they have.

✓ For children who may struggle with the tasks, consider whether they can be supported by a TA or another child or you as an opportunity to discuss the task and adapt it to suit their needs.

✓ When undertaking the journey map, children could download weather symbols from the internet. They could then add these to their journey map.

Teacher Tools and Techniques	
Emotional Literacy	Discussion about feelings during the work on the journey map
Developing Relationships	Constructive criticism Positive comments
Self-Development	Understanding their own journey map and how they felt about situations Celebrating difference
Skills for Learning	Planning and organisation of tasks
The Brain, Learning and Behaviour	Linking the journey map weather symbols with how they felt

PHSE LINK (PSHE ASSOCIATION PROGRAMME OF STUDY FOR PSHE EDUCATION – KS2)

About personal identity; what contributes to who we are (e.g. ethnicity, family, gender, faith, culture, hobbies, likes/dislikes).

That mental health, just like physical health, is part of daily life; the importance of taking care of mental health.

Recognising what makes them special.

Recognising the ways in which we are all unique.

Identifying what they are good at, what they like and dislike

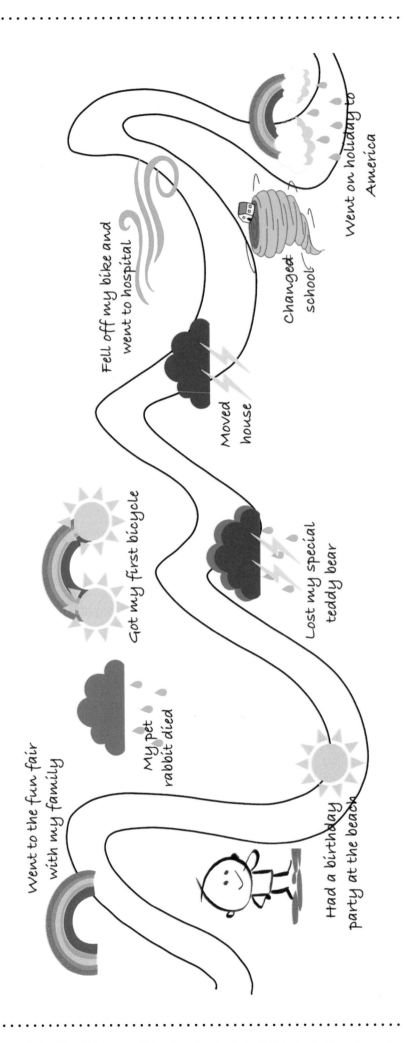

The following events appear along the winding path:

- Went on holiday to America
- Changed schools
- Fell off my bike and went to hospital
- Moved house
- Got my first bicycle
- Lost my special teddy bear
- My pet rabbit died
- Went to the fun fair with my family
- Had a birthday party at the beach

Diary Extract

Learning Objective: To narrate past experiences and convey emotion	
Success Criteria:	

- ◆ Identify and describe how different places make you feel
- ◆ Use past tense and present tense appropriately
- ◆ Chronological order
- ◆ Include emotive language
- ◆ Temporal (time) connectives
- ◆ Include figurative language – simile/metaphor/idiom
- ◆ Use colloquial language (informal)

Pupils Can...	Make links between their own experiences and the events and information they encounter in texts. Read and extract information that conveys emotions. Write informally, recounting personal or imagined experiences, swapping appropriately between past and present tense. Use emotive language and precise descriptive language.
	Express and articulate personal opinions, feelings and emotions, Write informally, swapping appropriately between past and present tense. Recount personal or imagined experiences using some emotive language to engage the reader.
	Recognise and use narrative language, e.g. 'Dear Diary'. Use emotive language. Write informally in the first person. Use past tense and present tense mostly correctly.

Emotive language is when certain word choices are made to evoke a strong emotional response in the reader, e.g. *The animal was killed vs The animal was slaughtered. Using emotive language persuades the reader to share the writer's point of view or experiences by rousing emotions/feelings.*

Descriptive language is used to help the reader visualise what a character or setting is like. It can engage the reader and help them feel part of the narrative and connect to the text. It often includes figurative language alongside adjectival phrases to help the reader to imagine in their mind's eye.

Resources *The Map of Good Memories* by Fran Nuño and Zuzanna Celej	Diary extract - Anne Frank - Malala Yousafzai

TASTER: HOW DOES THIS MAKE YOU FEEL?

Show the students a picture of a place many of them will have experienced. Ask the children to mind map the things they like the most about this place and how this place makes them feel, e.g. *'I enjoy the park because I love running through the leaves in autumn', 'When I'm at home, I feel safe and content'.*

Places could be – *The cinema*

- *The park*

- *The swimming pool*

- *A house (to imagine as their own home)*

BUILDING TASK: CONVEYING EMOTION

Explain to the students that there are many ways that people convey their emotion, e.g. *body language, facial expressions, posture, thoughts, internal sensations (fight, flight, freeze), dialogue, tone of voice, actions.*

Ask the students how they know when someone is angry, upset or happy.

Can they describe emotions using a range of narrative techniques? Ask the students to pick an emotion, or pick a random emotion from a hat, and ask each child to write or say a sentence to convey that emotion without naming the emotion.

Her heart was racing, her hands were sweating and her legs were shaking – Fear.

He felt like a weight had been taken off his shoulders – Relief.

She couldn't contain herself, she wanted to jump up and down and punch the air – Excitement.

She jumped out of her skin, her open hand clasped her heart and she let out a delightful squeal – Surprise.

Can the students name the emotions their peers are describing?

BUILDING TASK: ANNE AND MALALA

Anne Frank was a young girl of Jewish heritage, who decided to diarise the events she experienced throughout the Holocaust. Anne Frank's *The Diary of a Young Girl* is renowned for its emotive language. As a class, identify the adjectives and phrases which convey her feelings of fear.

October 20th, 1942: My hands still shaking, though it's been two hours since we had the scare… The office staff stupidly forgot to warn us that the carpenter, or whatever he's called, was coming to fill the extinguishers… After working for about fifteen minutes, he laid his hammer and some other tools on our bookcase (or so we thought!) and banged on our door. We turned white with fear. Had he heard something after all and did he now want to check out this mysterious looking bookcase? It seemed so, since he kept knocking, pulling, pushing and jerking on it. I was so scared I nearly fainted at the thought of this total stranger managing to discover our wonderful hiding place…

Malala Yousafzai has made many speeches about her beliefs on human rights and especially the education of women and children.

In 2008, she protested against the closing of girls' schools in her area of Pakistan. In 2012, she was shot because of her views. Despite being shot, Yousafzai survived and became even more determined to speak out about the importance of education of girls. In 2014, she received the accolade of becoming the world's youngest winner of the Nobel Peace Prize.

This inspirational young woman now travels around the world spreading her message and speaking on human rights.

As a class or with a learning partner, identify the adjectives and phrases which convey her feelings in the following extracts.

SATURDAY 3 JANUARY: I had a terrible dream yesterday with military helicopters and the Taleban. I have had such dreams since the launch of the military operation in Swat. My mother made me breakfast and I went off to school. I was afraid going to school because the Taleban had issued an edict banning all girls from attending schools.

Only 11 students attended the class out of 27. The number decreased because of Taleban's edict. My three friends have shifted to Peshawar, Lahore and Rawalpindi with their families after this edict.

On my way from school to home I heard a man saying, 'I will kill you'. I hastened my pace and after a while I looked back if the man was still coming behind me. But to my utter relief he was talking on his mobile and must have been threatening someone else over the phone.

Malala writes on the website https://malala.org/malalas-story:

2014: After months of surgeries and rehabilitation, I joined my family in our new home in the U.K. It was then I knew I had a choice: I could live a quiet life or I could make the most of this new life I had been given. I determined to continue my fight until every girl could go to school.

With my father, who has always been my ally and inspiration, I established Malala Fund, a charity dedicated to giving every girl an opportunity to achieve a future she chooses.

MAIN TASK: 'MAPPING YOUR MEMORIES'

In *The Map of Good Memories,* Zoe is having to leave the city she has lived in her whole life in order to take refuge in another country.

1. Zoe makes her own map of her favourite places.

Ask the students to draw their own map with all their favourite places on it.

2. Ask the students how they would feel if they had to leave the town they grew up in and not go to their favourite places again. Support the children to identify *why* they would feel this way by supplying them with a table to write down their feelings.

Favourite Place	How it makes me feel	Favourite memory there	How I would feel to leave
The park that has an oval-shaped lake. In the middle of the lake is a duck-house that has been built to look like a castle. Trees line a gravel path from the lake to the park's café, where customers can sit comfortably relaxing and watching the wildlife. There are friendly squirrels that cheekily steal your lunch if you are not looking.	It makes me feel relaxed because I like listening to the birds and looking at the trees. I feel calm and tranquil as I sit holding a hot chocolate in my hands and watch the ripples on the lake as the ducks swim to and from their castle home. It makes me feel joyful because I can run and play there. I love to run through the leaves in the autumn and listen to them rustle and crunch. I laugh out loud when I hear the screams of people shouting at the squirrels for taking their biscuits.	One day my mum took me to the park for a delicious picnic and she brought a flask of hot chocolate. We fed the ducks together. It was a special time together because we talked and talked about which secondary school I was going to go to and we made the important decision together. I remember thinking that my mum really wanted to know what I thought. My dog jumped into a pile of leaves and disappeared! He came bounding out from the other side of the pile covered in oak leaves like some Halloween creature.	I would feel saddened that me and my mum wouldn't be able to feed the ducks together. I would feel empty like the bread bag that had been used to hold the duck food. I would miss seeing my dog enjoying himself and watching his tail wag.

DIFFERENTIATION

◆ Basic map layout could be given to children.

◆ Give the children emotions they could describe.

◆ Give children specific adjectives for strengthening their vocabulary.

Teacher Tools and Techniques	
Emotional Literacy	Awareness of emotions in decision-making
	Recognising the feelings of others
	Dealing with failure as an opportunity to learn
Developing Relationships	Talking partners – agreement and compromise
	Cooperation
Self-Development	Thinking out loud, use of language/symbols to communicate, self-motivation, awareness of strength and areas for development
	Verbalising ideas
	Performance
Skills for Learning	Thinking out loud, use of language/symbols to communicate
	Grouping/sorting, decision-making, agreement, sequencing, identifying information, understanding cause and effect, synthesising
The Brain Learning and Behaviour	Targeting audience and purpose
	Communicating ideas

PHSE LINK (PSHE ASSOCIATION PROGRAMME OF STUDY FOR PSHE EDUCATION – KS2)

About different feelings that humans can experience.

How to recognise and name different feelings.

About ways of sharing feelings; a range of words to describe feelings.

About things that help people feel good (e.g. playing outside, doing things they enjoy, spending time with family, getting enough sleep).

Diary Extracts

Learning Objective: To narrate past experiences and convey emotion	

Success Criteria:

◆ Plan appropriately

◆ Identify and describe how different places make you feel

◆ Use past and present tense appropriately

◆ Use emotive and descriptive language

◆ Use temporal connectives

◆ Keep to chronological order

◆ Include figurative language – simile/metaphor/idiom

◆ Use colloquial language (informal)

Pupils Can...	Make links between their own experiences and the events and information they encounter in texts. Read and extract information that conveys emotions. Write informally, recounting personal or imagined experiences, swapping appropriately between past and present tense. Use emotive language and precise descriptive language to engage the reader.
	Express and articulate personal opinions, feelings and emotions. Write informally, swapping appropriately between past and present tense. Recount personal or imagined experiences using some emotive language to engage the reader.
	Recognise and use narrative language, e.g. 'Dear Diary'. Use emotive language. Write informally in the first person. Use past tense and present tense mostly correctly.

Emotive language *is when certain word choices are made to evoke a strong emotional response in the reader, e.g.* The animal was killed vs The animal was slaughtered. *Using emotive language persuades the reader to share the writer's point of view or experiences by rousing emotions/feelings.*

Descriptive language *is used to help the reader visualise what a character or setting is like. It can engage the reader and help them feel part of the narrative and connect to the text. It often includes figurative language alongside adjectival phrases to help the reader to imagine in their mind's eye.*

 Resources	*The Map of Good Memories* by Fran Nuño and Zuzanna Celej	Diary extract Diary planning template

TASTER: PURPOSE OF A DIARY

Divide the students into groups and give them each a copy of the diary extract.

Ask the groups to read together and answer the following questions:

◆ *What is this entry about?*

◆ *Why did the person write this?*

◆ *When was this written?*

◆ *Who may have written this?*

◆ *How is the writer feeling and how do you know?*

30th March 1991

Dear Diary,

Today was a great day, my mum came home with a new baby sister for me! I've always dreamed about having a baby sister. I'm 10 now and I wanted to start writing a diary so when she's older, we can read it together and we can laugh about all the fun things we did together!

I was a bit worried last night when Mum went to the hospital and it took me a while to get to sleep. Mum said I shouldn't worry and it wouldn't be long until she was back home for family cuddles. I cried a few times because I felt like my heart was beating really fast (it sounded like a loud ticking bomb ready to explode) but then I would just think about how great it was going to be when she got home.

My little sister is called Rebecca, but I'm going to call her Becky for short and she can call me Vixie.

I can just tell we are going to be best friends.

Love,

Victoria.

1st April 1991

My little sister has been here for two days now and she hasn't stopped crying! I'll be honest, I'm glad I'm not sharing a room with her. All she does is cry, have her nappy changed and drink milk.

I thought we'd be able to play together but she doesn't do anything! I think she might be broken!

I think I'll ask for a little brother next time.

Vix

BUILDING TASK: FEATURES OF A DIARY ENTRY

As a group discussion, ask the students what they believe the features of a diary are – write the suggestions on the board.

◆ *Uses past tense/mixture of tenses*

– *Uses first person*

　○ *Describes the writer's point of view, thoughts and feelings*

　○ *Includes opinions as well as facts*

　○ *Informal style*

　○ *Possibly reported speech*

Ask the students to write their own diary/recount writing skills checklist – what should a diary entry include? This will be used to encourage children to use their independent editing skills later on.

BUILDING TASK: MAP IT!

Referring to the previous activity 'Mapping your memories', ask the children to pick one of their favourite places to write a diary entry about.

Ask the children to write a plan for their entry.

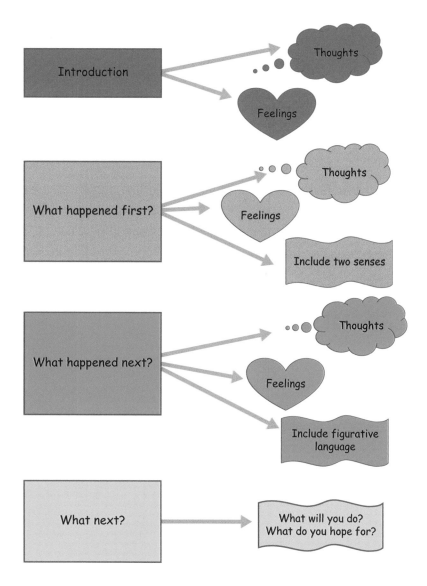

For example: I will… write about the park.

1. I will describe the park and set the scene. What was the weather like? Who was I with? What did the other person look like?

2. I will describe what happened and who I was with.

3. I will write about how I felt.

4. I will include my senses when describing the place.

MAIN TASK: 'MY DIARY'

1. Ask the children to write their diary entry, referring to their plan.

2. As they are writing, stop partway through and ask the children to find three feeling words. Can they make these words more emotive? Work with a learning partner to edit and improve these.

3. As they continue to write their diary, encourage the use of figurative language. Can they place a simile within their recount of an event?

4. Once they have written their diary entry, ask them to self-assess by referring to the checklist they created at the beginning of the lesson plan. This will encourage them to analyse their own work and encourage editing skills.

5. Children can also peer review – does their learning partner agree with their assessment?

6. Doodles and illustrations are also used in diaries as they can be a useful indicator of how the writer is feeling and can help explain events. Children could add these to their final presentation.

DIFFERENTIATION

✓ Children could be supplied with a plan layout giving prompts as to what to include.

✓ Discussions involving what events to write about or a potential fictional event.

✓ Give children specific adjectives to include, strengthening their vocabulary.

✓ Record the diary onto audio equipment or as a video presentation.

Teacher Tools and Techniques	
Emotional Literacy	Awareness of emotions in decision-making
	Recognising the feelings of others
	Dealing with failure as an opportunity to learn
Developing Relationships	Talking partners – agreement and compromise
	Cooperation
Self-Development	Thinking out loud, use of language/symbols to communicate, self-motivation
	Awareness of strength and areas for development
	Verbalising ideas
	Performance
Skills for Learning	Thinking out loud, use of language/symbols to communicate
	Grouping/sorting, decision-making, agreement, sequencing, identifying information, understanding cause and effect, synthesising
The Brain Learning and Behaviour	Targeting audience and purpose
	Communicating ideas

PHSE LINK (PSHE ASSOCIATION PROGRAMME OF STUDY FOR PSHE EDUCATION – KS2)

About different feelings that humans can experience.

How to recognise and name different feelings.

About ways of sharing feelings and a range of words to describe feelings.

About things that help people feel good (e.g. playing outside, doing things they enjoy, spending time with family, getting enough sleep).

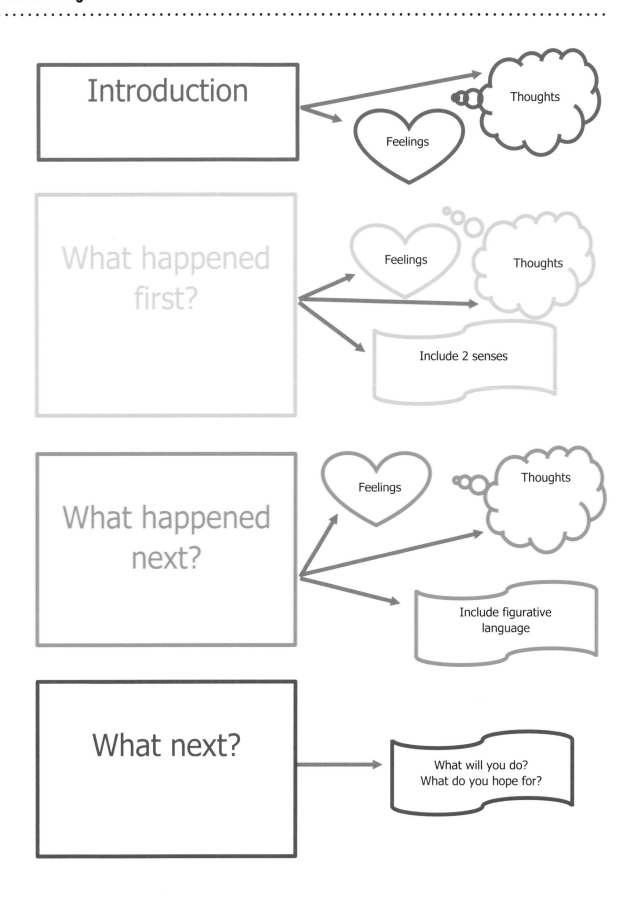

Special Memories Make Me Unique

Learning Objective: To understand that the experiences we have had make us who we are
Success Criteria:
◆ Share some of our happy past experiences
◆ Discuss the things we do that can change how we feel

Pupils Can...	Understand how experiences give us memories, which contain different emotions.
	Share a range of strategies that can shift change how we feel.
	Discuss how our experiences have made us a unique individual.

What do we mean by an internal map of the world?

An internal map of the world is *made up of our thinking and beliefs, which have been created; by the way we have perceived our experiences and interactions.*

Not only people but families, communities, cultures and societies have an 'internal map of the world' that affects how they both see and perceive the world. This internal map influences the choices they make and the perspectives they cherish, enforce and share.

Other elements that influence this internal map of the world include cultural beliefs and expectations, laws and customs and societally approved prejudices and/or rebellion against them. People understand who they are in the world and what their relationships are to others according to this internalised map. What are the rules and customs of behaviour that govern them, and does any given character as an individual obey them or not? Expectations about things like hierarchy, class, gender, sexuality, ethnicity and race will all be part of a character's internal map.

As an educational organisation, school welcomes many children who all have very different experiences of the world and the people in it and therefore have very different maps of the world. This gives schools an amazing opportunity to help children and young people both share their own map and share in the beauty and complexity of other people's worlds.

**Resources**	*The Map of Good Memories* by Fran Nuño and Zuzanna Celej Large sheets of paper	Pictures of buildings and houses Art materials Emotions wheel picture Emotions first aid box worksheet

TASTER: EMOTION WHEEL

1. Read the story to the children. Ask them to share their thoughts and ideas about the story – what has it made them think of? Explore the many emotions Zoe goes through during the story.

Read the story again and ask them to work in pairs to record the many emotions Zoe experiences. Ask the children to work in pairs and use the felt tip pens and/or pencil crayons to put together a colour palette for each of the emotions FEAR, SAD, HAPPY, ANGER. Discuss what they have created.

Ask them to create an emotion wheel for Zoe showing a picture of her emotions using the colour palette they have chosen.

BUILDING TASK: FIRST AID BOX

Share a first aid box with the children and discuss how it is used. It is needed when someone hurts themselves and need to be helped.

Ask the children to think of a time when they were sad and someone did something to make them feel better. Help them understand that the things people did to help them were like the things in the first aid box. Sometimes, they have been a little bit sad and so just need a quick hug, a bit like a plaster on a poorly finger. At other times, they may have been extremely sad and so needed to spend time with someone who they loved and who could care for them. Record their answers on the board. Support them to see that they are all different and that what may work for some will not work for others. Their experiences have all been different and they are unique. Ask the children to create a first aid box to show all the things they can use if and when they feel sad.

MAIN TASK: MEMORY PICTURE

1. Share with the children Zoe's map and talk about how she has different memories linked with different buildings and areas in the city where she lived.

2. Explain that their task is to draw a building that has been special to them and inside four of its windows draw four pictures that are special to them. Each picture needs to show an

event, which made them feel Happy, Sad, Angry and Frightened. Each window will cover the picture and so the audience has to open the window to see what is behind it.

3. Once completed, ask them to write what helped them during that time and hide it in the picture somewhere. This could be under the brickwork, in a window box or even behind the picture itself.

4. Once the pictures have been created, the children can share them in an exhibition. Parents could be invited to see what they have created and hear the children read the storybook.

DIFFERENTIATION

✓ For some children who are on the autistic spectrum, identifying feelings can be difficult. This is a great exercise to help them identify the signs that people give when they feel the four emotions discussed. It can be helpful to pair them with children who have a high emotional literacy level or with staff.

✓ For children with attention and concentration challenges, give them a task sheet to show the step-by-step approach to achieving what has been asked.

✓ For many children talking about emotions can be tricky, this may create a need to move to get rid of the excess energy they may feel. Observe their reactions and if you see them struggle and start to move around the class or distract others give them a reason to move or take a break. Support their emotional regulation.

Teacher Tools and Techniques	
Emotional Literacy	Empathy, discussion
Developing Relationships	Collaboration
Self-Development	Self-awareness – thinking about their own emotions and what they do to manage them
Skills for Learning	Planning Organisation
The Brain Learning and Behaviour	Understanding that their experiences are all different and it is this difference that makes them unique

PHSE LINK

About personal identity; what contributes to who we are (e.g. ethnicity,

family, gender, faith, culture, hobbies, likes/dislikes).

That mental health, just like physical health, is part of daily life; the importance of taking care of mental health.

Recognising what makes us special.

Recognising the ways in which we are all unique.

Identifying what they are good at, what they like and dislike.

My Self-Soothing First Aid Box

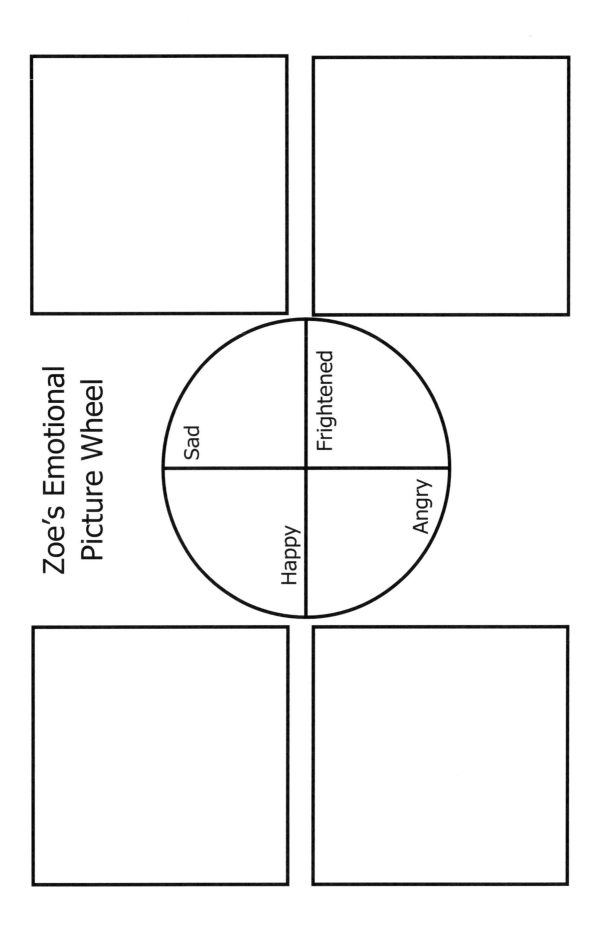

Zoe's Emotional Picture Wheel

Sad

Frightened

Happy

Angry

Precise Language

Learning Objective: To use clear and precise language to inform or explain	

Success Criteria:

Include at least one of the following

◆ preposition

◆ adverb

◆ adjective

◆ relative clause (which, who, when)

◆ appropriate verb choice

Pupils Can...	Make precise word choices that give the most accurate description possible, convey meaning and allow the audience to have the clearest picture of a desired outcome.
	Carefully choose words that most accurately convey meaning and give descriptions that enable the audience to fully understand and achieve a desired outcome.
	Carefully choose words that convey a desired meaning and outcome. Mod

*Preposition is a word that tells you where something is in relation to something else. Such as **in, on, under, inside and outside**. It can also be a position in time to something else such as **before** or **after**.*

*A **Relative Clause** is a **clause that can be used to give additional information about a noun. A relative clause includes a relative pronoun like** 'that', 'which', 'who', 'whose', 'where' and 'when'.*

Maybe by Kobi Yamada and Gabriella Barouch	Collection of pictures showing an action, e.g. running, eating, talking
Collection of pictures showing people/animals showing emotions	Illustrations from the book

TASTER: WHERE IS IT?

Place an item in the classroom somewhere and ask the students if they can tell you where it is without pointing. Explain that they have used a preposition to describe where the object is. Do this several times. For example, on top of the computer, under the chair, next to Kevin, etc. As an added challenge, tell the children they may not use the same preposition twice. Make a list of prepositions the children have used.

You could show them the Preposition song: *www.youtube.com/watch?v=byszemY8PI8*

Play The Meatball Song. Tell the students that, when they hear a preposition, they must stand up or pat their head: *www.youtube.com/watch?v=HgOdKV5jOcM*

Children could also sort a list of prepositions into groups of similar meanings:

Next to, alongside, adjacent, adjoining, beside

Under, beneath, underneath, below

BUILDING TASK: EXACTLY!

Show the children clips or pictures of people doing activities or displaying emotions. As a class decide the appropriate vocabulary to use. Discuss the strength of the word and its shade of meaning.

For example: *ate, munched, gobbled, devoured, gorged?*

pleased, happy, delighted, ecstatic?

With a learning partner, children use a thesaurus to choose exact verbs or adjectives to describe the pictures displayed. Illustrations from the book could be used.

For example, the illustration when the child fails – sad, forlorn, upset, thoughtful, despondent, downcast.

BUILDING TASK: WHAT'S THE DIFFERENCE?

I cut the pizza.

I sliced the pizza.

I sliced the pizza into quarters.

I sliced the pepperoni pizza into quarters.

I carefully sliced the pepperoni pizza, which was on the kitchen table, into quarters.

Using a pizza cutter, I carefully sliced the pepperoni pizza, which was on the kitchen table, into quarters.

Elicit from the children the changes that have been made and the difference this has made to the task completed.

Ask the children to be precise with one of the following sentences.

◆ *I washed my hair.*

◆ *I made toast.*

◆ *I wrote in a book.*

◆ *She made dinner.*

◆ *He ate crisps.*

MAIN TASK: DO AS I SAY?

1. Model the barrier game activity to the class. Using a picture that you have designed using shapes and lines (and possibly colours), describe the drawing to the children and ask them to replicate this on their paper.

Once you have completed your description and instructed them precisely where to position everything, share your example to compare with theirs. How good were you at describing? You could have been deliberately awful!

2. Discuss with the children what helped them with their drawing from your description… or what would have helped. Prepositions, size, colour? For example:
   Blue triangle
   Blue right-angled triangle
   Blue right-angled triangle with the right angle in the bottom left-hand corner

3. Children design their own pictures to describe to their learning partner. Children compare their drawings – what went well? What didn't go so well?

4. Nex, ask the children to verbally give instructions to their partner to complete a task such as making a paper aeroplane or building something out of playdough.

5. This activity could also be extended into the playground where students can build an obstacle course and can instruct a partner to complete an exercise activity. This will ensure the precise use of verbs.

DIFFERENTIATION

✓ Children given a range of drawings to describe from simple to more challenging

✓ Preposition vocabulary mats can be used

✓ Children given a drawing that has some dreadful instructions to follow – can they improve them?

Teacher Tools and Techniques	
Emotional Literacy	Awareness of emotions in decision-making
	Recognising the feelings of others
	Dealing with failure as an opportunity to learn
Developing Relationships	Talking partners – agreement and compromise
	Cooperation
Self-Development	Thinking out loud, use of language/ symbols to communicate, self-motivation
	Awareness of strength and areas for development
Skills for Learning	Thinking out loud, use of language/ symbols to communicate
	Grouping/sorting, decision-making, agreement
The Brain Learning and Behaviour	Targeting audience and purpose
	Communicating ideas

PHSE LINK (PSHE ASSOCIATION PROGRAMME OF STUDY FOR PSHE EDUCATION – KS2)

Recognise positive things about themselves and their achievements; set goals to help achieve personal outcomes.

Skills that will help them in their future careers (e.g. teamwork, communication and negotiation).

Personal identity: what contributes to who we are (e.g. ethnicity, family, gender, faith, culture, hobbies, likes/dislikes).

Identify personal strengths, skills, achievements and interests and how these contribute to a sense of self-worth.

How to manage setbacks/perceived failures, including how to re-frame unhelpful thinking.

Instructions

Learning Objective: To write a set of instructions	

Success Criteria:

◆ Include a catchy title that sets out the goal

◆ List equipment/resources

◆ Use bullet points or numbered steps

◆ Break down instructions into steps in chronological order

◆ Use time connectives

◆ Use imperative verbs

◆ Include precise language (adverbs, prepositions, adjectives, relative clauses) to clarify

◆ Use illustration/labelled diagrams

◆ Include an evaluative statement

Pupils Can...	Write a clear and detailed set of instructions that express time, place and cause using conjunctions, adverbs and prepositions. Use parenthesis and relative clauses to add additional advice and information. Adapt degrees of formality and informality to suit the form of the instructions. Use layout devices to provide additional information and guide the reader. Use evaluative statements to conclude writing.
	Write a detailed set of instructions that show time, place and cause using conjunctions, adverbs and prepositions. Use a catchy title, subheadings and a labelled diagram to aid presentation. Use parenthesis to add additional advice. Relative clauses can be used to add further information.
	Write a clear set of instructions that uses adverbs for time and place prepositions. Use a catchy title and subheadings and a labelled diagram to aid presentation.

Preposition *is a word that tells you where something is in relation to something else. Such as* **in, on, under, inside and outside**. *It can also be a position in time to something else such as* **before** *or* **after**.

A **Relative Clause** *is a* **clause that can be used to give additional information about a noun. A relative clause includes a relative pronoun like** *'that', 'which', 'who', 'whose', 'where' and 'when'.*

Evaluative Statements *are concluding sentences such as – 'Now, enjoy your delicious homemade pizza'.*

Conditional adverbial *shows the circumstances for the main idea/clause to come into effect. It can include the word 'if'. For example – 'If you prefer a crispier pizza base, roll the dough out thinner'.*

Resources	*Maybe* by Kobi Yamada and Gabriella Barouch	Students to bring in materials from home to make a dream jar Pictures of dream jars Example of instruction texts

TASTER: HOW WAS IT DONE?

Play the adverb game where children are given an activity and an adverb. They are asked to mime an activity and the class must identify the adverb.

For example: Have a stock of activities or have the class come up with their own activities to mine. Activities to mime could include:

◆ *Riding a bike*

◆ *Mixing a cake*

◆ *Swimming*

◆ *Dancing*

◆ *Blowing out candles on a cake*

◆ *Playing football*

BUILDING TASK: I HAVE A DREAM...

Remind the children of the BFG and how he caught dreams and kept them in jars to keep them safe. Show the children the illustrations from **Maybe** and how the character is using objects of reference in her jars and labels/text to represent her hopes and dreams. Can the children identify what the character's hopes and dreams might be?

Students discuss with learning partners what their hope and dreams might be. This could be an activity to think about goals for the end of the year and children could revisit this at the end of term six to see how far they have achieved these dreams/aspirations.

BUILDING TASK: BUILD A DREAM

Children should write a short paragraph on their hopes/dreams for the future. This could be what they would like to achieve by the end of the year; how they would like to improve themselves, changes they would like to see in the world, etc.

Children can design their own dream jar. What will it look like on the outside? Is there a label on the jar? What will be on the inside of the jar – objects, texts, pictures, photos? Children label their designs thinking about materials, etc.

Children to make their dream jar – making notes as they go or taking photographs at each step if needed.

MAIN TASK: HOW TO MAKE A DREAM JAR

1. Children refer to their notes and designs. They should make a list of resources they used.

2. As a class, share some examples of catchy titles they may wish to use or use as a prompt for their own.

3. Show children different examples of instructions. Are there any features that are similar? Point out the use of imperative verbs. Discuss features such as the importance of chronological order. Can the students think of parts of the process/procedure that will need added detail to help clarify meaning? Are there parts that would benefit from a diagram?

4. Children write a first draft of how to make their dream jar.

5. Using the success criteria, children re-draft, edit and improve their instructions.

6. Before a final version, students peer-evaluate their instructions.

7. Display dream jars and their instructions for all to admire!

DIFFERENTIATION

✓ Children can write instructions in a sequenced plan using photos or pictures

Photo/Picture	Photo/Picture	Photo/Picture	Photo/Picture	Photo/Picture
First...	Next...	Following this...		

✓ Children can be given a template to complete.

✓ Children can include Top Tips.

✓ Children can design on a computer and explore layouts.

Teacher Tools and Techniques	
Emotional Literacy	Awareness of emotions in decision-making
	Recognising the feelings of others
	Dealing with failure as an opportunity to learn
Developing Relationships	Talking partners – agreement and compromise
	Cooperation
Self-Development	Thinking out loud, use of language/symbols to communicate, self-motivation
	Awareness of strength and areas for development
Skills for Learning	Thinking out loud, use of language/symbols to communicate
	Grouping/sorting, decision-making, agreement
The Brain Learning and Behaviour	Targeting audience and purpose
	Communicating ideas

PHSE LINK (PSHE ASSOCIATION PROGRAMME OF STUDY FOR PSHE EDUCATION – KS2)

Recognise positive things about themselves and their achievements; set goals to help achieve personal outcomes.

Skills that will help them in their future careers (e.g. teamwork, communication and negotiation).

Personal identity: what contributes to who we are (e.g. ethnicity, family, gender, faith, culture, hobbies, likes/dislikes).

Identify personal strengths, skills, achievements and interests and how these contribute to a sense of self-worth.

How to manage setbacks/perceived failures, including how to re-frame unhelpful thinking.

What Sort of Person Would You Like to Be? You Have the Power to Choose

Learning Objectives: To identify a range of qualities and characteristics that make us unique

To develop a greater understanding of how we decide what to believe about ourselves

Success Criteria:

◆ Describe qualities or characteristics about themselves that they like and are proud of

Pupils Can...	Describe things that they can do.
	Share an object that has significance to them and explain why.
	Share a dream they have for their future.

Self-Concept is generally thought of as what we think about ourselves – our individual perception. This includes our behaviour, talents, abilities and our unique characteristics. Essentially, it is the mental picture we create of who we are as a person. For example, beliefs such as 'I am a good parent' or 'I am a kind person', 'I am a creative gardener' or 'I am a hard worker' are part of an overall self-concept.

Our self-concept is important because it influences how we think, feel and act in everyday life. Carl Rogers (1959) proposed that self-concept had three separate components: self-concept, self-image and ideal-self, and that it was the discrepancy between the self-image and the ideal-self that created our self-esteem or our overall sense of self-worth. If we have a positive self-concept, it acts as a shield to protect us from negative events, thus a positive self-image is one of the foundations for good MHWB.

In relation to school, children and young people can have a good self-image in relation to some subjects but a poor self-image in relation to others. It is what they believe that affects how they engage and make progress.

Resources	*Maybe* by Kobi Yamada and Gabriella Barouch	Labels sheet/luggage labels
	A special object that has a meaningful memory	Different packs of flower seeds
		Seed packet template
	Dream bubble	Paper and pens

TASTER: SHARE YOUR THOUGHTS

Read the story to the children. Discuss what the story has made them think about, or the questions they might like to ask the author or the child in the book. Ask each child to draw a dream – something they would like to do in the future on the dream bubble. Share a dream of your own with the children and then ask them to share theirs.

Share with the children an object that has a special meaning for you. It might be a shell from a holiday when you were little or a fossil you collected or the cork of a champagne bottle from a celebration. It can be an object that makes you sad such as the key from your first house or even an object that makes you cross like a piece of a special plate that your friend broke. A picture would work if you don't have an object. Ask the children to bring in an object/picture of an object that has a meaning for them that they would be happy to share with each other. Ask them to tell the story about how the object became theirs or why they chose it and why it is important.

BUILDING TASK: LABELS

Ask the children to work in pairs and write three things about their partner on three different post-it notes. Ask some of the pairs to share what they have written. As they share what they have said about their partner, take the post-it notes and stick them onto the young person. After sticking them on, ask the young person if these are labels they would like to keep or get rid of.

When the children have finished, explain that we are given labels by other people all the time. We accept them without question, especially if the people who are giving them are our family or friends or adults we trust. But sometimes they get things wrong!

Share a label you have been given by family or friends that isn't true. Explain how you got it and what you have done about it. Sometimes the labels we are given are useful – Anne is a dreadful cook – so Anne never gets asked to cook anything; she gets away with not having to make food for family gatherings! At other times, we are given labels that we don't like – Ben is bad-tempered and gets angry really easily on the football pitch. Ben may have been angry once but he has now been given the label.

Help the children see that they have the power to keep the labels, not accept them or take them off and throw them away.

Ask the children to draw a picture of themselves and stick labels around the picture – red labels for things they would like to get rid of, and blue ones for the ones they are happy to keep. Ask the children to then write three labels in green that they would like to collect over the next year.

MAIN TASK

1. Spread out the packets of seeds on the table and ask the children to look at them. What do they notice?

— *Seeds need different conditions*

— *The plants are all different*

— *They each have descriptions of what they are like*

— *They each have instructions about what they need*

2. Explain that you want them to create a seed packet for themselves. Share a packet you have made with the different headings on it.

— *Description of the plant*

— *What sort of conditions the plant needs*

— *How to look after the plant*

— *What to expect when it grows to maturity*

3. Ask the children to draw a picture of themselves to go on the front. Add a name – if they want, they might like to turn their name into a botanic or Latin equivalent – Alice might become 'Alyssum' or Rose might be 'Rosa'.

4. Ask the children to fill in the seed packet about themselves, for example:

Description

Rosa is a beautiful plant that is part of the Smith family. Also in the family are Ben, Sarah, Sally and Gus. Rosa is a young girl with blond hair and bright blue eyes and a sprinkling of freckles across her nose. She loves to play with Lego, constructing a range of houses and gardens for her toys to play in. Rosa also enjoys ballet and riding her bike. Rosa has been interested in fossils since she was three when she found her first fossil on the beach when she was on holiday. She has to hide her fossil collection under her bed so that her brother doesn't find it.

5. The last part of the packet is written about the future to show the sort of person they would like to be. For example:

What to expect when it grows to maturity.

Rosa when fully grown will be an archaeologist who travels the world discovering ancient civilisations. She will live in a castle with her pet dog Hettie and her family. Rosa will write books about her travels and all her discoveries and have her picture in lots of magazines. Rosa's friends will describe her as being happy and fun to be with and her children will describe her as being kind and the best mummy in the world.

6. Help the children include in the 'What to expect when it grows to maturity' – their dreams, how people will describe them and the things they would like to do or be known for. This enables them to start to understand that they have the power to choose what sort of person they wish to be.

DIFFERENTIATION

✓ For writing tasks, children can be paired and work together – use other adults or learning partners to scribe for them.

✓ For some children, you may wish to use the adapted seed packet that enables them to draw pictures about themselves and how to look after them.

✓ Be thoughtful of children who are living in sheltered accommodation such as a refuge or are refugees. They may not have access to personal items or pictures. If this is the case, you could offer for children to bring a picture of an object or a drawing of something they have that is special to them.

Teacher Tools and Techniques	
Emotional Literacy	Sharing personal thoughts, feelings and significant objects and explaining why they are important
Developing Relationships	Cooperation and collaboration Supporting others
Self-Development	Thinking about themselves
Skills for Learning	Planning and organisation Information processing Decision-making
The Brain Learning and Behaviour	Understanding that they have the choice and can be the person they want to be

PHSE LINK (PSHE ASSOCIATION PROGRAMME OF STUDY FOR PSHE EDUCATION – KS2)

About personal identity; what contributes to who we are (e.g. ethnicity, family, gender, faith, culture, hobbies, likes/dislikes).

That mental health, just like physical health, is part of daily life; the importance of taking care of mental health.

Recognising what makes us special and the ways in which we are all unique.

Identifying strengths, likes and dislikes.

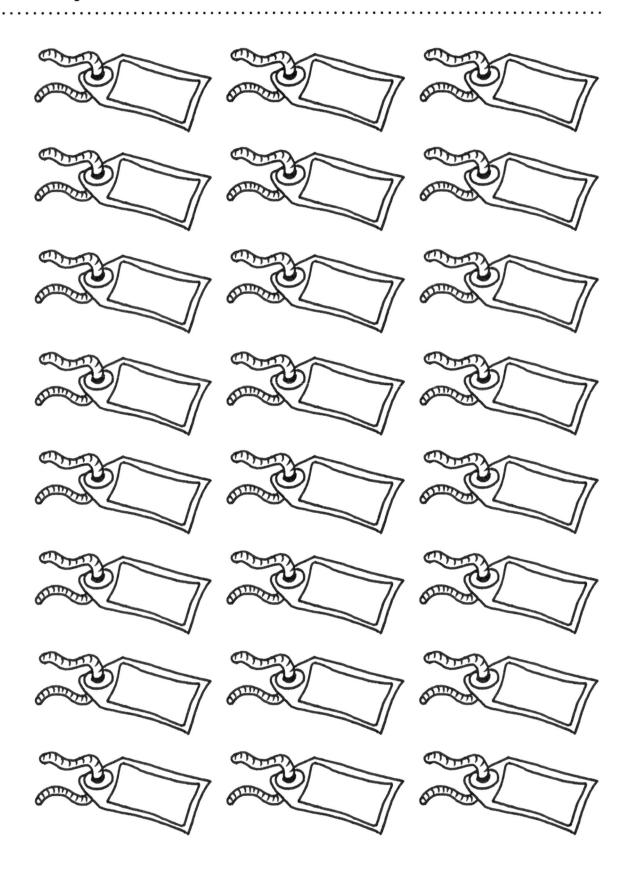

SUTTONS SEEDS

BEAUTIFUL FLOWERS FOR ALL GARDENS

NAME:

NEEDS CARE AND ATTENTION TO GROW WELL.

IF WATERED WITH LOVE, WILL FLOURISH AND THRIVE

FLOWERS:

Description

Conditions needed to grow

How to care for the plant

What to expect when it grows to maturity

Suttons Seeds
Paignton
England
www.suttons-seeds.co.uk

24   37940   29886

177

Description

Conditions needed to grow

How to care for the plant

What to expect when it grows to maturity

Suttons Seeds
Paignton
England
www.suttons-seeds.co.uk

24   37940   29886

0 36000 29145 2

Primary Assembly:

Who is the Assembly for?

Children in KS1 and KS2.

What is the Focus?

Positive and negative self-talk.

Objectives

To support children both identify and challenge negative self talk.

Involvement of Children

Two children to play the part of negative and positive self talk characters.

Children to show how they feel about a statement.

Resources

Your Thoughts Matter by Ester Pia Cordova and Mariya Elizarova.

Numbers 1–10.

Negative self-talk challenges to share amongst the classes.

Key Message

We can challenge the self-talk we experience.

Introduction

Hold up the statement 'Thoughts are really important and affect what we do.' Ask for 6–10 children to come out from their classes and stand on a line to show how true they feel this is. One end of the line is very true the other is not true.

Explain that after you have read the story you are going to ask them the question again.

Main Event

Read the story to the children with the actors playing the characters of negative and positive self-talk.

Ask the children who came out before to stand where they had chosen and then ask them if they would like to move. Allow them to move and chose a new position. When they have moved ask them why they chose to move.

Finale

Explain that we all have negative and positive self-talk going on in our heads and that a really good skill to develop is to challenge the negative ones. Explain that you have a couple of negative thoughts for people to practice on. Share them out across the classes and explain that when they have had time to chat about them you would really like to hear the challenges they have come up with.

Chapter 4
The Brain, Behaviour and Learning
KS2

KS2 BOOKS

A Tale of Two Beasts by Fiona Roberton

The Thinking Traps by Jessica Cortez

Silly Limbic by Naomi Harvey

ASSEMBLY

A Little Spot of Anxiety by Diane Alber

DOI: 10.4324/9781003322801-5

Two-Voice Poem

Learning Objective: To write a two-voice poem	

Success Criteria:

◆ Include two characters with a shared experience

◆ Use chronological order

◆ Have characters' opinions of the experience differ

◆ Use emotive words

◆ Use descriptive language (include use of senses)

◆ Create and follow a structured pattern

Pupils Can...	Identify how language, structure and presentation contribute to meaning. Make changes to vocabulary, grammar and punctuation to enhance effects and clarify meaning. Draw inferences such as inferring characters' feelings, thoughts and motives from their actions, and justifying inferences with evidence.
	Identify how language, structure and presentation contribute to meaning. Compose and rehearse sentences orally, progressively building a varied and rich vocabulary and an increasing range of sentence structures.
	Discuss words and phrases that capture the reader's interest and imagination. Recognise some different forms of poetry (for example, free verse, narrative poetry). Draw inferences and justify inferences with evidence. Compose and rehearse sentences orally, building up a varied vocabulary.

Opinion is a belief, a way of thinking or a judgement about something.

Chronological Order is the order of events happening one after the other in time. It is the order in which things happen.

Structured pattern is how a poem is set out visually and aurally in a repetitive or serial form. It might be that the first line always starts the same way, or the last line of a stanza is always the same.

Emotive language is the careful and deliberate choice of words that will evoke a strong emotion in the reader, e.g. slaughtered instead of killed or suffering rather than in pain.

Resources	*A Tale of Two Beasts* by Fiona Roberton	◆ Trip Advisor comments ◆ Photos, pictures of artwork, places ◆ Foods to taste, e.g. sour sweets (check allergies)

TASTER: WHERE DO YOU STAND?

Place the signs Agree/Like and Disagree/Dislike at opposite sides of the room. Ask the students to consider a variety of subjects and ask them to move to the sign that reflects their opinion. If they have no opinion or are undecided, they can remain still.

Show pieces of artwork, places and landmarks, fruit and veg, play music, give subjects such as spiders or ask them to taste food.

When students have made a choice and stood under their sign, ask one or two of them why they have chosen to stand there. Elicit from the children that everyone has an opinion and that there may be experiences or other reasons that have helped shape that opinion. We don't all have to agree, but we do have to respect others who may have a different point of view.

BUILDING TASK: FACT OR OPINION

Start by asking the students to decide whether the following statements are fact or opinion.

◆ *Julia Donaldson writes amazing storybooks for children.*

◆ The Gruffalo *is one of the world's most-read books.*

◆ *I hate it when the adverts come on the TV just at the good bit in the film.*

◆ *A kilogram of potatoes weighs the same as a kilogram of feathers.*

Distinguish between what is a fact and what is an opinion. Look carefully at the first example. It is a fact that Julia Donaldson writes storybooks for children. It is my opinion that they are amazing.

BUILDING TASK: FANCY A TRIP?

Look at some examples of reviews on Trip Advisor or other review sites. Can the students pick out the fact from the opinion? Choose two differing reviews from the same venue/event. How do they differ? Discuss why they may differ.

Can the students spot emotive words (strong feeling words)?

Not a pleasant stay

We stayed here for the first (and last) time on January 2nd. My husband and I are in our 70s and are not as agile as we once were. My husband has a mobility problem and finds it difficult to walk even short distances. On booking the hotel, we asked if we could have a ground floor room within a short distance of the car park and the restaurant. We were assured that they would arrange this for us. When we arrived, we were given a second-floor room at the rear of the building and miles away from the restaurant. Thank goodness the lift was working as the stairs would have given my husband a heart attack! We asked to be moved to a different room, but the horrendously rude and difficult staff were incredibly useless and we had to stay and suffer in the room we had been given.

The room was clean & tidy inside but when we went to retire to bed, we discovered that the door would not lock either inside or outside. This was fixed the following morning.

We will not be visiting again

Wonderful 4-night stay

We stayed in the hotel's ensuite double room which I can only describe as immaculate. The water pressure and temperature in the shower were even better than we've got at home. The room had a huge TV, coffee and tea-making facilities and lots of biscuits! The hotel has its own swimming pool. Although the pool is small, it was lovely for families with a lifeguard on duty.

The restaurant was OK, and the food was satisfactory. Lots of wonderful and adventurous things to do in the local area. The hotel staff were helpful in pointing us to nearby activities and events. We will be going back soon.

MAIN TASK: TWO-VOICE POEM

1. Read the book *The Tale of Two Beasts* by Fiona Roberton to the students. What do they notice about the character's differing points of view? They both remember the events, but both feel about them differently. They have two differing opinions.

2. As a class, pick out the events

Girl's opinion	Event	Squirrel's opinion
Poor thing is stuck in a tree	Squirrel hanging in a tree	Relaxing in my favourite tree
Squirrel is whining	Squirrel making a noise	Happily singing
I'll give him a name	Girl made a noise	She growled at me
I'll keep him safe and warm	Squirrel covered with a scarf	She tied me up!

3. The events can be written down in a two-voice poem. Model writing the first few lines of the poem using 'thinking out loud'. Especially thinking about emotive words and feelings. You could add techniques such as alliteration. Can the students spot the structure you are using?

    I was shocked to see the poor little suffering animal trapped in the tree.

    I was horrified to be dragged from my restful, relaxing recreation in the tree

    I'm a rescuer

    I'm a victim

    Deciding to care for him, I gave him a name

    She put her face in my face and growled

    He needs warmth and security, so I wrapped him up safely.

    She tried to suffocate me!

4. The class can complete the poem with a learning partner and take a character role each or they can create two new characters and their character's understanding of an event or events.

DIFFERENTIATION

✓ Give students a shorter version of events to describe in their two-voice poem.

✓ Students can be challenged to include alliteration or figurative language in their poem.

✓ Students can use a structure which always starts with 'I' or 'I felt… when'.

✓ Students can perform and record their role-play as the two characters.

Teacher Tools and Techniques	
Emotional Literacy	Recognition and awareness of emotions
	Exploring and explaining emotions
	Understanding everyone has a point of view and that they may not always agree with someone's opinion
Developing Relationships	Talking partners – agreement and compromise
	Sympathy and empathy
Self-Development	Thinking out loud, considering options, experiences, forming opinions
Skills for Learning	Thinking out loud, decision-making, agreement, collaboration, empathy
The Brain Learning and Behaviour	Experiences help shape our opinions
	Our opinions and points of view can change

PHSE LINK (PSHE ASSOCIATION PROGRAMME OF STUDY FOR PSHE EDUCATION – KS2)

Everyday things affect feelings and the importance of expressing feelings.

Personal behaviour can affect other people.

Discuss and debate topical issues; respect other people's points of view.

A varied vocabulary to use when talking about feelings and how to express feelings in different ways.

Personal identity: what contributes to who we are (e.g. ethnicity, family, gender, faith, culture, hobbies, likes/dislikes).

How to manage setbacks/perceived failures, including how to re-frame unhelpful thinking.

REVIEW EXAMPLES

Not a pleasant stay

We stayed here for the first (and last) time on January 2nd. My husband and I are in our 70s and are not as agile as we once were. My husband has a mobility problem and finds it difficult to walk even short distances. On booking the hotel, we asked if we could have a ground floor room within a short distance of the car park and the restaurant. We were assured that they would arrange this for us. When we arrived, we were given a second-floor room at the rear of the building and miles away from the restaurant. Thank goodness the lift was working as the stairs would have given my husband a heart attack! We asked to be moved to a different room, but the horrendously rude and difficult staff were incredibly useless and we had to stay and suffer in the room we had been given.

Wonderful 4-night stay

We stayed in the hotel's ensuite double room, which I can only describe as immaculate. The water pressure and temperature in the shower were even better than we've got at home. The room had a huge TV, coffee and tea-making facilities and lots of biscuits! The hotel has its own swimming pool. Although the pool is small, it was lovely for families with a lifeguard on duty.

The restaurant was OK, and the food was satisfactory. Lots of wonderful and adventurous things to do in the local area. The hotel staff were helpful in pointing us to nearby activities and events. We will be going back soon.

Review Writing

Learning Objective: To present opinion in a review
Success Criteria:
◆ State your point/opinion clearly
– Use connectives to link opinions and reasons
– (I think, I feel, In my opinion, In my view, It is widely believed that…)
◆ Give evidence/examples to support your point/opinion
– Use conjunctions to explain thinking (because, so, and, not only, but)
◆ Explain your reason (why do you feel this)
◆ Include a conclusion which summarises your view
◆ Use emotive language to show strength of opinion

Pupils Can…	Identify how language, structure and presentation contribute to meaning. Make changes to vocabulary, grammar and punctuation to enhance effects and clarify meaning. Draw inferences such as inferring characters' feelings, thoughts and motives from their actions, and justifying inferences with evidence.
	Identify how language, structure and presentation contribute to meaning. Compose and rehearse sentences orally, progressively building a varied and rich vocabulary and an increasing range of sentence structures.
	Discuss words and phrases that capture the reader's interest and imagination. Recognise some different forms of poetry (for example, free verse, narrative poetry). Draw inferences and justify inferences with evidence. Compose and rehearse sentences orally, building up a varied vocabulary.

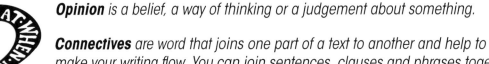

Opinion is a belief, a way of thinking or a judgement about something.

Connectives are word that joins one part of a text to another and help to make your writing flow. You can join sentences, clauses and phrases together using connectives, or joining words. Connectives can be conjunctions, prepositions or adverbs.

Conjunctions hold words, phrases and clauses together. There are three different kinds of conjunctions – coordinating, subordinating and correlative. Some common connectives include 'and', 'but', 'so' and 'then'.

Emotive language is the careful and deliberate choice of words which will evoke a strong emotion in the reader, e.g. slaughtered instead of killed or suffering rather than in pain.

 **Resources**	*A Tale of Two Beasts* by Fiona Roberton	Examples of optical illusions Opinion statement (at least two per child) List of connectives and conjunctions

TASTER: SAY WHAT YOU SEE?

Show the students examples of optical illusions. The duck/rabbit drawing is often used and is a good one with which to begin.

Discuss with students that we all see something different in things. We all have our own perspectives. Bring the students' attention to the Indian parable of the six blind men and the elephant. Discuss that each perception is different given the evidence they have. Sometimes we can see someone's opinion and why they might think it and sometimes not because they may have a totally different perspective with which we may not agree

Image and Poem *http://realityraiders.com/fringewalker/belief-systems/the-blind-men-and-the-elephant/*	Each of the blind men touched a part of the elephant and each exclaimed that the elephant was something different. Man 1 - the body: 'It's a wall!' Man 2 – the tusks: 'It's a spear!' Man 3 – the trunk: 'It's a snake!' Man 4 – the leg: 'It's a tree!' Man 5 –the ear: 'It's a fan!' Man 6 – the tail: 'It's a rope!'

BUILDING TASK: IN MY OPINION...

Give students two or three cards each that have an opinion statements. The students keep the cards that match their opinion but must pass on the cards that they don't agree with. However, they can only pass on their unwanted card to someone who agrees with the statement. They can do this through questioning and persuasion. Children could write examples to collect as a class. See Opinion Statement sheet.

Statements might include

◆ *Footballers are paid too much money*

◆ *Everyone should be a vegetarian*

◆ *Sport is boring*

◆ *Social media is good*

◆ *Harry Potter is over-rated*

BUILDING TASK: THE WHY CHAIN?

With the cards they have collected from the previous task or three statements of their own (two agrees and a disagree), students should prepare reasons why they agree or disagree with their statement. Share with their partner. Play The Why Chain? using connectives and conjunctions – there should be no repeats!

School should start at 8 am and finish at 6 pm

Why?

Because we need more time to learn and socialise

Why?

In order to help us achieve more

Why?

So that we can reach our potential

Why?

As a consequence, we will feel good about ourselves

Why?

MAIN TASK: WRITE A REVIEW

Show students a piece of artwork or a piece of architecture. Do the children like or dislike the work?

1. Students make a note of things they like/dislike about the art. As a class, think about points of note such as colour, topic/subject, shape, size, characters, feelings it evokes, things it reminds them of, etc.

2. With the class, share and model possible opinions backed up with evidence and explanation.

Frida Kahlo – Self Portrait with Monkeys

www.fridakahlo.org/self-portrait-with-monkeys.jsp

In my opinion this main character appears deep in thought as her eyes are looking off into the distance and she has an expressionless face. She does not seem bothered by the monkeys surrounding her or even clinging to her which suggests she is concentrating on her thoughts and the monkeys are not a distraction.

Point – Evidence – Explanation

I think the painting is interesting as she is surrounded by monkeys and it leaves me with lots of questions such as why the monkeys need to comfort Frida.

---

3. Students use their notes and connective prompt sheets to write their review.

4. Ensure the children have a conclusion that summarises their views.

DIFFERENTIATION

✓ Students give a point and evidence.

✓ Students complete a prompt sheet with

– I think that…

– The painting makes me feel…

– I dis/like the…

– My favourite part is…

✓ Students can include counter opinions or choose a piece of art.

✓ Students can listen and describe a piece of music before they continue their review.

✓ Students can include the subject's possible inner thoughts.

Teacher Tools and Techniques	
Emotional Literacy	Recognition and awareness of emotions
	Exploring and explaining emotions
	Understanding everyone has a point of view and that they may not always agree with someone's opinion
Developing Relationships	Talking partners – agreement and compromise
	Sympathy and empathy
Self-Development	Thinking out loud, considering options, experiences, forming opinions and justifying opinions
Skills for Learning	Thinking out loud, decision-making, agreement, collaboration, empathy
The Brain Learning and Behaviour	Experiences help shape our opinions
	Our opinions and points of view can change

PHSE LINK (PSHE ASSOCIATION PROGRAMME OF STUDY FOR PSHE EDUCATION – KS2)

Everyday things affect feelings and the importance of expressing feelings.

Personal behaviour can affect other people.

Discuss and debate topical issues; respect other people's points of view.

A varied vocabulary to use when talking about feelings and how to express feelings in different ways.

Personal identity: what contributes to who we are (e.g. ethnicity, family, gender, faith, culture, hobbies, likes/dislikes).

How to manage setbacks/perceived failures, including how to re-frame unhelpful thinking.

Opinion Statements

School should be open from 8 am to 6 pm	Sharing is caring
Harry Potter is over-rated	Social media is good
Sport is boring	Everyone should be a vegetarian
Camping is fun	Waking up early improves your day
Strawberry is the best flavour of ice-cream	Footballers are paid too much money
Movies do not need age ratings	London is the best city in England
Reality TV shows should be banned	Homework is important
Dogs are better than cats	Cats are better than dogs
Marmite is better than peanut butter	Primary schools should have Saturday detentions
There is life on other planets	Exploring space is a waste of money
Screen time should be limited to one hour a day	Spiders are not scary

Differing Points of View

Learning Objective: To explore the wants and needs of others and to strengthen the ability to empathise

Success Criteria:

◆ Make a perspectives poster

◆ Show the different views of two story characters

Pupils Can...	Describe how a character feels in the story.
	Describe how a character's behaviour is linked to how they feel.
	Describe how different people may feel and how this may influence how they behave.

Points of view: *The point of view, or POV, in a story is the 'eye' or narrative voice through which a story is told. When you write a story, you must decide who is telling the story and to whom they are telling it. A story can be told from the first-person, second-person or third-person point of view. Writers use POV to express the personal emotions of either themselves or their characters. The first-person point of view is identified by singular pronouns such as me, my, I, mine and myself or plural first-person pronouns like we, us, our and ourselves. Second-person point of view uses the pronoun 'you' to address the reader. This narrative voice implies that the reader is either the protagonist or a character in the story and the events are happening to them. This point of view allows the author to limit a reader's perspective and control what information the reader knows. It is used to build interest and heighten suspense. Third-person objective point of view has a neutral narrator that is not privy to the characters' thoughts or feelings. Third-person point of view, omniscient is where the story is still about 'he' or 'she' but the narrator has full access to the thoughts and experiences of all characters in the story.*

Differing perspectives *are where the same facts can have different meanings when seen from different perspectives. The perspective of each person is based on their beliefs, experiences, feelings and interpretations.*

	A Tale of Two Beasts by Fiona Roberton	Story mat/piece of material
Resources	Box People Pictures	If you want to act out the story, then you will need: small figure of a girl/squirrel/t rees/scarf/box/crayons/small bowl/hat and scarf/string/differing points of view sheet
	Shoe pictures	
	Match the correct sentences to the characters worksheet	

TASTER: POINTS OF VIEW

Read the book to the children. If you have small figures, you can ask someone to act it out on the story mat while you read it. When you have finished pose the question: 'Who was lying in the story the girl or the squirrel?'

Explore this concept with the children. Introduce the term differing points of view. Ask the question: 'What affects how we see and interpret situations?'

Collect all their views and ideas as a mind map on the board.

Give the children the differing points of view sheet to complete in pairs or individually.

MINI TASK: I CAN SEE...

Ask the children to work in pairs and choose a Box People picture. Ask them to:
i)   Identify the emotion the Box Person is experiencing in the picture.

ii) Identify how they would benefit from someone doing an action.

For example: *A Box Person is sad. What they would benefit from is someone giving them a hug/ asking them to play/asking if they can do anything to help.*

Help children to think about the fact that we are all different, and what is helpful to one person may not be to another. We base what we do on our own experience. If we were sad, and someone hugs us and we feel better, we may think that everyone will feel better if they have a hug. This is not always the case – some people don't like hugs! Teach the children to verbalise what they see and ask what they can do.

'I can see you are really upset. When I get upset, I like a hug would you like one?'

Ask children to come up with a range of scripts they might be able to use. Record them on the board. Create a display and observe and comment when you hear children using them. Try to model this yourself.

MAIN TASK: WHY THEY DID WHAT THEY DID!

1. Give each child a piece of paper and ask them to draw the shoes from a character in a Fairy Story – Cinderella, Sleeping Beauty, The Wicked Witch, The Wolf, Jack, The Giant, etc. Make sure they are all different.

2.   Lay all the pictures of shoes on the floor.

3. Ask the children to work in pairs and stand by one set of shoes. They must not be the shoes they have drawn.

    3. Once they have chosen a pair of shoes, they need to say what the person felt during the story (emotional) and why (reason) and what they then did linked to that feeling (behaviour). For example:

    Shoes: *Little Red Riding Hoods red boots*: **Emotion**: *Fear of being followed in the woods.* Reason: *The wolf was chasing her and she believed he wanted to eat her.* **Behaviour**: *Ran to safety at Grandma's house.*

4. Once they have shared the emotion that the owner of the shoes felt, the reason and the behaviour, they can then move onto the next one. You can make the activity a carousel type of game where you all move together. Ask the children to try and choose a different emotion from the ones that have already been identified for each of the characters. This helps demonstrate that we all experience a range of emotions each day. For example:

    Little Red Riding Hood: Excitement at seeing Grandma/Fear at being followed/Anxious about what might have happened to Grandma/Fear of the Wolf eating her/Relief at the Woodman arriving/Sadness at the wolf having to be killed.

5. Talk about the things they come up with as you move around the different shoes.

6. Ask the children to choose one of the stories and to write a postcard from two different people in the story demonstrating different points of view.

7. Create an example together on the board to give some ideas of sentences. For example:

    Cinderella. Postcard from the stepmother might contain how challenging she finds Cinderella's behaviour.

    'You will never guess what she has gone and done now! Not only did she not complete all her chores but she is constantly rude sulky refusing to help clear up around the house or help her step sister'.

    'I am at my wits end with her. It seems like nothing I do is good enough. I have now told her if her chores are not completed, she cannot go to the ball'.

    Postcard from The Stepsister:

    'I don't know what to do, Mama is so upset all the time. Cinderella just keeps winding her up'.

    'Cinderella is now not coming to the ball. Mama told her that if she got her chores all done, she could come but she hasn't. I don't know what she does all the time in the kitchen. Now she's spoilt everything. She is so selfish'.

DIFFERENTIATION

✓ Only ask children with their hand up to answer a question. Very anxious children struggle with the fact they may be picked on.

✓ Pair children with a learning partner who can support them in their groups.

✓ Give easily understood Box People pictures to children who struggle with naming emotions.

✓ Model how the shoe game is played.

✓ Use the 'Match the correct sentence' sheet for those children who need it.

Teacher Tools and Techniques	
Emotional Literacy	Sharing the different emotions of the characters
Developing Relationships	Working together in pairs
Self-Development	Making links between emotions and behaviours
Skills for Learning	Understanding points of view for writing
The Brain Learning and Behaviour	The link between emotions and how we feel, what we think and therefore how we behave

PHSE LINK (PSHE ASSOCIATION PROGRAMME OF STUDY FOR PSHE EDUCATION – KS2)

How to recognise what others might be feeling.

How feelings can affect people's bodies and how they behave.

Simple strategies to positively resolve arguments between friends.

The King

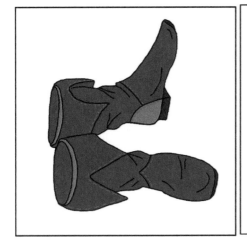

Rumpelstiltskin

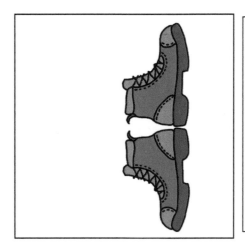

The Father

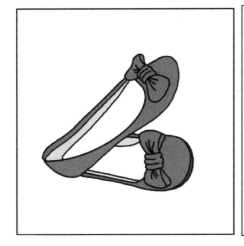

The Daughter

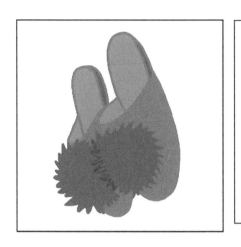

Grandma

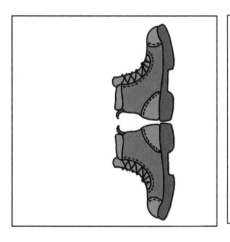

The Wood Cutter

The Wolf

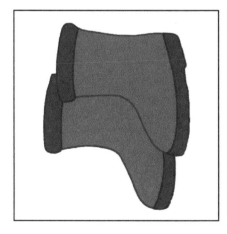

Little Red Riding Hood

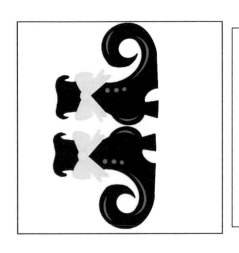

Wicked Stepmother

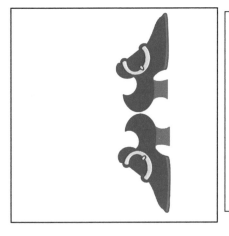

The Prince

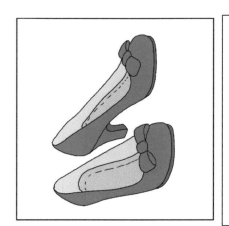

The Ugly Sister

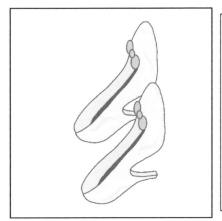

Cinderella

Differing Perspectives

Perspective of:

Perspective of:

Thoughts

Feelings

Feelings

Actions:

Actions:

Match the sentences with the characters

Cut out the names of the characters.

Stick them on separate pieces of paper and draw a small picture of them by their names.

Cut the sentences into strips.

Read each one.

Stick each sentence strip under the name of the person who said them.

Grandmother
Mother
Little Red Riding Hood
The Wolf
The Woodcutter

He was chasing me through the woods, I thought he would eat me.
When someone knocked on the door, I opened it thinking it was my granddaughter.
She said hello and let me into the house.
I don't know why she ran away from me, I just wanted to play catch.
He was a vicious beast and tried to bite me.
I thought she would be safe; she was just walking to her Grandmother's house to take her some cakes.
I was frightened when I got to Grandmother's house.
I don't know why Grandmother hid in the cupboard. I think she wanted to play hide and seek.
Yes I was hungry but I only wanted to have one of the delicious cakes she had in her basket.

| I was cutting down trees when I heard a scream; I know something bad had happened. |
| I was terrified, I thought he was going to eat me, so I hid in the cupboard out of sight and hoped he went away. |
| I was expecting my Granddaughter when I opened the door, but he barged into my house and threatened me. |
| Grandmother was in bed, but she looked different, she had funny ears. |
| The little girl was terrified, she was about to be eaten. |
| The wolf had been causing problems in the woods for years. |
| He grabbed me and threw me on the floor before tying me up. |
| The Woodcutter kicked in the door and grabbed the wolf tying him up so we were safe. |

Modal Verbs and Adverbs

Learning Objective: To show degrees of possibility using adverbs and modal verbs
Success Criteria ◆ Identify the verb ◆ Identify the modifier (modal verb or adverb) ◆ Decide how it changes the meaning of the sentence ◆ Decide whether it is likely or unlikely to happen

Pupils Can...	Understand modal verbs and adverbs that indicate degrees of possibility (possibility, obligation and ability). Identify which word in a sentence the adverb is modifying, explain how it alters the meaning and comment on how to choose adverbs carefully.
	Understand modal verbs and adverbs that indicate degrees of possibility (possibility, obligation and ability). Identify which word in a sentence the adverb is modifying and explain how it alters the meaning.
	Identify adverbs and explain how an adverb works in a sentence.

A **Modal verb** is a verb (such as can, could, shall, should, ought to, will or would) that is usually used with another verb to express ideas such as possibility, obligation and ability

An **Adverb or adverbial phrase** is a word or phrase that modifies a verb, expressing a relation of place, time, manner, cause or **degree of possibility.**

A **conditional sentence** is a sentence that has one event dependent upon another, e.g. *If it rains tomorrow, I will need a coat. Sports day may be cancelled if it rains tomorrow.*

	*The Thinking Traps* by Jessica Cortez	

TASTER: YES OR NO

Play the Yes or No game with students. The students must ask you a series of questions that you are not allowed to answer as Yes or No. This means you will have to think of alternative ways of responding. It may involve being creative! It will include having some of your responses involving adverbs and modal verbs.

Is your name Miss Smith – It is.

Did you have breakfast this morning – I did not have enough time.

Will we be having maths this morning? – We may have to miss maths if this questioning goes on too long!

Will you give us a longer break? – Definitely not.

Students can play against each other – Who has a winning technique/strategy that they are willing to share? Students may keep repeating 'maybe' or 'might' as part of their strategy. Make the game more challenging by having a no repeats rule.

BUILDING TASK: ON ONE CONDITION

Explain to the students that a conditional sentence contains the word 'If' and Should the sentence begin with If, it will need a comma.

If I win a million pounds, I will buy a house for my family and give the rest to charity.

The second clause in the sentence relies on the first part of the sentence happening. I could not buy a house for my family unless I had a million pounds. Ask the children to complete the following conditional sentences

If you don't brush your teeth,.........................

If you shout at your teacher, ...

If you are kind to someone, ...

If you are looking for someone to help you, ...

If you go to bed late, ...,

Identify with the children that there are likely to be two verbs in their answers.

If I win a million pounds, I **will buy** a house for my family and give the rest to charity.

One is the main verb and one modifies the verb. It gives a bit of extra meaning. It modifies it.

BUILDING TASK: ON ONE CONDITION AGAIN

For this task, give the students the main clause and ask them to write the conditional phrase. The students can place the conditional phrase at the beginning of the sentence or at the end.

I may miss the bus…

I may miss the bus if I wake up late. If I wake up late, I may miss the bus.

◆ He may be sad

◆ I might go to nan's house

◆ The teacher will be livid

◆ The netball team will likely lose

◆ The championship cup could be ours

MAIN TASK: HOW LIKELY IS IT?

1. Give the students some examples of events and how likely something is going to happen. They will have seen something like this in their maths probability lessons.

Display a line on the board with a definitive at both ends. Impossible to Certain. Alternatively, you could have a line across the floor in the classroom and have a sign for each end. Read out the following statements – where would the students place the statement on the line? Students could mark it on the board or, if the line is on the floor, stand in their proposed place.

Impossible/Never   Certain/Always

Tomorrow is Sunday. There will be rain this afternoon. The teacher will take register in the morning

Miss Smith will trip over her cat. Miss Smith will stop talking for five minutes.

2. Explain to the children that there are words in the English language that help us understand the possibility of something happening and which make our writing more precise. These are modal verbs and adverbs.

   Adverbs for possibility – definitely, perhaps, possibly, surely, maybe, obviously, rarely, certainly.

   Ask the students to use one of these adverbs in a sentence of their own. For example – '*I am possibly going to go to kickboxing this weekend*'. How likely is this to happen? Where would the student place themselves on the degree of possibility line?

   Repeat with a number of students' own examples.

3. Modal verbs for possibility – first look at the modal verbs: will/won't, may/may not, might/ might not, shall/shall not.

   Where would the students place these modal verbs on the degree of possibility line?

   Students could write their own statements to give to a partner to place on the line.

4. Give the children the following statements – what do these modal verbs imply or suggest about the event and whether it is likely to happen? Discuss with a partner where they might place these on the class degree of possibility line.

   I must do my homework tomorrow.

   I can do my homework tomorrow.

   I should go to the dentist as my tooth is painful.

   I ought to go to the dentist as my tooth is painful.

   Elicit from the students that these modal verbs suggest that there is a feeling of obligation or ability.

   I can do my homework tomorrow suggests that the person has time to do it tomorrow and is able to do it, but it may or may not happen.

   I should go to the dentist as my tooth is painful implies that the person knows it is a good idea as the pain will be gone but they may not go. They feel obliged to go to get the tooth sorted.

   Have the students changed their minds as to where they have placed these statements on the line?

5. Sort modal verbs into possibility, obligation and ability.

Will Could not Would Must Might May May not Can't Will not Should Shall not Must not Can Could Ought Should not Won't	Possibility	Obligation	Ability

6. Thinking about the book *The Thinking Traps* and looking at some of the negative traps that are described. How would children respond to the following statements using a modal verb or adverb in their answer?

I never get picked for the team, so I think I should quit. – You **could** use the self-talk tool that **will** help you think more positively about yourself.

◆ *It's going to be a bad day today as I've forgotten my PE kit, Dad has packed me awful jam sandwiches for my lunch, my friend is off school sick and, to top it all, I've got Spanish - and the teacher hates me!*

◆ *Nobody likes my artwork.*

◆ *I would like to go to my friend's party, but I bet my mum won't let me.*

◆ *I'll never be any good at football.*

◆ *Our maths investigation is going to be done my way or we won't do it at all.*

◆ *I can't ever get anything right.*

◆ *My PlayStation is broken! I'm so angry I feel like throwing it out the window!*

DIFFERENTIATION

✓ Students who are given the more common modal verbs to sort on a possibility line or into possibility, ability and obligation can be given statements to sort or come up with their own.

✓ Students can be challenged to come up with their own thinking trap example for a learning partner to respond to.

✓ Students can create a statement and response that includes a modal verb and an adverb for possibility – highlight/underline their evidence.

✓ With a partner, students can role-play their conversation on thinking traps and advice given.

Teacher Tools and Techniques	
Emotional Literacy	Recognition and awareness of emotions
	Exploring and explaining emotions
	Understanding that there are tools to help us manage our emotions
Developing Relationships	Talking partners – agreement and compromise
	Understanding actions have positive or negative consequences
Self-Development	Thinking out loud, considering options, experiences, forming opinions
Skills for Learning	Role-play, decision-making, agreement, collaboration
The Brain Learning and Behaviour	Some events are dependent upon others
	Cause and effect

PHSE LINK (PSHE ASSOCIATION PROGRAMME OF STUDY FOR PSHE EDUCATION – KS2)

Everyday things affect feelings and the importance of expressing feelings.

Personal behaviour can affect other people.

A varied vocabulary to use when talking about feelings and how to express feelings in different ways.

How to manage setbacks/perceived failures, including how to re-frame unhelpful thinking.

Strategies to respond to feelings, including intense or conflicting feelings; how to manage and respond to feelings appropriately and proportionately in different situations.

Information Leaflet

Learning Objective: To write a leaflet to inform
Success Criteria: ◆ Using layout devices to structure text such as <ul><li>– headings</li><li>– subheadings</li><li>– bullet points</li><li>– tables</li><li>– shout outs/bubbles</li></ul>◆ Include adverbials for time, manner, cause or place ◆ Include conditional sentences ◆ Use modal verbs and adverbs for degree of possibility ◆ Subordinate clauses (to add more detail or important information) ◆ Use relative clauses

Pupils Can...	Use grammatical structures appropriately for the audience and purpose of the text, e.g. modal verbs and adverbs to indicate degrees of possibility (possibility, obligation and ability). Manipulate sentence structure for effect. Use a range of devices to build cohesion within paragraphs, e.g. pronouns, adverbials of time and place.
	Use grammatical structures appropriately for the audience and purpose of the text, e.g. modal verbs and adverbs to indicate degrees of possibility (possibility, obligation and ability). Begin to manipulate sentence structure for effect. Use a range of devices to build cohesion within paragraphs, e.g. pronouns, adverbials of time and place.
	Use grammatical structures appropriately for the audience and purpose of the text, e.g. modal verbs and adverbs to indicate degrees of possibility. With support, draw on what they have read as models for their own writing. Extend the range of sentences with more than one clause by using a wider range of conjunctions, including when, if, because and although.

A **Modal verb** is a verb (such as can, could, shall, should, ought to, will or would) that is usually used with another verb to express ideas such as possibility, obligation and ability

An **Adverb or adverbial phrase** is a word or phrase that modifies a verb, expressing a relation of place, time, manner, cause or **degree of possibility.**

A **conditional sentence** is a sentence that has one event dependent upon another, e.g. **If it rains tomorrow, I will need a coat. Sports day may be cancelled if it rains tomorrow.**

Relative clauses are clauses that begin with a relative pronoun. It adds extra information to a sentence. A relative pronoun is a word like that, which, when, where or who. In the sentence 'The dog, who had the stubby tail, yapped all day', the relative clause is 'who had a stubby tail'.

Subordinating clauses are clauses that can be used to add more detail or vital information to the main clause. The location of the subordinating clause can vary in location within the sentence. Subordinating clauses begin with a subordinating conjunction, e.g. if, as, since, when, although, while, after, before, until, because.

 **Resources**	*The Thinking Traps* by Jessica Cortez	Pictures of people and/or animals to describe features and locations

TASTER: RELATIVELY SPEAKING

Show the students a collection of pictures/photos of different people and/or animals. Can they describe the person or animal using a relative clause so that others in the class can point out who they are describing? For example:

The man, **who** has a wooden leg, *is* standing by the lamppost

Remind students of the need for commas if the relative is embedded within a sentence.

The dog is next to the tree **that** *has the squirrel in it.*

BUILDING TASK: THERE'S MORE...

Subordinate clauses add more detail and some vital information to a sentence.

Subordinate clauses include if, as, since, when, although, while, after, before, until, because.

Subordinate clauses can be moved around the sentence to add variety and help with the flow of the writing.

Break a sentence that contains a subordinate clause into two parts. Have one student hold the main clause and one student hold the subordinate. Have the class identify the subordinate conjunction. Have the two students combine the main clause with the subordinate clause. Show that the subordinate clause can go at the end of the sentence or at the beginning. Ensure the students are aware that the correct punctuation is used if the subordinate clause is at the beginning.

◆ *She got her first horse* *when she was ten years old.*

◆ *You should wear a coat* *because it is cold outside.*

◆ *I held a snake around my neck* *although I was terrified of it.*

◆ *After I had watched the film,* *my friend asked me whether I had enjoyed it.*

◆ *While the cat watched them from the window,* *the hungry birds ate the food.*

Show the students the following sentences. Ask them to identify the subordinate conjunction and the subordinate clause.

The wild tiger devoured the gazelle *because it was starving.*

Because it was staving, *the wild tiger devoured the gazelle.*

This time, split the main clause and embed the subordinate – you will need a third student to help with this!

The wild tiger, *because it was starving,* *devoured the gazelle.*

Ensure the children are aware of the change in punctuation for an embedded clause. Will it always work? Try with the previous sentences.

BUILDING TASK: WHAT ABOUT LAYOUT?

Place a different example of an information leaflet on each table. In groups, students visit each table and, on a sticky note or A3 paper, write down the features they like; the parts they think are helpful; features that stand out as important; what might appeal to the audience, etc. A list of things to comment on could be created before this task or the students could explore the leaflets first and these features could be drawn out during discussion after the activity. Students can start to think about the layout they may use. Will it have speech bubbles, shoutouts, diagrams, borders, subheadings? Will it be a poster or a folded leaflet?

Information leaflet examples:

https://communitydentalservices.co.uk/wp-content/uploads/2019/07/How-much-sugar.pdf

https://campaignresources.phe.gov.uk/schools/resources/parents-healthy-eating-and-being -active-leaflet

https://www.internetmatters.org/resources/screen-time-tips-to-support-7-11-year-olds/

https://communitydentalservices.co.uk/wp-content/uploads/2019/07/How-much-sugar.pdf

MAIN TASK: LET ME INFORM YOU

1. Read *The Thinking Traps* with the class again.

2. As a class, identify each character with their negative thinking trap. What does the thinking trap involve and how might it affect someone?

3. With a learning partner, identify the cool tools and which negative thinking trap it might help.

4. Students decide which trap and tools they wish to include in their information leaflet. They decide on the layout and how they wish to structure their leaflet. They organise this as a draft in note form.

   – Do they want to include illustrations?

   – Would examples and scenarios help?

   – Could the character have a speech bubble?

   – Would they prefer headings and subheadings as questions?

5. Students design and create their draft leaflet. Explain to the students that they are writing for an audience that has no understanding of Thinking Traps.

6. Peer evaluate – have they included success criteria? Before finalising, students can think about colour, font, etc.

DIFFERENTIATION

✓ Students can choose just one or two thinking traps to write about in their information leaflet.

✓ Students can be given a template for the leaflet.

✓ Students explain why the cool tool would work. For example, why does blowing bubbles calm you down? Students may wish to write about regulating breathing and pulse rate.

✓ Design could be completed in Publisher or written as a PowerPoint presentation.

Teacher Tools and Techniques	
Emotional Literacy	Recognition and awareness of emotions
	Exploring and explaining emotions
	Understanding that there are tools to help us manage our emotions
Developing Relationships	Talking partners – agreement and compromise
	Understanding actions have positive or negative consequences
Self-Development	Thinking out loud, considering options, experiences, forming opinions, receiving and giving constructive feedback
Skills for Learning	Decision-making, agreement, collaboration, draft–write–improve, evaluating
The Brain Learning and Behaviour	Some events are dependent upon others
	Cause and effect

PHSE LINK (PSHE ASSOCIATION PROGRAMME OF STUDY FOR PSHE EDUCATION – KS2)

Everyday things affect feelings and the importance of expressing feelings.

Personal behaviour can affect other people.

A varied vocabulary to use when talking about feelings and how to express feelings in different ways.

How to manage setbacks/perceived failures, including how to re-frame unhelpful thinking.

Strategies to respond to feelings, including intense or conflicting feelings; how to manage and respond to feelings appropriately and proportionately in different situations.

Thinking Traps or Cognitive Distortions

Learning Objective: To explore how our thinking affects our feelings and behaviours
Success Criteria:
◆ Share and talk about one way in which our thinking can affect how we feel and behave

Pupils Can...	Describe the thinking feeling behaviour triangle.
	Discuss ways that our thinking can affect our behaviour.
	Share the types of cognitive distortions and give examples.

Thinking Traps or Cognitive Distortions *are patterns of thought – usually with a negative swing – that prevent us from seeing things as they really are. In other words, if we can change the way we think, we're going to change our behaviour, which has the power to alter our mood and the way we manage the world.*

Mind Reading *is a trap that happens when we believe that we know what others are thinking. This can lead to very negative assumptions being made.*

*A **Fortune-telling trap** occurs when we predict that things will turn out badly. When we believe the future is negative, this can lead us to act as if it is a self-fulfilling prophecy.*

Black-and-white thinking *is when we only look at situations in terms of one extreme or the other. A situation is either good or bad, success or failure – there is no middle ground. This therefore means that if we don't achieve our expectations, we start to view ourselves as a failure.*

Filtering *is similar to black-and-white thinking; filtering involves only paying attention to the negative aspects of a situation while ignoring all the positives. When we only focus on the negatives, we end up viewing the entire situation as negative and so, in our minds, everything is now negative.*

Catastrophising *involves imagining that the worst possible thing is about to happen and predicting that we won't be able to cope with it. In reality, the worst-case scenario usually never happens and even if it did, we would probably be able to cope.*

Over-Generalisation is when we conclude that a single negative event is actually part of a series of unending negative events. If something bad happens, we believe it's likely to happen again and again.

Labelling is an extreme form of generalisation; labelling occurs when we attach a negative label about ourselves or someone else rather than acknowledge it was just a single event or mistake.

Personalisation is a distortion where you believe that everything others do or say is some kind of direct, personal reaction to something we've said or done. We end up taking everything personally when in reality it's nothing to do with us.

Should Statements are when we have ironclad rules for how we, or others, should and shouldn't behave. When our expectations fall short, we feel disappointed, frustrated, anxious or even angry with ourselves. We might think that these should and shouldn't 'rules' are helping to motivate us but in reality, they end up preventing us from taking meaningful steps towards improving our lives.

Emotional Reasoning is one of the most common thinking traps we fall into. It is where we take our emotions as evidence for the truth. When we use emotional reasoning, whatever we're feeling at the time is believed to be true regardless of the evidence. This can be really harmful because it creates a loop: you think something negative, it makes you feel bad, so you think something negative, which makes you feel even worse – it's a dangerous, circular type of logic.

Control Fallacies involve two similar beliefs about being in complete control of pretty much everything in our lives. The first type is called external control fallacy, where we see ourselves as victims of fate with no direct control over our lives. The second type of control fallacy, internal control, occurs when we assume we are completely responsible for the pain and happiness of everyone around us.

The **Fallacy of Fairness** is when you often feel resentful because you think that you know what is fair, and no one is abiding by it. It may sound obvious, but 'life isn't always fair'. People who go through life assessing whether something is 'fair' or not will often end up feeling resentful, angry and unhappy because of it.

The **Always Being Right** trap is when we tend to put other people on trial to prove that our own opinions and actions are the only correct ones. If we use this distortion, being wrong is unthinkable and we'll go to any length to prove ourselves right. Often being right can be more important than the feelings of other people, even close family and friends.

 **Resources**	*The Thinking Traps* by Jessica Cortez Square breathing sheet Bubble breathing sheet	Box person triangle Box people pictures Thoughts, Feelings Actions Triangle Match the characters with their thoughts

TASTER: THOUGHT, FEELINGS ACTIONS TRIANGLE

Share the Thoughts, Feelings Actions Triangle with the children. Explain how they are all connected. Our thoughts affect our feelings, which affect our emotions, and our emotions make us think and behave in different ways.

Share the box person Thoughts, Feelings Actions Triangle.

How might the box person feel? – Frightened.

How might this feeling influence his thoughts? - He might question whether he could cross the bridge without falling in.

How might this feeling and thought influence his actions? – They might make him believe he couldn't do this and then he might wobble and fall, or it might turn back and not even try.

Ask the children to work in pairs. Give each pair one of the box people pictures and ask them to create their own Thoughts, Feelings Actions Triangle.

Explore the different things the children have come up with and highlight that we don't all feel the same or act in the same way. This is due to our many different experiences. Even children with the same pictures will come up with other things.

MINI TASK: THINKING TRAP CARTOONS

Ask the children to work in pairs/groups or small teams and draw their own different Thinking Trap Cartoons: Peddy (predicting); Ali (All or nothing); Spi (spiral); Tre (extremes); Maggy (magnifying); Reed (mind reading).

Share the thoughts sheets and ask them to work in pairs to match up the thoughts with the different characters.

Ask the children to come up with some of their own thoughts for each character. Share and discuss what they find.

MAIN TASK: COOL TOOLS

1. Ask the children to work in pairs and identify the different 'Cool Tools' that the characters try and use in the story: Flag it, Bubble Breathing, Self-Talk box, Imagination Creation, Distraction do-er, Energy Escape.

2. Can the class think of any other 'Cool Tools?' Collect these and write them on the board. These might include: Star Breathing, 5–4-3-2-1, meditation, yoga, etc. or can they come up with tools in the same group as the others. Distraction do-er could include colouring or playing computer games, card games or jigsaw puzzles.

3. Ask the children to work in pairs and create an information page on one of the different 'Cool Tools'. Each page will form part of a display to show the different cool tools that the children could use. These could also support an assembly on the topic to help share the ideas.

4. Discuss with the children the success criteria for their page:

   – A picture/symbol to show the category. This would need to be clear and easily understood.

   – A description of what it is and why it can help.

   – Examples of exercises or things from the category

   – A photograph showing some of them.

   – A comment from someone who finds this strategy useful.

   – Step-by-step instructions if needed

5. Once the children have finished you can create a display to show the different Thinking Traps characters and the Cool Tools to manage them.

DIFFERENTIATION

✓ Pair children who might struggle to record/read with children who could do this more easily.

✓ Set up groups so that they are balanced and supportive of each other.

✓ Use children's strengths in gathering the work for the display. This might be asking a pair of children to take the photos that you want of the children working, using the Cool Tools or drawing different cartoon characters or collecting and ticking off all the work that is needed for the display. Using children's strengths when working on a project can be a lovely way of helping other children see that we can all contribute in different ways.

Teacher Tools and Techniques	
Emotional Literacy	Talking about feelings and their links to how we behave
Developing Relationships	Working in groups or pairs
Self-Development	Understanding how our feelings may affect our behaviour and that if we change how we think we can affect the way we feel
Skills for Learning	Planning and organising the things we need to complete a task
The Brain Learning and Behaviour	The link between what we think and how we feel, and how both affect how we behave

PHSE LINK

About different feelings that humans can experience.

How feelings can affect people's bodies and how they behave.

About ways of sharing feelings; a range of words to describe feelings.

Different things they can do to manage big feelings to help calm themselves down and/or change their mood when they don't feel good.

That mental health, just like physical health, is part of daily life; the importance of taking care of mental health.

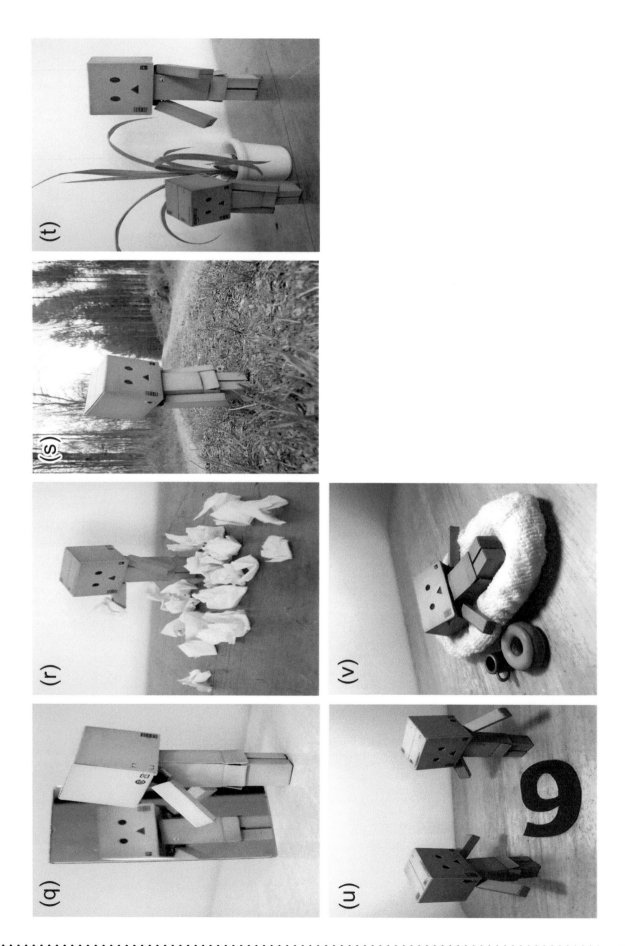

Thinking Trap Character

1. Put the picture of your Thinking Trap Character in the box.

2. Write the different thoughts that this character might have in the thinking bubbles.

3. Can you think of some thoughts this character might have?

Can You Find the Right Thought That Goes with Each Character?

'Oh no it is going to rain today and then Sports Day will be ruined.'

'The weather person said it will rain today, that means that we will have a huge storm and the road will wash away and then I won't be able to get to my club tonight.'

'I've forgotten my homework. The day is ruined everything is going wrong, I will never get chosen to be in the team today and I bet there are no sandwiches left at lunchtime when I go into the dining room.'

'This homework is way too difficult; I will never be able to do this. I must be really stupid I bet everyone else can do it.'

'Oh no I've fallen over. I've broken my arm, I will have to go to the hospital, then they will have to operate, and then I'll never be able to ride my pony again. You can't ride with one arm.'

'You must be really angry at me for getting that question wrong. That means you will never talk to me again'.

I will never be able to go to sleep, I'll have to stay awake all night.'

'My new teacher is really nice she never gets cross with us.'

'I hate rounders, I never get a turn to bat.'

'I will never be good at football, no one will ever choose me to be on their team, everyone will laugh at the way I play and then no one will talk to me ever again.'

'No one likes my drawings they all just laugh.'

'I bet the new supply teacher picks on me.'

'I always mess up and make mistakes in Judo, I'm useless.'

Today was dreadful. I forgot my homework, no one chose me for football, I missed chips for lunch and my best friend was off sick for the day'.

'I know my dad isn't going to let me go to the cinema with the others.'

'Ben always does better than I do in the spelling test I must be really stupid.'

Bill and Ned never get scared of the dark; I must be a real cry baby.'

This game of chase is going to be played by my rules or it won't happen.'

'I know no one will play with me if I go to the park so there is no point going.'

'If Mum won't let me make a chocolate cake then the whole party will be ruined.'

'Not only did I get a detention but my best friend played football at break instead of chess and Mr Smith kept picking on me in science and then everything went wrong in English.'

'There is no point revising for the test I always get everything wrong.'

'I hate school, the teacher picked on me, no one wanted to be my partner, I forgot my homework, the dinner lady made me wait until last and I left my football at home. The whole day is ruined.'

'I won't ever be able to play in the football team, I'm just totally useless.'

Plan a Play script

Learning Objective: To plan a play script	

Success Criteria:

◆ Decide on the scene and characters

◆ Consider the characters' emotions

◆ Consider the characters' language

◆ Consider the characters' positions, movements and actions

◆ Record dialogue and include character directions

Pupils Can...	Change and develop parts of a narrative text to create and rehearse a play scene, or they could create their own play based on the same theme.
	Create an outline of a scene that includes strong description through dialogue and action based on a narrative text.
	Edit a short scene from a narrative text for a short play scene; rehearse through role-play and adapt it to plan a script.

Character directions/asides are often written in brackets and in italics next to the piece of dialogue. They are directions to the actor showing how the dialogue is to be spoken or to instruct the actor to perform an action, e.g. Rolls eyes skywards and sighs (loudly).

Stage directions are given to any character, and it doesn't have to be the one speaking. 'Melanie moves to centre stage, drops to her knees and holds her head in her hands. A distance noise of an approaching aeroplane can be heard'.

Sometimes a narrator is used instead to explain the scene.

	*Silly Limbic* by Naomi Harvey	Equipment to make shoebox dioramas and puppets. Children may wish to bring some from home

TASTER: SAY IT LIKE...

Give children a generic sentence and ask them to say it in a variety of ways. For example:

I think I've left the iron on.

I love a walk in the park.

My brother ran away with the circus.

The dog ate my homework.

Tomorrow is Saturday.

Children are then asked to say the sentence in a variety of ways such as an opera singer, pirate, frightened mouse, rapper, ogre, parent, teacher, doctor or even a happy seal!

BUILDING TASK: MUSICAL STATUES

Play some music and, as the music stops, children are asked to stand still in a particular pose. For example, when the music stops, stand in a pose that suggests you are being chased by a bear.

Other examples could be

◆ *You are petting a cat*

◆ *You are petting a dragon*

◆ *You saw Father Christmas coming down the chimney*

◆ *You were tripped up by someone*

◆ *You have found £100 on the floor*

Ensure children are noticing their body language and facial expressions. All will be important as part of character directions and development for their play and play script.

BUILDING TASK: WHO SAID WHAT!

Starting with characters from books and films they might know,

ask the children who said the quote.

For example, who might say

That porridge was far too hot!	*To Infinity and Beyond!*
Toto, I've a feelin' we're not in Kansas anymore.	*To live would be an awfully big adventure.*
Anything is possible when you have inner peace.	*Some people are worth melting for.*
We are all connected in the great circle of life	*Hakuna Matata – it means – no worries.*
It takes a great deal of bravery to stand up to your enemies, but a great deal more to stand up to your friends.	*When life gets ya down, do ya wanna know what ya gotta do? - Just keep swimmin', just keep swimmin'.*

Thinking about the story *Silly Limbic* – who might say

What if the bus breaks down?	*It will be fine. It's perfectly safe,*
I'm scared that the rollercoaster will stop at the top and I won't be able to get down.	*Let's think about the positives and the fun we can have.*
It's best that I stay at home.	*You don't know if you don't try.*
Change can be exciting.	*Just need to slow my breathing down.*
Count to ten and try again.	*There is a monster in my wardrobe.*
We are all able to look out for each other.	*No one will talk to me at the party.*
There are more pros than cons.	

MAIN TASK: AND... ACTION!

1. With a learning partner or in a small group, decide on a short scene from the book. Think about the setting and create a shoebox diorama for their play – if they are going to use puppets/props to act out a scene.

2. Decide which characters are in the scene and make character puppets, or masks should the children choose to act out in person.

Puppets can be finger puppets, lolly stick puppets, wooden spoon puppets or even jelly babies on cocktail sticks!

3. Children decide on their character/s and think about their role in the scene. What might they say and how might they say it?

4. Children may wish to add a resolution to their scene.

5. Children may wish to have a narrator that explains the scene.

6. Children to note down what is said and how it is said. If acting out in person, they may wish to note who moves where and what actions are carried out. This could be recorded in a story map or film strip template.

7. Provide opportunities for reflection – is this what their character would say? Is this how their character might act? Does the character change?

DIFFERENTIATION

✓ Record on a cartoon strip or as a story map.

✓ Use pictures with speech bubbles.

✓ Record their role-play or speech on video or audio.

✓ Children can create a brand-new situation for the characters and add different elements.

Teacher Tools and Techniques	
Emotional Literacy	Recognising the feelings of others
	Recognising and naming feelings
	Empathy
Developing Relationships	Talking partners – agreement and compromise
	Cooperation and collaboration
	Constructive criticism and critical friend
Self-Development	Thinking out loud, modelling, self-motivation
	Awareness of strength and areas for development
Skills for Learning	Thinking out loud, annotation
	Grouping/sorting, decision-making, agreement
The Brain Learning and Behaviour	Targeting audience and purpose
	Communicating ideas

PHSE LINK (PSHE ASSOCIATION PROGRAMME OF STUDY FOR PSHE EDUCATION – KS2)

Everyday things that affect feelings and the importance of expressing feelings.

Varied vocabulary to use when talking about feelings and how to express feelings in different ways.

Strategies to respond to feelings, including intense or conflicting feelings; how to manage and respond to feelings appropriately and proportionately in different situations.

Predict, assess and manage risk in different situations.

Play script

Learning Objective: To write a play script	

Success Criteria:

◆ Include a cast list

◆ Include a descriptive scene setting – where, when, what it's like

◆ Speaker's name is to the left with a colon

◆ New speaker, new line

◆ Write dialogue without inverted commas (speech marks)

◆ Use character directions – include adverbs and actions to help the character express feeling, e.g. angrily, gently, roll eyes

◆ Place character directions in brackets *(usually in italics)*

Pupils Can...	Discuss the way that characters are developed in a play script through dialogue, character directions and action.
	Use a given narrative as a base and create a new scene in a play script, using their own ideas for strong characterisation through dialogue, directions and action.
	Re-tell part of a given narrative as a play script and include character directions to show characters' emotions and development.
	Re-tell a part of a story, turning prose to play script.

Character directions/asides are often written in brackets and in italics next to the piece of dialogue. They are directions to the actor showing how the dialogue is to be spoken or to instruct the actor to perform an action, e.g. *Rolls eyes skywards and sighs (loudly).*

Stage directions are given to any character, and it doesn't have to be the one speaking. 'Melanie moves to centre stage, drops to her knees and holds her head in her hands. A distance noise of an approaching aeroplane can be heard'.

Sometimes a narrator is used instead to explain the scene.

 Resources	*Silly Limbic* by Naomi Harvey	Examples of play scripts

TASTER: SAY IT TWO WAYS

Share the following short play script with the students. Do not set the scene or explain how the script should be spoken.

Melanie: Good Morning!

Victoria: Morning.

Melanie: How are you feeling?

Victoria: I've had better days.

Melanie: I could have guessed – you don't look great.

With another adult, or a student that has been prepared and rehearsed, act this scene in two ways. One angrily and one sympathetically. Discuss with the children the difference this makes to how they feel about the characters. Elicit from the children that character directions would be helpful. As a class, using thinking-aloud techniques, amend the script with character directions. For example:

Melanie: *(looking at her watch)* Good Morning!

Victoria: *(Sullenly)* Morning.

Melanie: *(Sharply and sarcastically)* How are you feeling?

Victoria: I've had better days.

Melanie: *(Huffing)* I could've guessed – you don't look great.

Melanie turns her back and storms out of the room.

BUILDING TASK: WRITE IT ANOTHER WAY

Students take the following script and decide how they want their characters to be feeling/acting. They may even include stage directions. Characters could be angry, sympathetic, delightfully happy, jokey, tired/worn out, etc.

Person 1: What have you drawn?

Person 2: Can't you tell?

Person 1: Tell me about your drawing. I want to hear all about it.

Person 3: Maybe it would be best to talk about it later.

Person 2: No, It's OK – I don't mind.

Person 3: No, really. I don't think now is a good time.

Person 1: I think now is a perfect time.

Person 2: OK. It's a drawing of......

Children can perform their short scenes for the class. Can the class guess the stage and character directions used?

BUILDING TASK: ANNOTATE

Using examples of play scripts, ask the children to note and highlight any instances of character or stage directions. Discuss what they might tell us about the character and how they are feeling.

Students can use different colours to highlight features of play scripts. They should include a key with their work stating which colour corresponds to which key feature. Key features should include stage direction, character direction, scene setting, names on the left of the page followed by a colon and the cast list. If there are features missing, such as scene setting, the students could add this to the example.

MAIN TASK: AND... ACTION!

1. Remind the children of the story *Silly Limbic* and the role-play/dramas they rehearsed in the previous sessions. Explain that, using these plans, they will be writing their own scene following the layout and features of the play script examples they have explored.

2. Model with the class how to start their play script with a cast list and a scene setting. An example of one of the student's plans could be used, e.g. Characters: Daisy, Daisy's father, Oscar, Limbic. Oscar's front doorstep on a bright sunny afternoon. There is a knock at the door. Waiting patiently outside is Daisy and her father.

3. With a learning partner, children draft their scripts following the features and layout modelled. Include reflection and check-in stops to identify good examples and areas for improvement.

4. During the writing process, provide opportunities for students to practise/rehearse their plays aloud – possibly with another pair of learning partners. This will allow students to think about unnecessary dialogue or to see whether enough character direction (or too much) has been given. Ask the students whether their character has developed through the play, e.g. Has Oscar become braver – how have they shown this? Is Limbic under control – how have they achieved this?

5. Children can record or perform their plays for the class.

DIFFERENTIATION

✓ Give children a template to follow.

✓ Children can create a completely new scene using the characters from the story, *Silly Limbic*.

✓ Children to be given a piece of prose to turn into a play script.

Teacher Tools and Techniques	
Emotional Literacy	Recognising the feelings of others
	Recognising and naming feelings
	Empathy
Developing Relationships	Talking partners – agreement and compromise
	Cooperation and collaboration
	Constructive criticism and critical friend
Self-Development	Thinking out loud, modelling, self-motivation
	Awareness of strength and areas for development
Skills for Learning	Thinking out loud, annotation
	Grouping/sorting, decision-making, agreement
The Brain Learning and Behaviour	Targeting audience and purpose
	Communicating ideas

PHSE LINK (PSHE ASSOCIATION PROGRAMME OF STUDY FOR PSHE EDUCATION – KS2)

Everyday things that affect feelings and the importance of expressing feelings.

Varied vocabulary to use when talking about feelings and how to express feelings in different ways.

Strategies to respond to feelings, including intense or conflicting feelings; how to manage and respond to feelings appropriately and proportionately in different situations.

Predict, assess and manage risk in different situations.

Fight or Flight: How the Brain Helps Us Survive

Learning Objective: To explore anxiety, how it makes our bodies feel and why To identify strategies to manage anxiety	
Success Criteria: ◆ Describe how anxiety makes us feel and why ◆ Describe strategies that manage it	

Pupils Can...	Explain one strategy they can use to help them when they are anxious.
	Explain how our brain shuts down thinking and problem-solving abilities to help it focus on ways of surviving.
	To explain the hand model of the brain and ways to calm the system and manage anxiety.

Anxiety is a feeling of unease, such as worry or fear that can be mild or severe. Everyone experiences feelings of anxiety at some point in their life. For example, you may feel worried and anxious about sitting an exam, going to the dentist or starting at a new school or job. When you feel anxious, your body goes on high alert, looking for possible danger and activating your fight or flight responses. Common anxiety signs and symptoms include having a sense of impending danger, panic or doom, increased heart rate, breathing rapidly (hyperventilation), sweating, feeling sick or needing to go to the toilet, trembling and having trouble concentrating or thinking about anything other than the present worry.

Daily stressors like bullying or missing your train can cause anxiety. However, it is the long-term nature of chronic stress that can lead to more harmful health problems. Stress can also lead to behaviours like skipping meals, drinking alcohol or not getting enough sleep. Toxic stress can occur when a child or young person experiences strong, frequent and/ or prolonged adversity – such as physical or emotional abuse, chronic neglect, caregiver substance abuse or mental illness, exposure to violence and/or the accumulated burdens of family economic hardship – without adequate adult support. Stress is harmful because it reduces the ability to metabolise and detoxify. It can also increase your toxic load by increasing your cravings for high fat, high sugar foods. High levels of stress for prolonged periods of time, particularly in early life, have an impact on brain development and our ability to manage stress in the future.

	*Silly Limbic* by Naomi Harvey Mini Book instructions The Anxiety Thermometer The Hand Brain poster Upstairs Downstairs Teams	Challenge the Worries worksheet Worry Monster Description sheet The hand brain video: www.youtube.com/watch?v=f-m2YcdMdFw

TASTER: WORRY MONSTER

Pose the question 'What is a worry?' Explore definitions with the children.

Support them in collecting different words that stand for worry.

Collect examples of worries or situations/things that make the children worry.

Ask the children to imagine Worry as a monster. What would it look like? Where might it live? For some children, they may think of it inside their body. For others, they may experience it outside and it just appears when they are worrying. What does it like to eat?

Ask the children to draw or make a Worry Monster out of a variety of materials. It could be a junk project, clay, plasticine or a drawing.

MINI TASK: CHALLENGE WORRY

Working with the children as a group, explore the many things that can cause them to worry or feel anxious. Look at the words that the children collected that are linked with worry.

Anxiety, worry, nervousness, panic, overwhelmed, concern, unease, angst, fretfulness, apprehension, disquiet, etc.

Ask the children to work in pairs and rank the words from strongest to weakest. In their pairs, ask them to think of situations that might make them experience the level of feelings.

Children to complete Let's Challenge the Worries Sheet. On the sheet, they list the words they have come up with in order of power. By each word, they draw or write a situation that might evoke this feeling and the negative self-talk that might go with it. In the last box, they should come up with the thought that challenges the worry. It is important to make this kind and thoughtful so that it might be the words you would say to a friend who has shared a worry. For example:

Word – *Worry*

Situation – *Having a new teacher for PE*

Self-talk – *Oh no, they look mean, they are bound to pick on me. I hate PE*

Challenging Thought – *Hey come on, remember the last new teacher we had was great and you really love PE*

MAIN TASK

1. Explain to the children that their brain is an amazing organ, more powerful and complex than the best computer ever made. Explore some of the amazing things their brain can do.

2. Ask the children to imagine that their brain is a house with an upstairs and downstairs. It is useful to illustrate this when you are talking. (See upstairs downstairs house illustrated sheet.) The idea of the upstairs-downstairs house comes from the book *The Whole Brain Child* by Dr Dan Siegel and Tina Payne.

3. Expand this house analogy by adding characters to both parts of the house. Explain that the upstairs house is the thinking brain or the Neocortex. The downstairs brain is the emotional brain or the Limbic System.

4. The Upstairs Team are the logical thinkers and the problem solvers. They are sensitive, understanding and perceptive of other people's feelings and can adapt quickly to different needs.

5. Ask the children to give the Upstairs people names that can help them remember what they do. Problem-Solving Peter or Adaptable Alice, Calming Claire, Logical Leonard and Artistic Arthur, Sensitive Susan and Observant Oliver.

6. Ask the children to fill in their Upstairs Team on their diagram. They can change the names of the team and draw them as people or cartoon characters.

7. Move to talking about the people who live downstairs The Downstairs Team. They are more linked to emotions. They have very strong instincts and intuitions. They are the team that keeps us safe and makes certain that we get what we need to survive. Our survival instincts come from the team downstairs. This team alerts us to danger, is always on guard and helps us flee or fight to survive. This team is made up of Warning Wilson, Gary the Guardian, Survival Sarah, Isabelle Instinct and Alerting Alan.

8. Ask the children to complete the Downstairs Team.

9. Draw in the stairs that connect the two teams. Explain that when the two teams are able to work together, the brain can make the best decisions and help us the most to think, make the right choices, develop positive friendships and get along with others. When both teams are working well, we can be creative and invent new games, relax and if we get too excited or worried the teams can figure out how to calm us down and work out what to do.

10. If Warning Wilson senses danger, he lets the others know and Surviving Sarah starts to organise everyone so that they can keep us safe. Alerting Alan sets off the alarm, which tells the body that there is danger and it needs to be ready to fight, freeze or run. Gary the Guardian then takes over and tells the Upstairs Team that the Downstairs Team is now in charge. When this happens, the gate at the bottom of the stairs that link the Upstairs Team and the Downstairs Team shuts. No one from the Upstairs Team can come to help – they are all shut out.

11. When this happens, the brain has 'Flipped its lid' – this describes the Upstairs Team as being out of action and the Downstairs Team as being in control.

12. Ask the children to think about why this might be a good way to manage things. In addition, how it might help the person survive.

    Example: if a tiger was to appear out of the woods on your way to school one day. The Upstairs Team might try to think about this – maybe it's a friendly one, it might not be able to run very fast, maybe we could outrun it, how fast does a tiger run? This thinking and the questions could be dangerous. The Downstairs Team needs to take over and decide what to do NOW.

13. When the body senses danger, the Brain House will be agitated and confused from all the information coming in from the senses and all the noise from the characters trying to talk at the same time and work out what to do.

14. When this happens, the Downstairs Team need to be able to focus, concentrate, and get the body ready to deal with the danger.

15. Gary the Guardian gives the order for the heart to beat faster so that more blood is pumped to the muscles. He tells the lungs to work faster so that the body has enough oxygen to feed the muscles and gets the muscles ready to fight.

16. Gary the Guardian prepares the body to keep it safe.

17. Help keep the metaphor light so that the children don't get too frightened.

18. Ask the children to think about what would happen in the two teams if they went to the park and suddenly a dragon flew up from the woods towards them.

19. Help the children understand that everyone 'flips their lid' at one time or another, even the adults. Share a story to help the children understand this. One such story might be about the time when you were running late and needed to go and pick up someone. You went to run out of the house but couldn't find your car keys. You kept running around, looking in the bowl where you always put the keys but couldn't find them. The more worried you became at being late, the more you ran around looking in the same place. (Your Upstairs Thinking Team had been shut out. The Downstairs Team knew there was a big problem and that they needed to be in control and had closed the gate.)

20. Support the children in understanding that when we 'flip our lids' we can't get the help of Calming Claire or Problem-Solving Peter, which isn't helpful as we need them. In children and young people, Gary the Guardian panics easily and presses the Panic Button and can set off meltdowns and tantrums really easily. That is because the Upstairs Team hasn't learnt all the strategies they need until they are in their mid-20s. To help children understand this point, it can be really helpful to ask them if they have ever seen an adult fall to the floor and roll about shouting and having a tantrum because they want a bar of chocolate?!

21. It is really important to keep the metaphor light and playful.

22. By the time you are an adult, you will have worked out how to get the two teams to work together and keep you safe – most of the time!

23. Share with the children a range of activities they could do linked to the Upstairs Downstairs Teams. Put the children into groups and set up a carousel of tables with the different activities on them for the children to work on in their teams.

    Table 1: *Create a Strategies to Calm Booklet.*

    This booklet needs to show a range of different ways to keep calm. This might include star breathing or 5-4-3-2-1 or thinking about their favourite place.

    Table 2: *Create a puppet show to demonstrate the Upstairs Downstairs Teams flipping their lids.*

    Ask the children to use their Upstairs Downstairs Teams to show what can happen when the Downstairs Team notices a potential danger.

    Table 3: *Create a comic strip to show what happens when danger is sensed by the body.*

    Table 4: *Draw the Upstairs Downstairs Teams and write descriptions about them OR make them out of plasticine*

    Table 5: *Make a poster to show the Upstairs Downstairs Teams and explain what happens when the brain senses danger.*

    Table 6: *A short play sketch to show what happens in the brain when we flip our lid.*

24. Share the video clip of Dan Siegel talking about the hand brain model and ask the children to share this with their parents at home.

   www.youtube.com/watch?v=f-m2YcdMdFw

DIFFERENTIATION

◆ You know the children within your class and are therefore aware of their needs. You can support them by using other children as scribes or readers or learning buddies.

◆ Some children struggle with sharing their ideas and answering questions. Help them to understand that you won't pick on them and that you will only ask them to answer a question if their hand is up or you might ask them quietly when the other children are working.

◆ Keep a watchful eye on those children who are anxious or who have experienced trauma. If you notice any distress, then they can be supported by an adult.

Teacher Tools and Techniques	
Emotional Literacy	Talking about anxiety and putting words in order
Developing Relationships	Working in pairs and small groups
Self-Development	Understanding how they feel in different situations and exploring strategies that may be helpful
Skills for Learning	Planning and organising work
The Brain Learning and Behaviour	Understanding how the different parts of the brain help us keep safe.

PHSE LINK (PSHE ASSOCIATION PROGRAMME OF STUDY FOR PSHE EDUCATION – KS2)

About different feelings that humans can experience.

How feelings can affect people's bodies and how they behave.

About ways of sharing feelings; a range of words to describe feelings.

Different things they can do to manage big feelings, to help calm themselves down and/or change their mood when they don't feel good.

That mental health, just like physical health, is part of daily life; the importance of taking care of mental health.

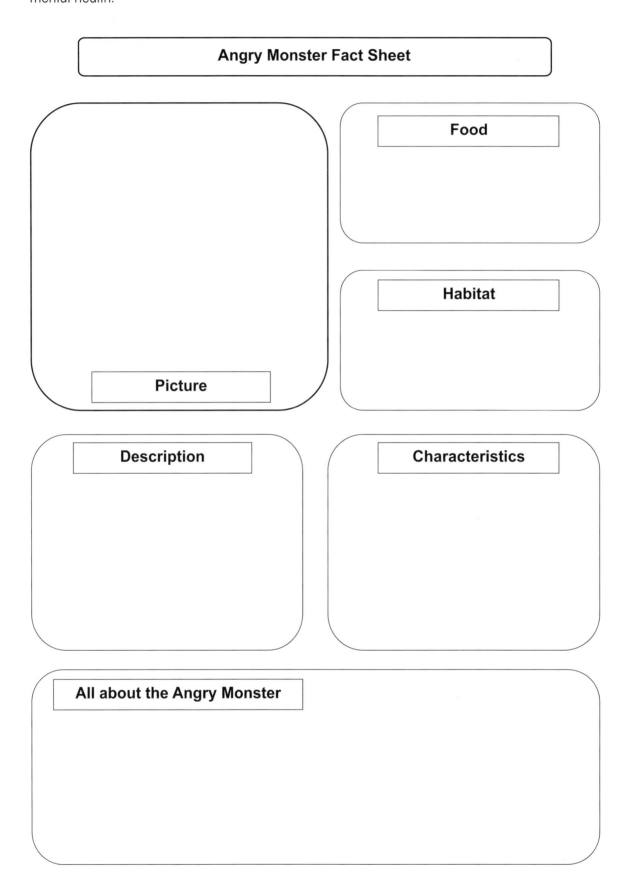

Angry Monster Fact Sheet

Food

Habitat

Picture

Description

Characteristics

All about the Angry Monster

How to Tame the Angry Monster

Resources

Step one

Step Two

Step Three

Step Four

Challenge the Worry

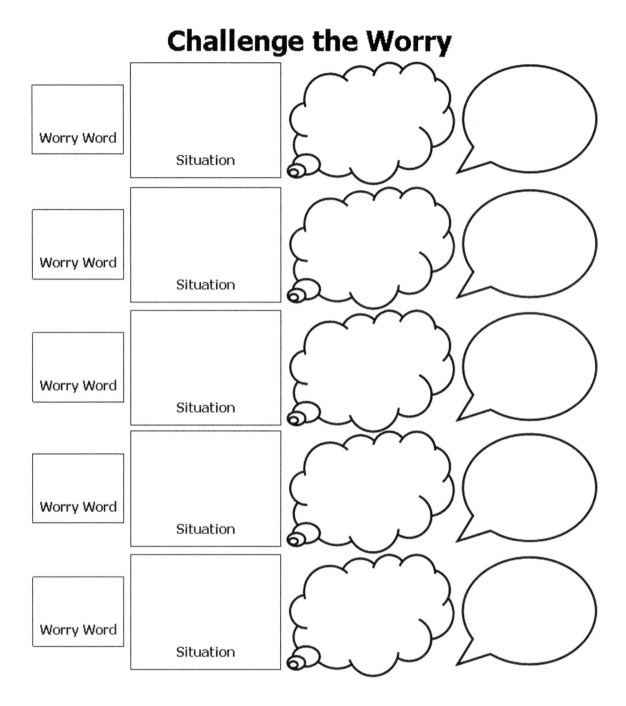

Whenever we experience anxiety or worry our mind starts to race with thoughts that are not always true. Anxious thoughts are often focused on the worst possible outcomes. These thoughts can have the power to make us believe that things are much much worse than they really are. This then makes us doubt whether we are able to manage.

1.   In the first box write one of the Worry words you have come up with.

2.   In the cloud draw or write what might have caused this worry.

3.   In the thought bubble write the negative self-talk that might happen

4.   In the speech bubble write the Challenge to the thought.

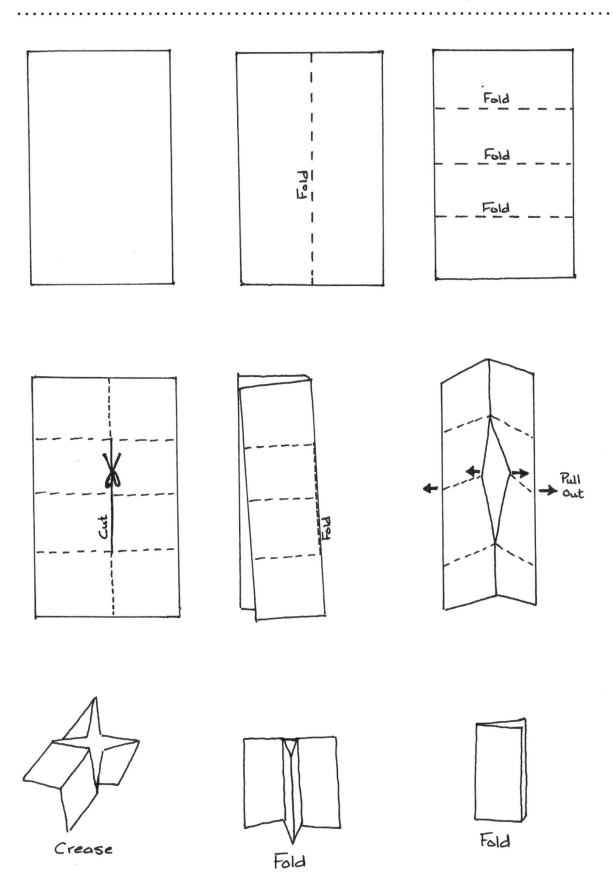

Upstairs Downstairs Teams

Upstairs Team

Downstairs Team

Flipping your Lid

Upstairs Downstairs Teams

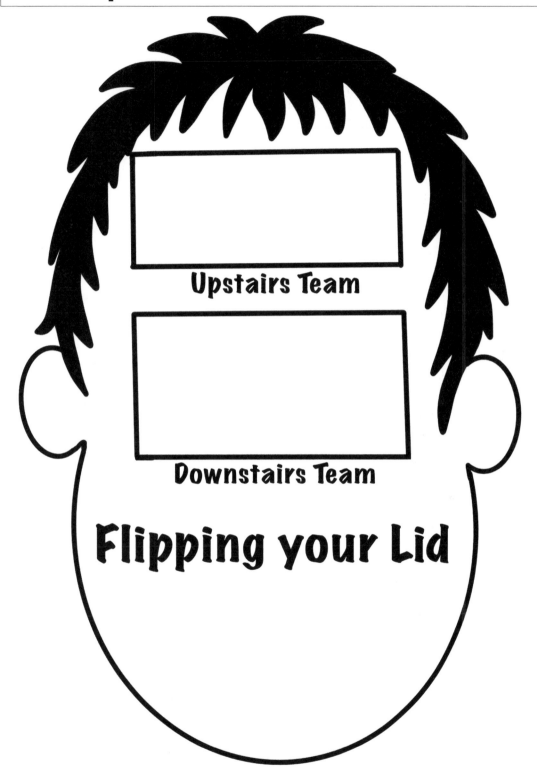

Upstairs Team

Downstairs Team

Flipping your Lid

Ways to manage Anxiety

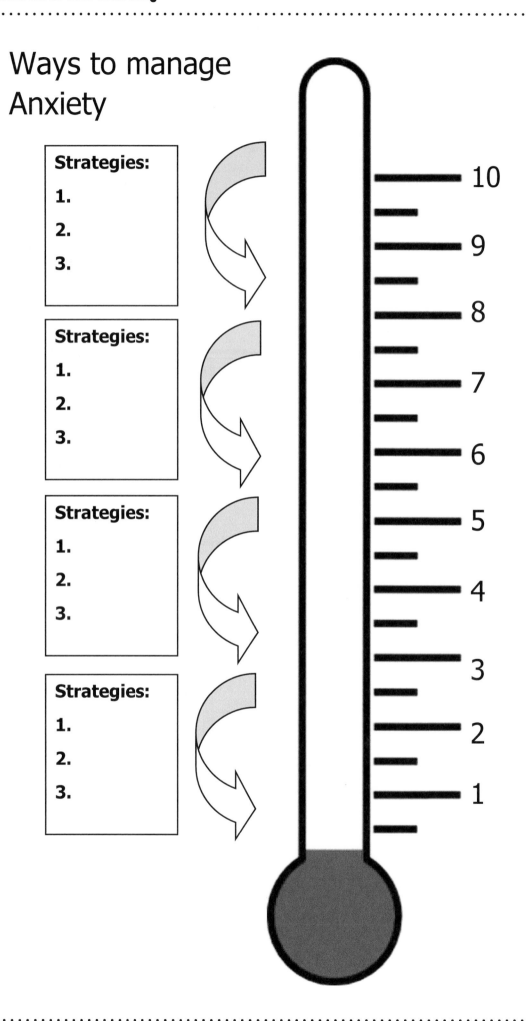

Strategies:

1.

2.

3.

Strategies:

1.

2.

3.

Strategies:

1.

2.

3.

Strategies:

1.

2.

3.

10

9

8

7

6

5

4

3

2

1

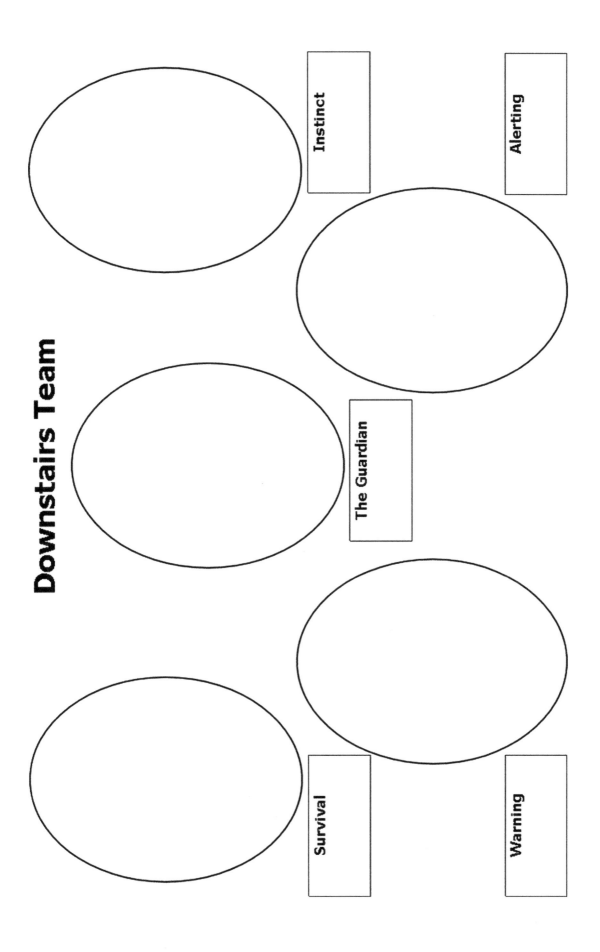

Downstairs Team

Instinct

Alerting

The Guardian

Survival

Warning

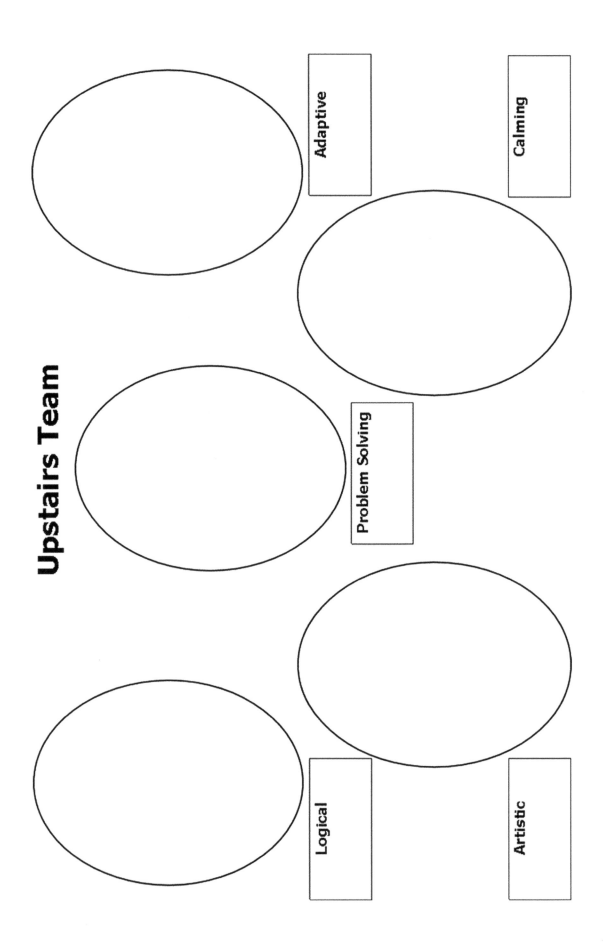

Upstairs Team

Adaptive

Calming

Problem Solving

Logical

Artistic

Primary Assembly:

Objectives

To help children understand that worries or anxiety are very natural and that strategies can be learned to make them more manageable.

Introduction

Introduce the Emotions Spots.

Ask the children to share a time when they feel worried. Where is that feeling – everyone is different.

What do they do to help manage the feeling? These actions are called strategies.

Main Event

Read the story about Spot.

Discuss the many things that can make us worry. Link them to What if.......

Share the response in the book. I can do this.

What things do children enjoy doing that helps them manage their worries?

Finale

Introduce the hand and the 5 Grey Spots.

Share the strategy to collect them and then blow them away.

Help children to understand that they can learn to trick their brain by making their breathing deep and regular. Their brain then calms down and they can think and problem solve better.

Key Message

We can manage our anxiety by focusing on our breathing and tricking our brain.

Who is the Assembly for?

Children in KS1 and KS2.

What is the Focus?

To enable children to understand that worries or anxiety are part of life and their function is to keep them safe. Sometimes they grow too big. When worries grow too big then you can use the blow away strategies to get rid of it.

Involvement of Children

Children to take the roles of the different Spots.

Children to learn the Grey Spot strategy.

Resources

A Little Spot of Anxiety by Diane Alber.

Large picture of a hand with spots on.

Chapter 5

Skills for Learning
KS2

KS2 BOOKS

Inside My Imagination by Marta Arteaga and
    Zuzanna Celej

The Tale of Two Fishes by Juliette Ttofa and
    Julia Gallego

Going Places by Peter and Paul Reynolds

ASSEMBLY

What Do You Do with a Chance? by
    Kobi Yamada and Mae Besom

DOI: 10.4324/9781003322801-6

Imaginary Setting

Learning Objective: To describe an imaginary setting	

Success Criteria:

◆ Decide on a narrative voice

◆ Use adventurous and precise vocabulary

◆ Use senses to help immerse the reader in the setting

◆ Varied sentence structure (such as short sentences to build tension and longer sentences for description)

◆ Figurative language (similes, metaphors, personification, onomatopoeia, alliteration)

◆ Include character reactions to the settings

◆ Adverbial phrases for time, place, manner or reason

Pupils Can...	Describe setting and atmosphere through precise vocabulary choices, e.g. adverbs, adjectives, nouns, expressive verbs and figurative language. Use all the senses when imagining and then describing the setting. Edit, proofread and amend their writing based on self and peer evaluation.
	Describe setting and atmosphere through precise vocabulary choices, e.g. adverbs, adjectives, nouns, expressive verbs and figurative language. Edit, proofread and amend their writing based on self and peer evaluation.
	Describe settings that use adverbials for time and place. Language choices for nouns and adjectives are more precise. Edit, proofread and amend their writing based on self and peer evaluation.

Narrative Voice is the perspective a story is told from. Stories are usually told in the first or third person. First person is used when the character is telling the story. Third person is when an external narrator is telling the story.

Similes are phrases that compare one thing to another thing of a different kind. It helps the reader understand the characteristics or qualities of the object/character/feeling they are describing. Similes can involve comparative words – 'like' and 'as', e.g. The puppy had eyes like chocolate buttons. He was as quiet as snowfall at night.

A Metaphor is a word or phrase that compares one thing to another thing of a different kind. It helps the reader understand the characteristics or qualities of the object/character/feeling they are describing. It can be directly compared using 'is', e.g. The moon is a shiny marble against a sea of black night sky.

Personification is when something non-human is given a human quality, ability or emotion. It is a type of comparison and helps the reader understand a description by giving it recognisable behaviours and feelings, e.g. The daffodils danced and turned their happy faces towards the sun.

*Onomatopoeia is a word or phrase that evokes the actual sound of the thing they describe, e.g. The **tick-tock** of the clock could be heard. The dolphin **splash**ed.*

 **Resources**	*Inside My Imagination* by Marta Arteaga	Selection of pictures of imaginary settings
		https://pixabay.com/images/search/fantasy %20world/
		Music to inspire an imaginary setting

TASTER: SYNONYM SPEED SEARCH

Split the class into small groups/teams. Each team should have a thesaurus or access to an online thesaurus. Have a list of ten words (these could have been gathered as a class) that involve the use of senses and character feeling. Words may include:

◆ *Sound* – bang, cry, whisper, noise

◆ *Sight* – large, horrid, ugly, pretty

◆ *Smell* – smelly, odour, pungent

◆ *Taste* – spicy, salty, delicious, awful

◆ *Touch* – distinguish between feeling an object or surface (bumpy, soft, smooth, cold) and feeling something on your skin (cold, hot, damp)

◆ *Feeling* (inside) – worried, scared, hesitant, joyful

Students race to find, agree and choose a synonym to replace the given words. Award points for speed or number of words found in a given time. Points can be awarded for justifying the choice or for the most adventurous word.

BUILDING TASK: CATEGORIES

This game will not only help build general knowledge but will help students to replace common nouns used in a description with more precise words. Decide with the class a list of six to seven categories that they can use. Examples of categories might include the following:

Tree, Bird, Fruit, River, Animal, Flower, Vegetable, Boy's name, Girl's name, Country, Town, Fish, Author.

The class is split into groups and given a list of categories. They are then given a letter of the alphabet and must find a noun that begins with that letter for each of the categories.

Tree – Ash

Animal – Aardvark

Bird – Albatross

Fish – Angel

And so on.

There could be a time limit given or the first group to finish shouts STOP.

Ten points are awarded for a word that is unique. Five points for a word that another group may have.

For an extra challenge, the students can be asked to place an adjective, verb and adverb, making the answer alliterative.

Ancient Ash

Ancient Ash appearing alone

BUILDING TASK: LOOK CAREFULLY

Show the children the page in the book *Inside My Imagination* where the young girl simply describes her 'amazing paradise'.

Model with the class on one piece of the illustration to describe fully. Include at least one sense in the description.

Which part of the illustration am I describing?

◆ *Proudly striding across the floor of lush green flora, the magnificent beast raised its noble head and inhaled deeply the pleasant perfume of paradise.*

◆ *Thin, fragile stems held aloft the colourful flower heads that swung like bells in the summer breeze.*

The children could be given an alternative illustration from the book to work on.

MAIN TASK: LOOK AT MY WORLD

1. Show children a variety of pictures/drawings of imaginary settings. Can they think of a word that describes the atmosphere most appropriate for the setting? Why do they think this?

2. Students listen to a piece of music a couple of times. On the second listening, ask the children to think about a setting that this piece of music suggests. As they listen again, the students could draw the imaginary setting that the music brings to mind. Can they imagine themselves walking through the setting? Are there any inhabitants and/or creatures? What is the climate like?

    Gustav Holst's The Planets could be useful. There are snippets from Jeff Wayne's War of the Worlds which could be used. If using YouTube, a search for 'Fantasy Music' provides a large selection of music with some wonderful pictures to accompany.

3. Using either a given setting or the one they have created from their own imagination, students write a first draft of their setting.

4. Revisit the success criteria – have the children included the narrator's reaction to the setting? Is there a variety of sentence openers and lengths? What is the overall atmosphere – has this been achieved? Students edit and improve.

5. Students share their descriptive setting with a partner – can the partner guess which setting has been described or draw the setting themselves from the description?

DIFFERENTIATION

✓ Children could use images from the internet to edit using software.

✓ A variety of images can be used to collate and create a collage for a new setting. Ensure children are aware of online searches and safety. School policies and internet protective controls should be in place when searching images.

✓ Link to artwork. Ink marbling art makes a fabulous background for imaginary settings.

✓ Interaction between inhabitants and narrator could be included.

✓ Template/plan for the five senses could be used to help mind map ideas.

✓ Role-play question and answer session. Interviewing an explorer that has been to a new world. Elicit information through questioning as an interviewer.

Teacher Tools and Techniques	
Emotional Literacy	Self-motivation and determination
	Positive attitude
Developing Relationships	Talking partners – agreement and compromise
	Cooperation and collaboration
	Constructive criticism and critical friend
Self-Development	Thinking out loud, modelling, self-motivation
	Awareness of strength and areas for development.
Skills for Learning	Thinking out loud, annotation
	Grouping/sorting, decision-making, agreement
	Imagination and creativity
The Brain Learning and Behaviour	Targeting audience and purpose
	Communicating ideas

PHSE LINK (PSHE ASSOCIATION PROGRAMME OF STUDY FOR PSHE EDUCATION – KS2)

Identify personal strengths, skills, achievements and interests and how these contribute to a sense of self-worth.

Everyday things that affect feelings and the importance of expressing feelings.

Varied vocabulary to use when talking about feelings and how to express feelings in different ways.

Manage setbacks/perceived failures, including how to re-frame unhelpful thinking.

Listen and respond respectfully to a wide range of people, including those whose traditions, beliefs and lifestyles are different to their own.

Reasons for following and complying with regulations and restrictions with reference to internet use. What to do if frightened or worried by something seen or read online and how to report concerns, inappropriate content and contact.

Free Verse Poem

Learning Objective: To write a free verse poem
Success Criteria:
◆ Keep to the topic/theme
◆ Use repetition
◆ Use similes and/or metaphors
◆ Use at least one line of personification
◆ Include alliteration
◆ Include onomatopoeia

Pupils Can...	Understand the terminology and techniques used in free verse.
	Use alliteration, repetition, onomatopoeia and the five senses to compare ideas to an abstract theme. Identify and use personal experiences to help describe and explain ideas within the free verse poem.
	Define free verse. Use alliteration, onomatopoeia, figurative language and the five senses in a free verse poem.
	Understand the term 'free verse' and write a free verse poem on a theme using alliteration and similes. Use the senses to help with descriptions.

Free verse is a form of poetry that doesn't have a particular rhyme or rhythm pattern. There are no obvious rules. The writer is 'free' to write on their theme.

Similes are phrases that compare one thing to another thing of a different kind. It helps the reader understand the characteristics or qualities of the object/character/feeling they are describing. Similes can involve comparative words – 'like' and 'as', e.g. The puppy had eyes like chocolate buttons. He was as quiet as snowfall at night.

A *Metaphor* is a word or phrase that compares one thing to another thing of a different kind. It helps the reader understand the characteristics or qualities of the object/character/feeling they are describing. It can be directly compared using 'is', e.g. The moon is a shiny marble against a sea of black night sky.

Personification is when something non-human is given a human quality, ability or emotion. It is a type of comparison and helps the reader understand a description by giving it recognisable behaviours and feelings, e.g. The daffodils danced and turned their happy faces towards the sun.

Onomatopoeia is a word or phrase that evokes the actual sound of the thing they describe, e.g. The *tick-tock* of the clock could be heard. The dolphin *splash*ed.

|  Resources | *Inside My Imagination* by Marta Arteaga | Collection of objects or pictures of objects for a connection game. |

TASTER: ONOMATOPOEIA CATEGORIES

With the class, make a list of animal noises. Explain that these are onomatopoeic words as they are words that sound like the word it describes, e.g. honk, twit-twoo, warble, bark, growl, hiss, meow, purr, oink.

Give the children another category. Can they think of three examples? For example:

People noises (giggle, achoo, hiccup, burp)

Weather noises (pitter-patter, drip-drop, crash, rumble)

Vehicle noises (honk, vroom, purr, beep)

Make a noise in the class. This could be scraping something along the board, dropping an object on the floor, snapping something in half or whipping something through the air. Can the children make up their own onomatopoeic words to describe the noise it makes?

BUILDING TASK: ONLY CONNECT

Explain to the children that our mind likes to make connections. Show the children the illustration from the book *Inside my Imagination* where the character breathes in her story and you could see how it worked inside her mind. There are cogs and wheels all working with each other leading from one thing to another and, in turn, connecting to something else.

Show the children a collection of four random objects. Can they find a connection? For example:

◆ *a pair of glasses, a brick, planks of wood, a hat.*

Children might make connections such as glasses and hats being worn. Bricks and planks of wood are used in construction.

◆ *a sunflower, a giraffe, a church spire, the sun.*

Connections might be to do with nature, height or living things.

What was the most interesting and creative connection made? Can the children think of two random things that cannot be connected?

BUILDING TASK: FIGURE IT OUT

Students are given two nouns to link using figurative language. This could be a simile, metaphor or personification.

For example:

leaf and sugar. A leaf is like sugar, sweetening our lives.

door and policeman. The policeman was a sturdy, huge, wooden door that barred our escape.

More obvious nouns to connect can be given. For a greater challenge, place nouns on lollipop sticks to be taken at random.

MAIN TASK: FREE VERSE

1. Re-read the book *Inside my Imagination* with the class. The character describes her imagination in similes. Can they spot them?

    — *My imagination is like a sea of thoughts that float and glide over each other.*

    — *My imagination is like a land of clouds of different shapes.*

    — *My imagination is like a meadow full of shooting stars.*

    — *My imagination is like an enormous music box, where I keep everything I see and hear.*

2. Look at the illustration of the cogs and wheels. Can the children think of figurative language to describe imagination using this picture? Collect examples from the class or ask them to help create a class one.

    My imagination is a collection of clicks, whirrs and buzzes, making connections and paths to a new world.

    Children can use other illustrations from the book to describe imagination.

3. Explain to the children that they will be writing a 'free verse', which means that they are gathering thoughts on the theme of 'Imagination' and putting them on paper. There is no rhyme or rhythm to follow. They can set the poem out how they like. Agree on success criteria with the children and what a good free verse poem might look like.

    Show the class an example of a free verse and explain some of the techniques that make it successful and a couple that need improving. For example:

— *Imagination is a bubbling brook that grows and grows into a vast, deep ocean.*

— *It is like a whirling wind that whooshes around your mind.*

— *It shouts, cries, giggles, runs.*

— *My imagination tells fibs and embellishes facts.*

— *It has superpowers!*

— *Hot.*

Point out the alliteration, onomatopoeia, simile and metaphor. Point out that the fourth line might need further explanation. On the fifth line – what is the superpower? Does it need to be named or should it be left with the exclamation mark? What about the repetition of grows and grows, could this be improved?

4. Ask the children to create their own free verse. Can they link imagination to a movement, an object, a smell, a sound? They can use the illustrations from the book or share ideas with a learning partner.

5. Display draft poems for students to read. Children can leave sticky notes remarking on parts of the poem they like. They could also indicate an improvement opportunity, e,g. with the above example, improvement opportunities might be

— *'An alternative word for grow'.*

— *'Can you explain a little more about telling fibs?'*

 ## DIFFERENTIATION

✓ Allow for a template plan that includes the senses. If imagination was a sound, what would it be? If imagination was a smell, what would it be?

✓ Challenge the children to think about layout, shape, colour, font style and size to further develop the free verse and present their ideas.

✓ Children can perform, record and critique their poems.

Teacher Tools and Techniques	
Emotional Literacy	Self-motivation and determination
	Positive attitude
	Being a critical friend and receiving constructive criticism
Developing Relationships	Talking partners – agreement and compromise
	Cooperation and collaboration
	Constructive criticism and critical friend
Self-Development	Thinking out loud, modelling, self-motivation
	Awareness of strength and areas for development
	Constructive criticism
Skills for Learning	Thinking out loud, annotation
	Grouping/sorting, decision-making, agreement
	Imagination and creativity
	Performing
The Brain Learning and Behaviour	Targeting audience and purpose
	Communicating ideas
	Constructive criticism

PHSE LINK (PSHE ASSOCIATION PROGRAMME OF STUDY FOR PSHE EDUCATION – KS2)

Identify personal strengths, skills, achievements and interests and how these contribute to a sense of self-worth.

Everyday things that affect feelings and the importance of expressing feelings.

Varied vocabulary to use when talking about feelings and how to express feelings in different ways.

Manage setbacks/perceived failures, including how to re-frame unhelpful thinking.

Listen and respond respectfully to a wide range of people, including those whose traditions, beliefs and lifestyles are different to their own.

Let's Play with Our Imagination

Learning Objectives: To describe a range of emotional words
To define imagination
Success Criteria:
◆ Use imagination to create an emotion creature
◆ Give a variety of words that describe an emotion

Pupils Can...	Name a variety of emotions.
	Give a variety of words that describe similar emotions.
	Describe how their imagination can be developed and looked after.

 ***Imagination*** *is thought of as the action or thinking of new ideas, images or concepts not present to the senses. It is a time when the mind is creative and can form mental images or phonological passages and narratives. When working with children, it can be really fun to help them think of things that are not there and then imagine what might be there or what someone might be saying or doing.*

 *Inside My Imagination* by Marta Arteaga

Pictures of scenes or landscapes

Emotions word list

Thesaurus

My imagination instruction sheet

 ## TASTER: IMAGINE!

Read the book to the children and discuss the thoughts and ideas it causes.

Ask the children to work in pairs.

Write the word imagination on the board and ask them to discuss a definition of what it means. Share the different definitions and create a class one that everyone feels is the best way of describing the word.

Give each pair one of the pictures and ask them to look at it and 'imagine' something that could be in the picture. Ask them to either draw a simple picture of what they have imagined or write a description of it. Share what they have come up with and discuss how amazing our ability to create is.

MINI TASK: EMOTION CHARACTERS

Ask the children to listen to the story again and write down any words they hear that they like or interest them.

Share the words they have chosen and help them explain why they are words that interest them. Ask the children to choose one of the emotion words from the list and find other words that mean the same or similar.

Show the children how to use a thesaurus or the synonyms link on the computer. Once the children have found four or more words, ask them to rank them from strongest to weakest. For example:

Happy – joyful – ecstatic – blissful – glad – delighted

Order the words: ecstatic – delighted – blissful - joyful – happy – glad

Ask the children to choose one of the words that they have just discovered and add it to the list. Display the list and see how many times the different words can be used in the week. Children can look through the book and choose a sentence that they find interesting that describes imagination. Ask the children to write a sentence of their own that describes their imagination. For example:

I entered my imagination. It was an amazing paradise

My imagination is like a sea of thoughts that float and glide over each other.

Ask the children to use their imagination and create a character that is an emotion.

Angry is a bird that lives in the jungle of Borneo. It is bright red with black beady eyes and a very sharp beak. It flies around the jungle jumping out on other birds and trying to peck them.

Calm is a small fish that lives in the warm sea around the shores of Australia. It is small and gentle and likes to float on the waves. The males are mainly blue with the females being a turquoise colour. The females have long floaty fins that gently float in the water around them.

MAIN TASK: LET YOUR IMAGINATION GO WILD

1. Give the children the phrase:

   My imagination is like an amazing plant that must be looked after in a very special way so that it keeps creating new things.

2. Ask them to draw their imagination as a unique and special plant.

3. Share the My Imagination sheet with them and ask them to write about their imagination plant and what it needs to thrive and grow.

4. When complete, set up an exhibition to show the different imagination plants and how the children look after them so that they can be imaginative.

5. Discuss how they need to use their imagination within a range of lessons over the following weeks.

6. Collect sayings about using their imagination, e.g. *Just leave it to your imagination. Let your imagination go wild.*

DIFFERENTIATION

✓   Ask the children to support each other within their pairs or groups.

✓   Ensure that children who may struggle with literacy have support from an adult when needed. This could be achieved with a supported group.

✓ For those children who may struggle with recording their ideas on paper, allow access to voice-activated software or let them work with another person/child who can record their work.

✓ For some children completing the My Imagination Plant sheet may prove too much of a challenge. They might be asked to make their plant and then add labels or share how it works with a talk to others.

Teacher Tools and Techniques	
Emotional Literacy	Expanding the use of emotional language
Developing Relationships	Working in pairs or small groups
Self-Development	Developing an understanding of their imagination and how they believe it works

Skills for Learning	Developing expressive language in relation to their imagination
The Brain Learning and Behaviour	Developing a greater understanding of themselves and how they learn

PHSE LINK (PSHE ASSOCIATION PROGRAMME OF STUDY FOR PSHE EDUCATION – KS2)

How to recognise and name different feelings.

How feelings can affect people's bodies and how they behave.

How to recognise what others might be feeling.

About ways of sharing feelings and a range of words to describe feelings.

Emotions

happy	sad	angry
frightened	disgust	surprise
trust	jealousy	loneliness
anticipation	amusement	boredom
calmness	frustration	sympathy
interest	excitement	horror
guilt	shyness	shame
relief	peace	worry
stress	hate	confused
tender	tired	meh
love	inspired	curious
cheeky	excluded	embarrassed

The Imagination Plant

Drawing of the Imagination Plant

Habitat (where it likes to live)

Properties (How it behaves and what it is made up of.)

Food (What it needs to grow)

Care (How to look after the plant)

Special Characteristics (What makes it unique)

How to Train your Plant (What do you have to do to get the Imagination Plant to work?)

Interview

Learning Objective: To formulate and ask questions of a character
Success Criteria:
◆ Decide what you would like information about
◆ Use clues from the story and illustrations
◆ Decide on formal or informal language (think about the interviewee)
◆ Use open-ended questions
◆ Clarify with further questions if responses are unclear
◆ Make notes of interviewees' responses

Pupils Can...	Ask effective questions that will help them clarify their understanding of a character. Establish what is known about characters, events and ideas in the narrative. Understand what is implied about characters through the way they are presented, Note and develop initial ideas on characters, drawing on reading and research.
	Identify and discuss key sentences and words in texts that convey important information about characters. Ask questions to clarify their understanding of a character. Understand what is implied about characters and make judgements about their motivations and attitudes from the dialogue and descriptions. Note and develop initial ideas on characters, drawing on reading and research.
	Locate, retrieve and collect information from texts about significant or important aspects of characters. Deduce the reasons for the way that characters behave from scenes across a short story. Ask questions to develop an understanding of characters' feelings and actions.

Closed questions are questions that can be answered with either one word or a very short phrase.

Open-ended questions are questions that allow a longer response, allowing the respondent to reflect on and voice opinions and feelings.

Resources	*The Tale of Two Fishes* by Juliette Ttofa and Julia Gallego	Illustrations from the book
		Images that evoke questions
		Jeopardy type questions

TASTER: 20 QUESTIONS

Play 20 questions with the class. One person (the answerer) thinks of a vegetable, animal or mineral. This 'answer' is recorded secretly so that the rest of the class cannot see it. The students must ask questions that will enable them to narrow down the options to discover the answer. The answerer can only answer yes or no, therefore, the questions need to be thought through carefully using deductive reasoning. They only have 20 questions to discover the answer. The answerer can state at the beginning of the game whether it is an animal, vegetable or mineral. Explain to the class that these are examples of closed questions.

I am thinking of an animal.

Is it a mammal? Yes

Is it domesticated? No

Does it live on land? Yes

Is it larger than a tiger? Yes

Is it carnivorous? No

…and so on.

BUILDING TASK: THE ANSWER IS…

Play the game of 'What was the question?' This is sometimes called 'Jeopardy'.

The students are given an answer and they must decide what the question could have been. For example:

A little girl with arachnophobia.

Who is Little Miss Muffet?

Mercury

Which planet is closest to the Sun?

Several fun, interactive Jeopardy games are available on the internet to play with the class:
https://jeopardylabs.com/play/kid-trivia22

Alternatively, children can make up their own games. This could be linked to the class topic, books and authors, science or history lessons.

BUILDING TASK: OPEN AND SHUT

Show the children an illustration – this could be an illustration from the book *The Tale of Two Fishes* or any drawing that might elicit lots of questions! With a learning partner, the students must come up with five questions that they would like to find out about the picture. Collate these questions. Can any of the questions be answered with a simple yes, no or a one-word answer? Do some questions require a longer answer? Sort the questions into closed and open. What do the children notice about how the questions/requests start?

Explain/Tell me more about/How/Why versus *How many/Can/Do you?*

Explain how the car ended up here.

Do you like the colour red for a car?

How many accidents have you had?

How did you get out of the car?

Do fish only swim in circles?

What type of fish are these?

Are these fish tasty?

How are these fish suited to their environment?

As a class, take a couple of the closed questions and change them to open-ended questions. For example:

'Are these fish tasty?' **could be changed to** *'Which recipe would you recommend for eating these fish?'*

MAIN TASK: I'D LIKE TO GET TO KNOW YOU

1.   Read the book with the class again. What questions are asked in the book – are they open or closed? Do the questions get answered?

2.   What questions do the children have about the story? What questions do they have about the main character? Discuss these in small groups and then as a class.

3. Explain to the children that they will have an opportunity to interview the main character to ask her about her experience with the fish and what she has learnt. With their learning partners, students draft questions that will draw out as much information about the girl and her experience as possible.

4. With the teacher in the role of the main character, children pose interview questions and take notes of the answers. Questions should be mostly open-ended. As teacher-in-role, questions can be closed down or obstructed, if necessary, in order for more open questioning to be considered.

5. Students can use their notes to write up an article on the character's experience. They will need to consider the order in which the article is written.

   – Background of character

   – Why she was feeding fish

   – What she learnt about the fish

   – What she has learnt about herself

6. As an extra challenge, the students could play the part of the interviewee as a fish!

DIFFERENTIATION

   ✓ Children could be given a template for the article that includes headings and then think of open-ended questions that will give the information they need.

✓ Intervies could be recorded, allowing the students to play back rather than use notes.

✓ Students can be given roles – interviewer, note-taker.

✓ Students could play the role of the main character.

Teacher Tools and Techniques	
Emotional Literacy	Empathy
Developing Relationships	Talking partners – agreement and compromise
	Cooperation and collaboration
Self-Development	Thinking out loud, modelling, self-motivation
	Awareness of strength and areas for development
	Questioning to understand self and others
Skills for Learning	Questioning and note-taking
	Thinking out loud, annotation
	Grouping/sorting, decision-making, agreement
	Imagination and creativity
The Brain Learning and Behaviour	Targeting audience and purpose
	Communicating ideas

PHSE LINK (PSHE ASSOCIATION PROGRAMME OF STUDY FOR PSHE EDUCATION – KS2)

Identify personal strengths, skills, achievements and interests and how these contribute to a sense of self-worth.

Everyday things that affect feelings and the importance of expressing feelings.

Varied vocabulary to use when talking about feelings and how to express feelings in different ways.

Manage setbacks/perceived failures, including how to re-frame unhelpful thinking.

Listen and respond respectfully to a wide range of people, including those whose traditions, beliefs and lifestyles are different to their own.

Personal behaviour can affect others.

Non-Chronological Report

Learning Objective: To write a Non-Chronological Report
Success Criteria: ◆ Include a catchy heading which highlights what the report is about   ◆ Include an introductory paragraph (general classification)   ◆ Include subheadings to organise factual information (may use wordplay or questions)   ◆ Use comparative language   ◆ Use technical language (may include a glossary)   ◆ Use passive voice   ◆ Use present tense   ◆ Include a rhetorical question   ◆ Include fact boxes, diagrams or charts/tables

Pupils Can...	Develop the introduction and conclusion using all the layout features. Describe the topic in a technical and accurate manner. Categorise and sort information for the reader. Inform the reader and describe the way things are. Engage the reader using rhetorical questions. Vary sentence length and use a wide range of subordinate conjunctions.
	Write a clear introduction and conclusion. Organise their information correctly into key ideas. Write interesting and catchy subheadings using wordplay and alliteration. Inform the reader and describe the way things are. Write sentences that move from a general idea to being more specific.
	Write a clear introduction. Organise their information under subheadings. Include some technical vocabulary. Include a relevant diagram or picture. Write simple sentences that include extra description and adverbial phrases.

Technical language is a word or phrase that is used and known in a particular topic. For example, when writing about birds, technical vocabulary might include *aviary, incubate, migrate*.

Passive voice is when the subject of the sentence appears after the verb. The verb acts upon the subject. For example, 'The bird ate the wriggling worm' uses the active voice. 'The wriggling worm was eaten by the bird' uses the passive voice.

A **collective noun** is a word or phrase that denotes a group of things as one entity. For example, a *pride* of lions, a *pod* of whales, a *crowd* of people.

	*The Tale of Two Fishes* by Juliette Ttofa and Julia Gallego	List of collective nouns
Resources		Pictures of animals
		Non-Chronological Report examples

TASTER: COLLECTIVELY SPEAKING

Using a variety of pictures of animals or using animal names, can the students identify the well-known collective noun? Follow this with some lesser known and more unusual collective nouns for animals such as *sleuth of bears, caravan of camels, dazzle of zebras.*

Display the collective noun – can the children deduce which animal group it might be?

There are origins of collective nouns that can be researched by the students, or they could try and interpret why the collective noun is so named. For example:

A family of sardines – is this because they are so tight together when they are packed in a tin?

A shiver of sharks – does this describe how you would react if you came face to face with one?

A murder of crows - ?

Students can come up with their own collective nouns. What might they call a group of maggots?

BUILDING TASK: COMPARATIVELY SPEAKING

In the book *The Tale of Two Fishes*, the fish are described comparatively using similes. *Their teeth were as sharp as spears. Their eyes were as big as boulders. And their tails were as giant as a whale's.*

In report writing, it helps the reader to understand the characteristics of a subject if it can be compared with something else.

Comparative adjectives could be used such as *'taller than a double-decker bus', 'sharper than a knife', 'whiter than snow'.*

Comparatives using similes are useful. *'The blackbird's shiny feathers are as black as polished ebony'.*

Give students a picture of an animal. They should write sentences which describe the animal using comparatives.

BUILDING TASK: COLLECT AND CONNECT

Give the children a non-chronological report with the heading and subheadings removed. Can they read the information, ascertain the purpose of this part of the text and write a suitable heading or subheading? Encourage the children to write interesting titles/headings. These could be in the form of a question or could use wordplay, puns or alliteration.

Give the children parts of a non-chronological report with no headings. Can they place the information into a new layout and include headings?

MAIN TASK: WHAT IS IT?

1. Read the book *The Tale of Two Fishes*. Have the students ever seen fish like these? Ask them to think of their own creature that lives in or by a pond. The students could draw the new creature and even label it.

2. With their drawing, children should now think about the information that the reader will need to know about their creature. Its name (they could make up a Latin classification), habitat, appearance, diet, etc. They could write notes alongside their drawing to use for their report. Alternatively, a template could be created as a class.

3. Students draft their reports under headings and subheadings. They think about layout, such as diagrams, pictures and 'Did you Know?' boxes. They should also think about technical vocabulary – it might be fun to make up new words. What is their collective noun? What are parts of the body named – new terminology?

4. Once the first draft is written, students should share it with their learning partner to peer evaluate against the success criteria. They could also look at any information they think might be missing or ask further questions about their partner's animal to clarify understanding.

5. Once the final editing of information is complete, students can explore the use of font, colours and layout.

6. Create a class book of animals. This could include a contents page, etc.

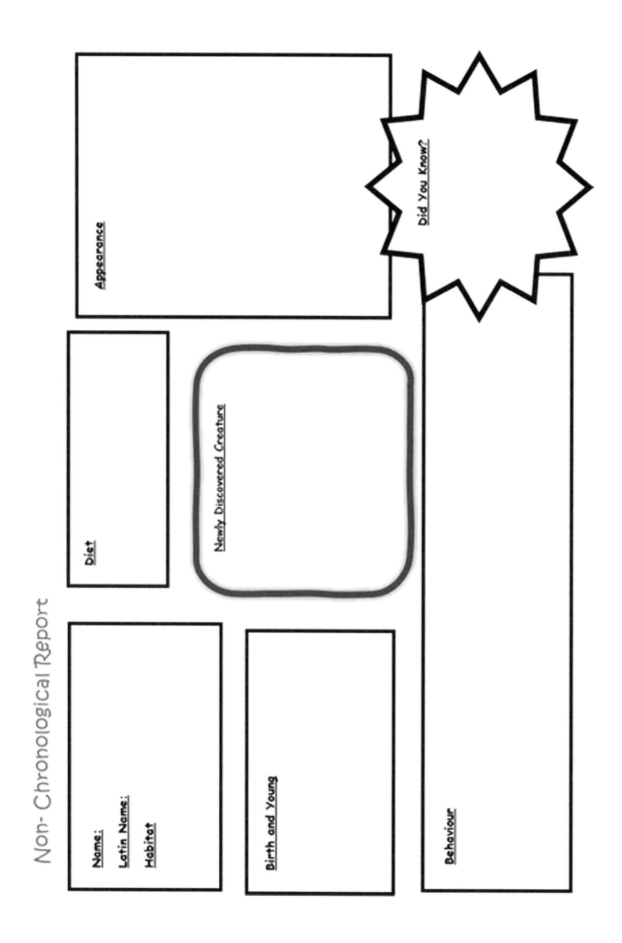

Non-Chronological Report

Appearance

Diet

Newly Discovered Creature

Did You Know?

Name:

Latin Name:

Habitat

Birth and Young

Behaviour

DIFFERENTIATION

✓ Give children a template to use.

✓ Give vocabulary mats and sentence starters.

✓ Use IT programmes such as Publisher and digital art.

✓ Present the newly discovered animal to the class in David Attenborough style.

✓ Provide exemplars to model writing.

Teacher Tools and Techniques	
Emotional Literacy	Constructive criticism and critical friend
	Giving and receiving feedback
Developing Relationships	Talking/learning partners
	Cooperation and collaboration
Self-Development	Thinking out loud, modelling, self-motivation
	Awareness of strength and areas for development.
Skills for Learning	Questioning and note-taking
	Thinking out loud, annotation
	Grouping/sorting, decision-making, agreement
	Imagination and creativity
The Brain Learning and Behaviour	Targeting audience and purpose
	Communicating ideas

PHSE LINK (PSHE ASSOCIATION PROGRAMME OF STUDY FOR PSHE EDUCATION – KS2)

Identify personal strengths, skills, achievements and interests and how these contribute to a sense of self-worth.

Everyday things that affect feelings and the importance of expressing feelings.

Varied vocabulary to use when talking about feelings and how to express feelings in different ways.

Manage setbacks/perceived failures, including how to re-frame unhelpful thinking

Listen and respond respectfully to a wide range of people, including those whose traditions, beliefs and lifestyles are different to their own.

Personal behaviour can affect others.

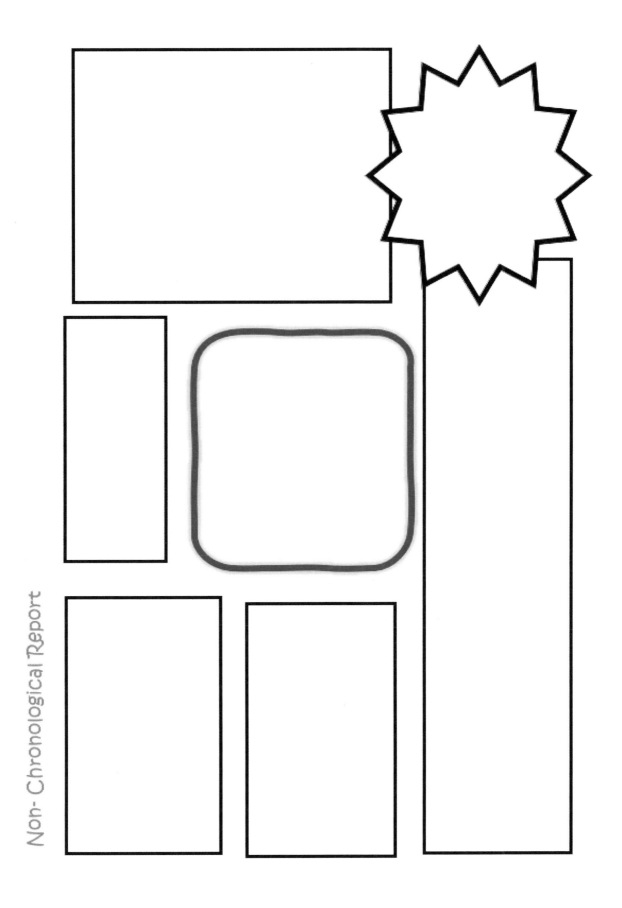

Non-Chronological Report

Have You Ever Wondered Why?

Learning Objectives: To develop an understanding of how our thinking can affect our mood	
To develop an understanding that thoughts are just that – thoughts and not facts	

Success Criteria:

◆ Explain what a thought is and that it is not a fact

◆ Explain how to catch good thoughts and let negative ones go

Pupils Can…	Tell you what a positive thought and a negative thought are.
	Explain how thoughts can affect their moods or their behaviour.
	Explain how to watch for thoughts and how to challenge negative ones.

Curiosity is a quality associated with inquisitive thinking or wanting to find out more. It leads to behaviour such as exploration, investigation and ultimately learning. Curiosity can be observed in humans and other animals. Curiosity is often linked with aspects of human development, in which it is connected to the process of learning and a wish to acquire knowledge or skills.

The term curiosity can also be used to denote the behaviour or emotion of being curious. This behaviour is linked to the desire to gain knowledge, information or skills. Curiosity as a behaviour and emotion is attributed as the driving force behind not only human development, but developments in all areas of knowledge, understanding, information and skills.

Curiosity was one of the seven areas identified by the Effective Lifelong Learning Inventory Team when they explored the key areas that people needed to be effective learners. They described Effective Learners who have a strong aspect of curiosity as having the energy and desire to find things out. They enjoy getting below the surface and asking questions to find out more. They are likely to come to their own conclusions and enjoy taking ownership of their own learning and enjoy a challenge. The ELLI Team highlighted that each learning dimension has both a positive aspect – an emergent pole – and a contrast pole, which tends to inhibit learning. The contrasting pole to Curiosity is Passivity. This they describe as learners who are more likely to accept what they are told without question and don't challenge ideas or information that they come across. They are less able to 'think' and 'explore' concepts or ideas and rarely engage in spontaneous exploration or discussion.

Resources	*The Tale of Two Fishes* by Juliette Ttofa and Julia Gallego YouTube: You are not your thoughts. https://www.youtube .com/watch?v=0QXmmP4psbA	Examples of posters Instruction card sentences Feeding the Fish Positive Thoughts worksheet

TASTER: POSITIVE AND NEGATIVE

Read the story to the children and discuss it. What was the little girl feeding the fish? Why do they think the red fish grew so much? Why did the blue fish disappear? How did the little girl get the blue fish back? What will you take away from this story? How will it change what you do or how you may behave?

Ask the children to work in pairs and draw/paint/collage the two fish.

Share the video 'You are Not Your Thoughts'. Support the children to explore what sort of thoughts might have fed the red fish and what sort of thoughts might have fed the blue fish. Ask the children to show in 'Thought Bubbles' what the little girl was thinking and put the different thoughts around each fish. Positive thoughts make us feel good and negative thoughts make us worry or not feel so good.

MINI TASK: INSTRUCTION CARDS

Ask the children to work in their pairs and discuss the sort of sign or poster that they could put by the pond to warn people about what happens when they feed the fish.

Explain to the children that you want them to write an instruction card to put under the sign to help people think about the types of thoughts they may be having. The card needs to show how to hold onto the positive thoughts and ignore the negative thoughts. Before they write, discuss the different ways that they might do this.

For example, identify if the thoughts they are having are positive or negative. (Would they say these things to their best friend?) If they are positive, they might be allowed through the Thought Police Barrier. If they are negative, the Thought Police might blast them. Get the children to be creative as this will help them remember to challenge their thoughts.

Record all their ideas on the board. Have fun and maybe draw a few cartoons.

Help the children to focus on how to encourage people to find good thoughts to feed the fish,

e.g. if you have a positive thought cut it up into words and let each word create a new positive sentence.

'Wow my story is really exciting'.

Wow – I used really good words

My – idea was really interesting

Story – stories can be great fun to do

Really – I worked hard on my punctuation

Exciting – the ending was really exciting

MAIN TASK: PLAY SCRIPTS/ROLE-PLAY

1. Re-read the story to the children.

2. Focus on the conversation between the girl and the snail.

3. Explore with the children what the snail may have said to help the little girl understand that her thoughts were feeding the fish.

4. Explore with the children how the fish explained to the little girl about the different fish and her different thoughts. Remind the children of the positive and negative thoughts they had put around their fish.

5. Ask the children to write the conversation between the little girl and the snail. Agree on what the story needs to contain and write this as a checklist on the board to help the children as they are writing.

6. Ask the children to read or act out their play scripts.

7. The play scripts could be used in an assembly to help share how our thoughts can affect how we behave and feel.

DIFFERENTIATION

✓ Pair the children with sensitivity so that children who need support are able to be supported either by another child or an adult.

✓ Use the Instruction card sentences sheet for those children who need support with making the card.

✓ Differentiate the work with the sorting of positive or negative thoughts exercise.

✓ Use the Feeding the Fish Positive Thoughts Worksheet for those children who would benefit from this sort of support.

✓ For children who struggle to record ideas use voice-activated software for the play script or an adult to enable them to record their ideas.

✓ For other children, using a cartoon format may be the better way of getting them to show the conversation between the snail and the little girl.

Teacher Tools and Techniques	
Emotional Literacy	Positive and negative self-talk
Developing Relationships	Working and listening to each other's ideas
Self-Development	Aware of the power of positive or negative self-talk
Skills for Learning	Creativity
The Brain Learning and Behaviour	The link between thinking and how we behave

PHSE LINK (PSHE ASSOCIATION PROGRAMME OF STUDY FOR PSHE EDUCATION – KS2)

How feelings can affect people's bodies and how they behave.

About ways of sharing feelings and a range of words to describe feelings.

About things that help people feel good (e.g. playing outside, doing things they enjoy, spending time with family, getting enough sleep).

Different things they can do to manage big feelings, to help calm themselves down and/or change their mood when they don't feel good.

To recognise when they need help with feelings and that it is important to ask for help with feelings and how to ask for it.

Explanatory Diagrams

Learning Objective: To explain using labelled diagrams

Success Criteria:

◆ Use straight lines/arrows pointing to parts of the diagram

◆ Number/alphabetise the parts of the diagram to indicate in which order the explanations should be read

◆ Use present tense

◆ Use causal connectives

◆ Include technical vocabulary

Pupils Can...	Compose, edit and refine explanatory texts and diagrams, focusing on clarity, conciseness and impersonal style.
	Summarise processes carried out using flowcharts or diagrams.
	Write explanatory texts, after oral rehearsal, using a diagrammatic plan.
	Explain processes orally ensuring relevant details are included. Create diagrams to summarise or make notes of stages in a process ensuring items are clearly sequenced or organised.

Explanatory Texts are more than a description as they include information about how and why. They explain causes and reasons. Explanatory texts are found within or alongside other text types.

Causal connectives are words or phrases in a sentence that show a reason for an action or result, e.g. 'as a result', 'consequently', 'due to'.

Technical vocabulary is vocabulary used specifically for a particular 'field' or 'study', e.g. the technical vocabulary for a vehicle would include 'ignition' and 'axle'.

Resources

Going Places by Peter and Paul Reynolds

Heath Robinson contraption illustrations

Explanation text with an unlabelled diagram

TASTER: LABEL IT

Show the children an unlabelled diagram. Then give them a piece of text to read. Using the text, can they label the diagram?

Unlabelled diagrams could be – inside of a volcano

◆ parts of an ant

◆ the water cycle

◆ parts of the body

BUILDING TASK: WHAT CAUSED IT?

Explain to the children that explanatory texts will use causal connectives.

Causal connectives show the cause! There will be a main clause with a causal connective showing the result or cause, e.g. <u>I banged my leg on the corner of the table</u>, *as a result* *I have a massive purple bruise.* <u>I lost the race</u> *because* I had not trained hard enough.

Can the children think of other causal connectives to replace 'as a result'?

Collect these as a class. Using a random connective generator (this could be a die where the number represents a connective, an interactive spinner, connectives written on lolly sticks, connectives in a hat), students have a connective with which to write or complete a sentence.

I missed the bus…

My homework was late…

The plant died…

The teacher was shattered…

My handwriting has improved…

Can the students use two different causal connectives for the same sentence?

Students can also try repositioning the connective to start the sentence.

As a result of banging my leg into the table, I have a massive purple bruise.

BUILDING TASK: HEATH ROBINSON CONTRAPTIONS

Heath Robinson was a cartoonist, illustrator and artist. He was known for his drawing of funny and very detailed contraptions that were used for completing simple tasks. 'Heath Robinson contraption' became an entry into the dictionary in the early 1920s. There are many different illustrations. These are our favourites – *The Tabby Silencer, The Wart Remover and Eating Peas.*

Children look carefully at the diagrams. With learning partners, children discuss how the contraptions work. Learning partners can then display the Heath Robinson illustration to the class and present their oral explanation. They can point to the various parts as they say what is happening and the effect this has, e.g. *A rope is attached to the handle of the water jug and runs to a turning handle underneath the window. The turning handle is turned clockwise, which extends the rope and lowers the water jug.*

MAIN TASK: THE HOW AND WHY OF IT

1. Look at the numbered diagram of the go-kart where Rafael is hammering, glueing and nailing his kit. Why are the arrows numbered?

Are they just labels that say 'wheel' or could they include more detailed information as to how and why? For example:

Number 4 – Wheel is placed on the side of the main chassis in front of the passenger entry. This wheel, when attached to a wheel on the other side, allows the passenger to steer and turn the Go-kart in any direction.

2. Children continue to label the diagram with the name of the part and how it is used and why it is needed. As a class, this could be discussed beforehand.

Arched body of the Go-Kart allows room for passengers' legs, consequently increasing passenger comfort.

The Go-kart has a curved body like an arch as this is a strong structure and therefore makes a sturdier vehicle.

Rear wheels for balance. Four wheels give extra stability rather than three, as a result turning a corner is safer and the chance of overturning is reduced.

3. Alternatively, use the design that Maya created.

4. Children, for a greater challenge, can use a Heath Robinson contraption to label and include explanations.

5. Children could design their own vehicle to enter the race, label it and add explanations for parts of the design.

DIFFERENTIATION

✓ Give children a range of labelled diagrams to explain.

✓ Own designs could be drawn, labelled and explained.

✓ Give the children technical terminology they could include.

✓ Give children specific conjunctions to include, strengthening their vocabulary.

✓ Wallace and Gromit clips could be used: www.youtube.com/watch?v=K7gdWIY9R4s

Teacher Tools and Techniques	
Emotional Literacy	Awareness of emotions in decision-making
	Recognising the feelings of others
	Dealing with failure as an opportunity to learn
Developing Relationships	Talking partners – agreement and compromise
	Cooperation
Self-Development	Thinking out loud, use of language/symbols to communicate, self-motivation
	Awareness of strength and areas for development
	Verbalising ideas
	Performance
Skills for Learning	Thinking out loud, use of language/symbols to communicate
	Grouping/sorting, decision-making, agreement, sequencing, identifying information, understanding cause and effect, synthesising
The Brain Learning and Behaviour	Targeting audience and purpose
	Communicating ideas

PHSE LINK (PSHE ASSOCIATION PROGRAMME OF STUDY FOR PSHE EDUCATION – KS2)

Recognise positive things about themselves and their achievements; set goals to help achieve personal outcomes.

Skills that will help them in their future careers (e.g. teamwork, communication and negotiation).

Personal identity: what contributes to who we are (e.g. ethnicity, family, gender, faith, culture, hobbies, likes/dislikes).

What constitutes a positive healthy friendship – support with problems and difficulties.

Identify personal strengths, skills, achievements and interests and how these contribute to a sense of self-worth.

Explanation

Learning Objective: To write an explanation	

Success Criteria:

◆ Include a catchy title – possibly a question

◆ Use present tense

◆ Use time connectives

◆ Use causal conjunctions

◆ Include technical vocabulary

◆ Use passive voice

◆ Include diagram or flowchart

Pupils Can...	Compose, edit and refine explanatory texts and diagrams, focusing on clarity, conciseness and impersonal style.
	Summarise processes carried out using flowcharts or diagrams.
	Write explanatory texts, after oral rehearsal, using a diagrammatic plan.
	Explain processes orally ensuring relevant details are included. Create diagrams to summarise or make notes of stages in a process ensuring items are clearly sequenced or organised.

Explanatory texts are more than a description as they include information about how and why. They explain causes and reasons. Explanatory texts are found within or alongside other text types.

Causal connectives are words or phrases in a sentence that show a reason for an action or result, e.g. 'as a result', 'consequently', 'due to'.

Time/Temporal connectives are words or phrases that show when an action is happening, e.g. 'before', 'first', following this'.

Passive Voice is a way of writing sentences that the action comes first and is 'done' to the subject. It makes the writing more objective, e.g. The ball was *kicked by Tayla* – Passive. *Tayla kicked* the ball – Active.

Technical vocabulary is vocabulary used specifically for a particular 'field' or 'study', e.g. the technical vocabulary for a vehicle would include 'ignition' and 'axle'.

	*Going Places* by Peter and Paul Reynolds	Examples of explanation flowcharts
		Examples of explanation texts
		www.literacywagoll.com/explanation.html

TASTER: ACTIVE OR PASSIVE

Using sentences from the book, can they change active sentences to passive ones?

Rafael hammered, glued and nailed his kit.

She was watching the bird intently.

She sketched the bird.

The children laughed at Maya and Rafael.

She put down the pencil and stared at the bird dreamily.

Maya and Rafael crossed the finish line

The rest of the class watched enviously as Rafael walked back to his seat with a kit.

BUILDING TASK: TIME CONNECTIVES

Ask the students to find a time connective or time phrase for each letter of the alphabet… or as many of the letters of the alphabet as they can. Were some letters of the alphabet easier than others? Children could use search engines or thesauruses for this activity.

Giving the class a starter sentence, can the students add another sentence that starts with a time connective?

This morning, *the dog started tearing up my homework.*

As soon as *I saw this, I chased my dog round the house.*

Eventually, *I caught up with my dog.*

During *the chase, my dog consumed my homework.*

After *eating my homework, my poor dog was sick.*

Following this, …

Next,

BUILDING TASK: TAKE NOTE

Show the children the following sentences about go-karts.

A go-kart is a motorless vehicle which is raced on a downhill road against the clock or against another competitor. Originally, go-karts were built from wooden crates and roller-skate wheels.

Ask them to read it and then erase it or cover it. What can they remember? It is easier to remember short pieces of information, but what if it were a longer text? This is where highlighting or taking notes is useful.

Display the sentences again but this time with keywords taken out.

A go-kart is a which is on a downhill road against the clock or against another competitor.

Originally, go-karts were built from and

How helpful is this? The key words are missing.

Show the children the key words: *motorless vehicle, raced downhill, clock, competitors, wooden crates, roller-skates.* Can the students now turn these words into a sentence or two?

Show the children the first 50 seconds of the following clip that shows how the brake on a go-kart works. Children can make notes as the clip is played. The clip can be played a couple of times if needed.

www.youtube.com/watch?v=5i9VfUnloYA

Using their notes, children should write two or three sentences to explain how the brake on this go-kart works.

MAIN TASK: EXPLAIN IT

1. Children to watch a video clip or read texts explaining how something is made, why something happens or how something works.

Such as:

— *Why does popcorn pop?*

— *How is popcorn made?*

— *Why do bees dance?*

>   – *How do toilets work?*

>   – *How do tsunamis form?*

BBC's 'Maddie's How Is It Made' has some very simple and basic explanations as clips.

BBC's Bitesize Science and History also have clips such as 'How Fossils Are Made' or 'How Did Vikings Make Decisions'.

Students are to make notes from the text or video clip. These notes can then be used as part of their plan for an explanation text.

2. Children will need to think of a catchy, attention-grabbing title for their explanation. It could be in the form of a question. It could use alliteration or wordplay.

3. Children draft their notes into a chosen format. This could be a flow chart or prose using headings and subheadings. A labelled diagram could be included in their text.

4. Students use their notes to write a formal explanation of their chosen topic considering the key features needed and then present to the class

Title of Work E.g How is Popcorn Made

Labelled Diagram

Water inside in kernel gets hot and expands.

POP!

Water turns into steam

Kernel turns inside out

Explanation

Include time connectives

Technical vocabulary

Causal connectives

Introduction

Interesting Facts

Glossary

DIFFERENTIATION

✓ Give children a template to make notes on using a shorter clip or simpler text.

✓ Children are given explanation prose to place in the template.

✓ Sentence starters with time connectives can be given.

✓ Connective mats available.

✓ Children incorporate a flowchart and prose into their explanations.

✓ Notes could be recorded on audio recording devices rather than written notes.

Teacher Tools and Techniques	
Emotional Literacy	Awareness of emotions in decision-making
	Empathy
	Dealing with failure as an opportunity to learn
Developing Relationships	Talking partners – agreement and compromise
	Cooperation
Self-Development	Thinking out loud, use of language/symbols to communicate, self-motivation
	Awareness of strength and areas for development
Skills for Learning	Thinking out loud, use of language/symbols to communicate
	Grouping/sorting, decision-making, agreement, sequencing, identifying information, understanding cause and effect, synthesising
The Brain Learning and Behaviour	Targeting audience and purpose
	Communicating ideas

PHSE LINK (PSHE ASSOCIATION PROGRAMME OF STUDY FOR PSHE EDUCATION – KS2)

Recognise positive things about themselves and their achievements; set goals to help achieve personal outcomes

Skills that will help them in their future careers (e.g. teamwork, communication and negotiation).

Personal identity: what contributes to who we are (e.g. ethnicity, family, gender, faith, culture, hobbies, likes/dislikes).

Identify personal strengths, skills, achievements and interests and how these contribute to a sense of self-worth. How to manage setbacks/perceived failures.

Skills for Learning

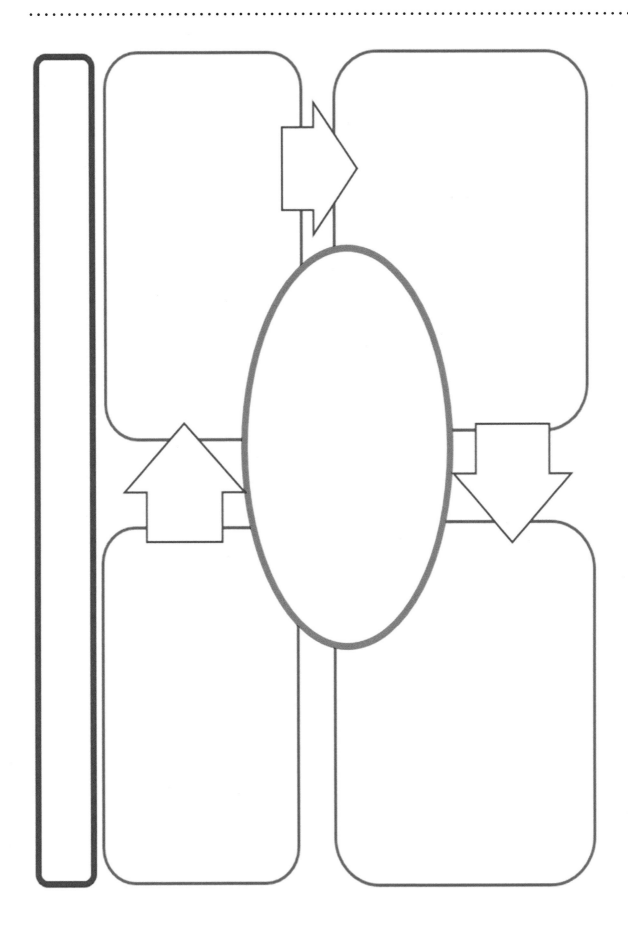

Let's Get Learning

Learning Objective: To explore and discuss learning and understand that we all learn in different ways	

Success Criteria:

◆ Talk about the way they learn

◆ Give examples of the way they learn best

Pupils Can...	Explain what learning is
	Give examples of a variety of things that have been learnt and how this learning was supported
	Explore and discuss their learning profile spider diagram

Human learning starts at birth and continues until death. Learning is the result of interactions between people and their environment. Learning has been studied by many different people and includes the fields of educational psychology, neuropsychology, experimental psychology and pedagogy. The research carried out has identified different sorts of learning. This includes learning occurring as a result of habituation or classical conditioning, operant conditioning or as a result of more complex activities such as play. Play is only seen in relatively intelligent animals.

Each and every time we learn something new our brain forms new connections and neurons and makes existing neural pathways stronger or weaker. Some experts call these changes 'plasticity' in the brain.

Research has now shown that learning is learnable and that it changes throughout our lifetime. Professors Patricia Broadfoot CBE and Guy Claxton sought to determine the essential attributes that govern learning, especially among schoolchildren. They set up a research team at the Graduate School of Education, University of Bristol. They identified seven specific areas that make a good learner: Curiosity, Resilience, Learning Relationships, Creativity, Meaning Making, Changing and Learning and Strategic Awareness. They developed the Effective Lifelong Learning Inventory – known as ELLI, which can assess and measure these different abilities.

Resources	*Going Places* by Peter and Paul Reynolds. Learning Timeline Learning Wheel Fleas in the jar video: www.youtube.com/watch?v=TK2Hd9aO5HM	Spider diagram blank Spider diagram example Origami instruction sheets www.origami-fun.com/printable-origami.html Learning Dimensions descriptions

TASTER: RAG RATE LEARNING

Ask the children to work with a partner and discuss what the word learning means. Ask them to come up with a definition.

Share the different definitions children have come up with and discuss. As a class, use the different ideas to come up with a class definition.

Give the children the Learning Timeline sheet and ask them to show some of the many different things they have learnt over their life. Ask them to colour code them: green – easy to learn, amber – a bit tricky to learn and red – really difficult.

Share and discuss the different things they come up with and create a class list of Easy, Tricky and Difficult. Support the children to understand that we are all different and that things that are easy for some are difficult for others. When looking at the things children felt were hard to learn, explore with the children what helped them. For example:

Really Hard – Learning to ride my bike. What helped? I really wanted to go out with my dad and brothers riding in the forest. Dad helped me practice every day.

Help the children see that we are all different and that we each find some things difficult and others easy. If we like something or really want to do it, then we are prepared to put the effort in and work at it. Link how we learn to do something with a sporting activity. Share some of the sports coaches that help our top athletes. Children could list ten skills a coach may need to support someone. How could they start to coach themselves?

MINI TASK: BOOKMARK LEARNING.

Give the children the Learning Wheel and ask them to complete it. Share their wheel in pairs. Ask each partner to present the Learning Wheel of their partner to the class. Make it fun as if they were introducing their partner to a game show.

Share the fleas in the jar video with the children.

How does this story make us think about:

◆ Learning

◆ How do our past experiences affect our thinking about learning now?

◆ How can we remind each other to take the lid off?

Now they have this new piece of information, how will it affect their learning? Ask the children to make a bookmark or a poster to help them to think about the many ways they could be their own Learning Coach.

MAIN TASK

1. Explain to the children that you are going to run an experiment about learning to identify what happens and how they learn best.

2. Give each of the children an instruction sheet for making an origami animal. Explain to the children that they are going to have a go at following the instructions to make the animal, and while they are doing this, they are going to record what they are thinking and how they are feeling.

3. Share the Learning Timeline example sheet with them to illustrate what you would like them to do.

4. Explain that you will stop every 60 seconds for them to record their thoughts and emotions on the sheet.

5. After five minutes stop the children and collect what they have experienced. Discuss the difficulty of doing this on their own. Offer them different options:

   − *Talk to a partner*

   − *Watch a guide to show them how*

   − *Access a coach to help them when they need it*

   − *Keep going on their own*

6. Set up the different groups or ways of working and carry on the learning timeline.

7. Discuss what they have found out about themselves and how they learn best.

8. Share the spider diagram with the children. Explain that a group of researchers at Bristol University identified seven different dimensions that had an effect on how we learn. The stronger we are in each dimension, the stronger learner we are.

9. Share the Learning Dimensions description sheets with the children and explore what each area is about together.

10. Share the spider diagram with the children and explain that you are going to ask them to rate how good they believe they are for each of the different dimensions.

   – *Working with others*

   – *Creativity*

   – *Resilience*

   – *Curiosity*

   – *Meaning making*

   – *Changing and learning*

   – *Strategic awareness*

11. See the definitions sheet and discuss each area with the children.

12. Share the Learning Dimensions example spider diagram to help the children understand how it will look.

13. Once they have their learning profile, ask them to identify the areas that they would like support to develop the most. Engage with each child and have a learning conversation afternoon with them.

DIFFERENTIATION

✓ Children can be supported in a range of ways. This may include working with a partner who can scribe or read.

✓ Sheets to support vocabulary including emotions or faces with emotions.

✓ For children with high levels of anxiety, the thought of being asked to answer a question can be very challenging to manage. For some children, knowing that the adult will not ask them unless their hand is up is a great way to give them control and manage the situation. For other children, having a conversation with them if you have noticed they have a good point to make, asking if they are able to share or if you can share their idea is another positive way to ensure they are included.

✓ Use a variety of origami instructions so that children with visual processing challenges or reading challenges do not have to be overwhelmed by what they are given.

Teacher Tools and Techniques	
Emotional Literacy	Discussing the emotions linked to learning
Developing Relationships	Working in groups and pairs
Self-Development	Understanding the learning process for them
Skills for Learning	Developing their own learning profile
The Brain Learning and Behaviour	Developing an understanding of how emotions affect learning and behaviours

PHSE LINK (PSHE ASSOCIATION PROGRAMME OF STUDY FOR PSHE EDUCATION – KS2)

Different things they can do to manage big feelings to help calm themselves down and/or change their mood when they don't feel good.

About everyday things that affect feelings and the importance of expressing feelings.

Problem-solving strategies for dealing with emotions, challenges and change, including the transition to new schools.

Learning Timeline

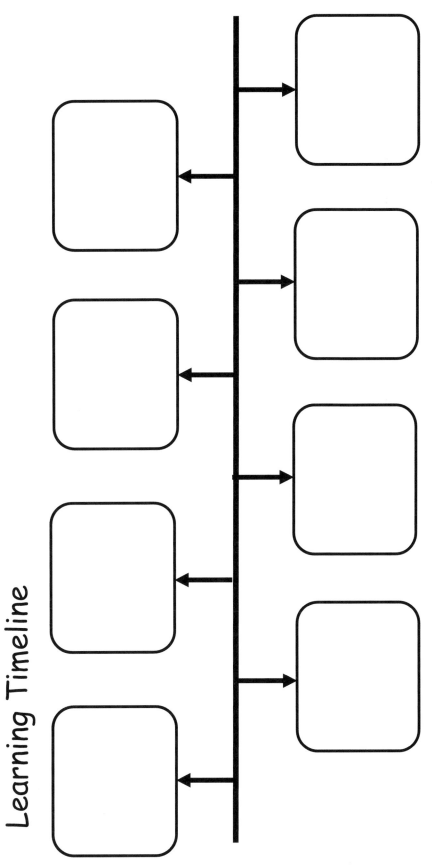

Draw in the boxes things you have learnt to do as you have grown up. Start with the box on the left and draw one of the first things you learnt to do. Work your way along the boxes so that you end up with something you have only recently learnt to do.

Learning Wheel

The wheel segments read (clockwise from top right):

- I learn information best by ...
- I learn spellings best by ...
- 3 things I like to learn with others
- 3 things I do when I get stuck with my learning
- 3 things I have found easy to learn
- The hardest thing I have ever learnt
- Things I like to learn by watching someone
- Things I like to learn quietly on my own

Learning Dimensions Spider Graph

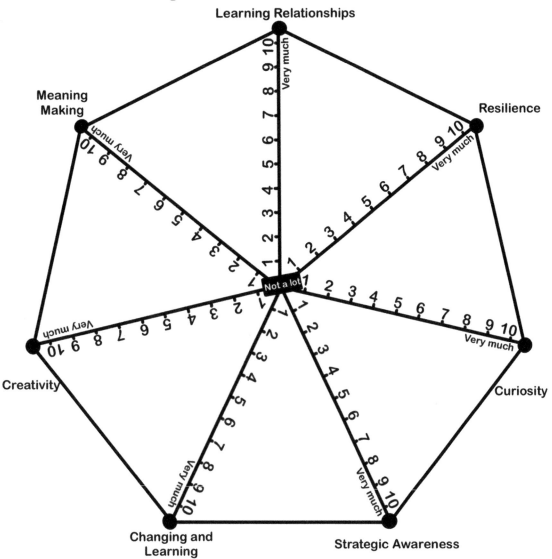

Example

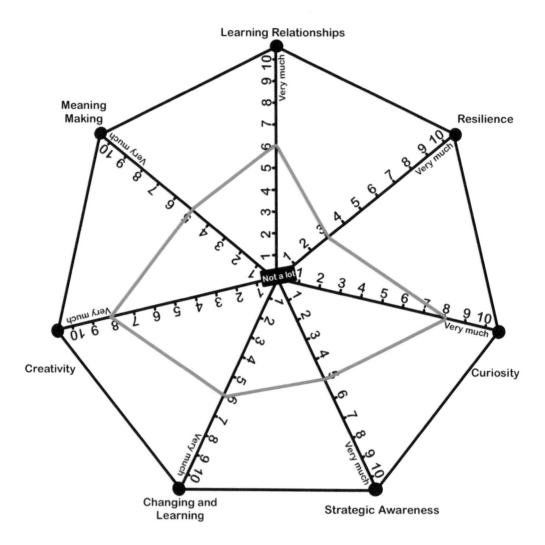

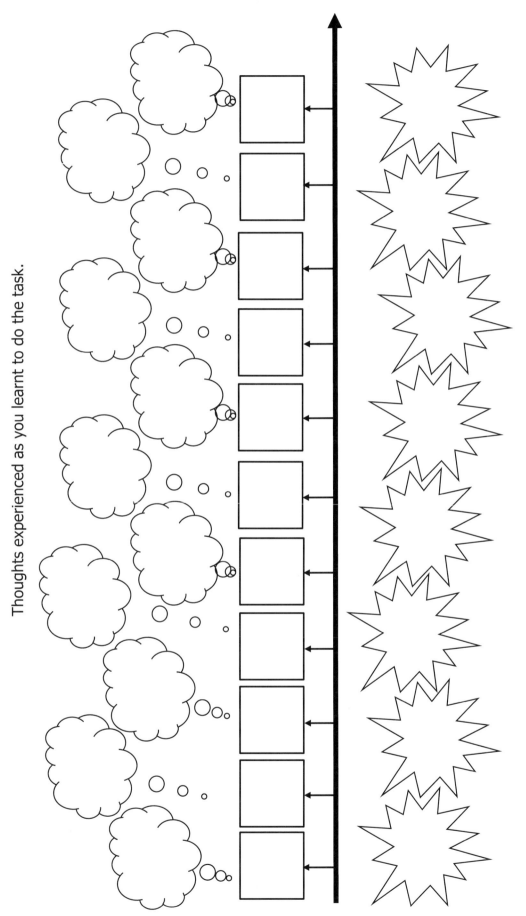

Thoughts experienced as you learnt to do the task.

Emotions experienced as you learnt to do the task.

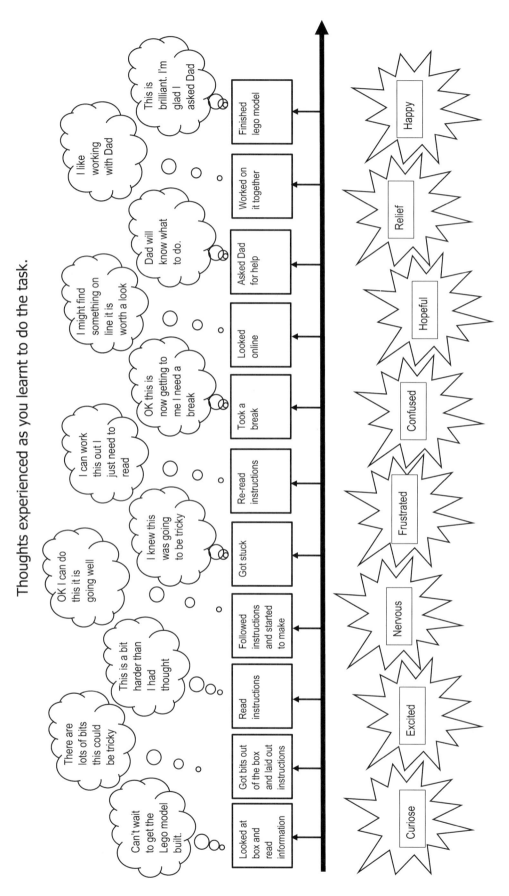

Thoughts experienced as you learnt to do the task.

Emotions experienced as you learnt to do the task.

Primary Assembly:

Who is the Assembly for?

Children in KS1 and KS2.

What is the Focus?

Learning sometimes needs you to be brave and have a go or take a chance.

Objectives

To understand that learning needs you to be brave and that sometimes you have to take a chance.

Ways to support others be brave and have a go or take a chance.

Involvement of Children

To come up with suggestions about what to do to enable them to take a chance or support others take a chance.

Key Message

We can be brave and take a chance. We can be supportive of others so that they can be brave enough to take a chance.

Resources

What Do You Do with a Chance? by Kobi Yamada and Mae Besom.

What if...... banner.

Introduction

Read the first 2 pages. Ask the children if they have ever wanted to do something but didn't have the courage to take the step and do it.

Find out some of the things children had not been able to do. Share a time when you were not able to take a chance and have a go.

Read the rest of the story.

Main Event

Ask the children to identify all the things that prevent them from taking a chance? Hold up the What if banner.

What if........

Share a range of what ifs......

What if I fail? What if I look silly? What if they don't like me? What if they don't think it is a good idea? Ask others to come up with their own what ifs

Finale

Ask the children to come up with a range of things that they might need to enable them to 'Take a chance'.

Courage/try/prepared to fail/prepared to make a mistake/ the knowledge that mistakes help you learn/belief in yourself/friends around you to support you/family who support you.

Can they think of ways that they can support others take a chance?